D1429969

CULTURES OF SOLIDARITY

CULTURES OF SOLIDARITY

Consciousness, Action, and Contemporary American Workers

RICK FANTASIA

UNIVERSITY OF CALIFORNIA PRESS
BERKELEY   LOS ANGELES   LONDON

University of California Press
Berkeley and Los Angeles, California

University of California Press, Ltd.
London, England

© 1988 by
The Regents of the University of California

First Paperback Printing 1989

Library of Congress Cataloging-in-Publication Data

Fantasia, Rick.
  Cultures of solidarity.

  Bibliography: p.
  Includes index.
  1. Labor and laboring classes—United States—History
—20th century. 2.   Trade-unions-—United States—History—
20 century. 3.   Labor disputes—United States—Case
studies. 4.   Class consciousnesss—United States—History—
20th century. I.   Title.
HD8072.5. F36   1988   331.8′0973   87–16748
ISBN 0-520-06795-9 (alk. paper)

Printed in the United States of America
      4   5   6   7   8   9

The paper used in this publication meets the minimum
requirements of American National Standard for Information
Sciences—Permanence of Paper for Printed Library Materials,
ANSI Z39.48-1984. ∞

To my brother, Nick

Contents

Preface   ix

Part One: Theoretical Directions and the Historical Terrain

1. Culture and Consciousness in Action   3

2. Corporate Action and the Bounds of Solidarity   25

*Part Two: Contemporary Expressions of Consciousness
          and Action*

3. The Internal Dynamics of Wildcat Strikes: Routinization
    and Its Discontents   75

4. Union Organizing and Collective Interaction: "Like a
    Thief in the Night"   121

5. The Strike as Emergent Culture: Community and
    Collective Action   180

6. The Limits and Possibilities of Trade Union Action   226

    Appendix
      The Measures Taken: Some Notes on Methodology   247

    Notes   255

    Bibliography   283

    Index   297

Preface

Though an earlier version of this book served as my Ph.D. thesis, its origins actually extend back several years before my time as a graduate student. In 1975, partly out of curiosity and partly out of necessity, I took a job in a steel-casting foundry, where I worked as a furnace operator in the finishing department. This experience, the subject of one of the three case studies that comprise the empirical foundation of this book, profoundly influenced my approach to the formal sociological training I subsequently received. Besides influencing my decision to attend graduate school in the first place, it provided me with an important set of empirical reference points from which to understand and criticize the discipline of sociology. What this meant was that my life as a graduate student was largely spent thrashing about trying to reconcile that experience with an immense body of literature that found American workers somehow immunized from the impulses, concerns, and conflicts which had punctuated that period in the factory. Perhaps if I had instead gone to work there *after* my formal academic training, I might have pursued a more standard methodological approach to issues of class consciousness and collective action (see Appendix), but I am not persuaded that that would have made me a better thinker, or this a better book.

Although I take full responsibility for any errors of logic or presentation here, there are, however, a number of people who have made this a better book by their comments and criticisms at various stages of its development. I am indebted to Lewis M. Killian, chairman of my doctoral committee, who in countless intellectual exchanges (often impassioned, always valuable) helped me relax my dogmatic impulses and recognize the richness, complexity, and dignity of human behavior. I also owe a great debt to Dan Clawson, who treated this project with the care and thoughtfulness he has shown in his own work, and who was always completely magnanimous in making himself available to me. He consistently prompted me to consider the political implications of my thinking and the necessity of taking opposing theoretical ideas seriously. In the formative stages of the work, Gerald M. Platt offered a sharply critical eye and served as a model of intellectual integrity, Michael Lewis tempered my sometimes unwarranted optimism with a perceptive and informed pessimism, and Bruce Laurie's comments helped me appreciate the art of historical scholarship.

As the project progressed beyond the dissertation stage, the wisdom, encouragement, and editorial advice of many others helped along the way. Among these were Kathleen Daly, whose suggestion that women in collective action would be different was too slowly, but fruitfully, taken; Michael Schwartz, whose extremely insightful perspective helped me develop my theoretical arguments more thoroughly and thoughtfully; and V. L. Allen, T. B. Bottomore, Mary Ann Clawson, Kai Erikson, John Ether, Philip Green, Vivien Hart, Gordon Marshall, Christiane Metral, Charles Page, Richard Parmentier, George Rudé, Richard Sanders, John Schall, Naomi Schneider, Peter Stallybrass, Kay Warren, and an anonymous member of the University of California Press Editorial Board. All have helped make this a better book than it would otherwise have been.

I wish to thank the Smith College Committee on Faculty Compensation and Development for its generous assistance at various stages of this work, the Smith College Project on Women and Social Change for several opportunities to test ideas in early stages of their development, and my students and colleagues at Smith College for the intellectually stimulating atmosphere in which I have been fortunate to work. The Leverhulme Trust provided support for a Visiting Fellowship in England in 1985–86 that allowed me some time and, more important, access to a stimulating group of colleagues in the School of English and American Studies at Sussex University. Thanks to Norma Lepine, Linda Mugridge, and Karen

Saenz for typing various portions of the manuscript, and to Melissa Niswonger for her valuable and patient computer assistance.

Most of all, I want to thank the workers documented here, as well as those in Westfield, Massachusetts, and the South Wales coalfields, who shared their experiences of struggle with me in one way or another. If this book does any justice to their cause, it will only serve as partial repayment for the many lessons they have taught me.

Part One

Theoretical Directions and the Historical Terrain

Chapter One

Culture and Consciousness
in Action

Early in the 1980s the news media began to devote an unusual amount of attention to the issue of working-class consciousness. Two compelling, yet contrasting, developments fascinated the press. The first was the extraordinary labor upheaval in Poland, which appeared to shake a social order many had thought immutable. Forged out of the solidarity displayed in general strikes and buttressed by the threat of still more general strikes, the "class consciousness" of Polish workers riveted the attention of the Western press for months. The second development was the American labor movement's seeming unresponsiveness toward President Reagan's brazen assault on the air traffic controllers union, PATCO. Indeed, the contrast between these two events did not go unnoticed. The *New York Times* bluntly stated in its Labor Day editorial in 1981 that "solidarity and purpose are words to describe labor in Poland, perhaps, but not in this country."[1] And in an allusion to the actions of their Polish colleagues, one commentator remarked that had other union workers honored PATCO picket lines, "It would have been over in five minutes."[2]

When asked to explain the relative quiescence of American labor in the face of the unmistakable union-busting tactics employed against PATCO, Lloyd Ulman, then director of the Institute of Industrial Relations at the University of California, Berkeley, cited the "lack of traditions of solidarity" in the American labor movement.[3] Just as class consciousness is considered an almost "natural" phenomenon among workers abroad, so a *lack* of class consciousness has often been deemed inherent in the character of the American working class. From the "Commons school" of industrial relations and Selig Perlman's *A Theory of the Labor Movement,* to Daniel Bell, Seymour M. Lipset, and the "end of ideology" thesis, to two generations of Critical Theorists, the view that class consciousness is a sensibility alien to American society has been an overwhelming theme in the sociology of the American working class.[4]

Yet the extraordinary degree of working-class solidarity expressed in the labor wars of the 1930s has served as a virtual ideal-typical model of class consciousness, and the general strike has at times punctuated relations between capital and labor in American history.[5] In 1981 few commentators seemed surprised that thousands of union and non-union workers crossed PATCO picket lines, whereas in 1934 the ethos of "an injury to one is an injury to all"

> had soared to a general acceptance by local unions the country over. When one union's picket lines were attacked by police all unions in a given locality threatened general strike. This happened again and again in 1934 and 1935. . . . Everywhere workers were saying to police and goons, "If you smash that picket line every union in the city is going out."[6]

In the 1930s general strikes and factory occupations seemed unambiguously to embody a powerful working-class consciousness in the same ways that the evident disunity over PATCO in 1981 seems to underscore its absence. However, although anecdotal evidence is abundant, actual research by sociologists into working-class consciousness in the United States has been extremely limited in scope and depth.

American sociology's study of working-class consciousness has almost invariably treated class consciousness as workers' conceptions, images, attitudes, and ideational and verbal responses to the social arrangements in which they find themselves. The basic approach has been to develop a survey schedule designed to measure worker attitudes on a range of issues: class identification, work satisfaction and dissatisfaction, class animosities, and political preferences. These attitudes are then correlated with any number of independent variables, such as skill level, racial or ethnic identifica-

quantitative

tion, religion, age, sex, and so on. Armed with such data, sociologists then assess the degree of "class consciousness" in a given population of workers. Some have found indications of working-class consciousness employing this methodology, although most "have turned up precious little of it."[7]

But whether or not one "finds" class consciousness is akin to the problem of whether the glass is half-empty or half-full; it may reveal more about the relative optimism or pessimism of the sociologist than about the existence of class consciousness. Survey research methodology entails some highly questionable assumptions when used in analyses of class consciousness. The measuring of attitudes demands that an individual's response be recorded as his or her fixed views about an issue. Although people's responses and expressions must indeed be taken seriously by social science, part of doing so means recognizing that the world may be a paradoxical and contradictory place to those negotiating it.

In historical and ethnographic accounts, discontinuities and paradoxes in consciousness emerge frequently, offering the most difficult, as well as the most potentially rewarding, problems for solution.[8] The sociological survey, in contrast, largely precludes one from discovering contradictory lines of thought, as well as from exploring the methods by which individuals synthesize contradictions. This issue was raised succinctly by a factory worker in a warning to a social research team, "There's no use asking people what they think; they'll tell you something different."[9]

This problem was also recognized by a pair of British scholars who, employing the method, were struck by its limitations. Robin Blackburn and Michael Mann found British workers "confused by the clash between conservatism and proletarianism, but touched by both," and they thoughtfully conclude that no image other than a contradictory one is possible in an industrial society that generates contradictions between "normal affluence," "sensible" industrial relations, "intermittent redundancy," and "authoritarianism." Moreover, they advance the view that "if the workers in our sample are 'confused' then they have every right to be, for that is an accurate reflection of the reality that confronts them."[10] The survey reveals its own limitations in this case; in general those not burdened by the limitations of surveys seem better able to recognize "ambivalences" in working-class consciousness.[11] For example,

sounds like C. Perron

Frank Parkin argues the existence of a dual value system that provides different moral frames of reference in different situations, and Howard Newby's deferential farm worker is "torn between the contractual elements of his relationship to the farmer and the personal, particularistic loyalties inherent in that same relationship . . . [and] often ambivalent in his moral assessment of the social and economic position of his employer."[12] Analyses pointing to paradoxes and oscillations in working-class consciousness that are largely precluded by the standard survey technique have issued from scholars as diverse as John R. Commons, Jean-Paul Sartre, and Kai Erikson.[13]

Survey research generally overlooks paradoxes in consciousness by recording responses as fixed and static. It also precludes a collective dynamic in class consciousness by supposing that collective consciousness can be gleaned from the sum of separate individual attitudes. A sum of the opinions of individual respondents recorded at a given moment in time may appear wholly different from the "consciousness" expressed by those same "respondents" in the midst of collective action and interaction. The issue is not whether one form or the other represents the "true" consciousness, but rather that individual attitudes and collective interaction somehow must both be taken into account if we are to take the notion of class consciousness, or any group consciousness, seriously.

By relying so heavily on survey methodology, American students of class consciousness have biased their analyses by overlooking potentially illuminating evidence. Some of this evidence can be found in the collective actions of workers, in the "explosions of consciousness" that erupt periodically and sometimes contradict the results of surveys.[14] For example, the Lubell Poll of 1959, conducted among steelworkers, showed that they were overwhelmingly opposed to the strike being threatened by their union leaders in contract negotiations and would not support the strike if it was called. These findings, an encouragement to the steel industry management, put the union leaders in a difficult situation. They, too, believed the poll and were unnerved by its results, but were forced to declare a strike when negotiations broke down. According to Charles Spencer:

> The workers, contrary to the poll, gave the strike call spontaneous
> and enthusiastic support. The strike lasted 116 days . . . the longest

qualitative good!

in the history of the industry. The militancy of the strike confounded the Steelmasters, and the officials of the union were slow to understand the feelings of their union members.[15]

A similar phenomenon took place at the Vauxhall automobile plant in Luton, England, only months after Vauxhall workers had been interviewed by John Goldthorpe and his associates in the *Affluent Worker* research project.[16] The results showed that Vauxhall workers were firmly integrated into the system and held no deeply felt grudges. Although they were satisfied with their wages, they considered their jobs a boring, albeit inevitable, part of their lives. Goldthorpe concluded that class consciousness was practically nonexistent at Vauxhall. His workers were acting according to middle-class patterns.

However, while the study was still at the printer, some union militants handed out summaries of its conclusions. A week later, the *Daily Mail* published a report showing Vauxhall's profits (amounting to £900 per worker), and this, too, was circulated throughout the plant. An eruption ensued for the next two days, which *The Times* reported as follows:

> Wild rioting has broken out at the Vauxhall car factory in Luton. Thousands of workers streamed out of the shops and gathered on the factory yard. They besieged the management to come out; singing "The Red Flag"; shouting "string them up." Groups attempted to storm the offices and battled police which had been called to protect them.

Other examples could be offered to show similar "practical critiques" of survey research.[17]

One would not want to conclude from this that such collective "explosions of consciousness" represented the "true" class consciousness of the workers and that the survey results were therefore incorrect. But it does suggest some things to be considered in relation to survey research on class consciousness: (1) the survey did not predict—indeed, could not have predicted—the results of the collective "chemistry" among workers; (2) the impact of the explosion at Vauxhall was at least as important for labor-management relations, the internal dynamics of the workplace, and the mutual solidarity among the workers as the "consciousness" de-

picted by the Goldthorpe survey; (3) class consciousness may encompass more than the day-to-day attitudes compiled by researchers; and (4) almost no attention has been paid to collective action in
the empirical study of class consciousness by sociologists. If a
method is employed that only measures individual attitudes at a
specific moment, analyses of class consciousness are severely constrained. Such approaches may capture some important attitudinal
trends, but crucial dynamics of collective interaction are lost, and
thus what is being measured may not represent the *collective* class
consciousness that studies purport to show.

I would argue, however, that the limitations and problems are
not simply methodological but derive primarily from theoretical
assumptions on which the method is based. It is not that the survey
is never a useful technique; rather, what it tends to reveal about
class consciousness is so narrow that the most important and interesting dimensions of class relations and experience are often
missed. In the study of class consciousness, attitudes and ideation
have been abstracted from the only context in which they can be
properly understood—the world of class practices in which they are
embedded. As Gordon Marshall has argued:

> An overemphasis on class imagery at the expense of class action
> can perhaps be attributed to the widely held belief among aca-
> demic observers that it is somehow necessary for men and women
> to encompass society intellectually before they can attempt to
> change it. This premise is not confirmed by the history of class
> action on either a revolutionary or on a more modest scale. . . .
> Consciousness is generated in and changed by social action. . . .
> Experience has shown that it is the relationships between attitudes
> and actions that are important and that these can only be studied
> contextually.[18]

Many have borrowed Marx's seemingly dichotomous notion of a
class "in-itself/for-itself" as the key problematic in the study of class
consciousness, but the centrality of action and process in the formulation has largely been ignored.[19] In the oft-cited phrase from *The
Poverty of Philosophy,* the increasing socialization of production
brings a class into being "as against capital, but not yet for itself. In
the struggle . . . this mass becomes united, and constitutes itself as
a class for itself."[20] By extracting the expression "in-itself/for-itself"

from its active context, the dynamic quality of the concept of class consciousness has been lost.

In Marx's formulation, the working class is "in struggle," "becomes united," "constitutes itself"; and these activities of "struggling," "uniting," and "constituting" ought to be considered *processes* of class consciousness. Too often, however, the notion of a class "in itself" is reduced to an "objective" matter of determining the relative size of the labor force, the concentration of workers in various industries, the occupational characteristics of a workforce, or the level of union membership. Concomitantly, the notion of a class "for itself" becomes a "subjective" problem of determining to what extent class members are conceptually aware of a class structure, whether or not they employ a language of class, or whether they identify themselves as belonging to one class or another. The latter has become *the* problem for most American sociologists.

In Marxist epistemology, "objectivity" and "subjectivity" are conjoined, not abstracted from each other. When Marx wrote about nineteenth-century working-class movements, his focus was neither on the reading habits of workers nor on how thoroughly they had been imbued with certain ideas, but rather on the extent to which their processes of internal organization and their activities as workers represented a revolutionary consciousness. That is to say, Marx sought to ground consciousness in life activity, in social being. He criticized the idealism of Hegel, who maintained the primacy of subjectivity and relegated social transformation exclusively to the ideational realm: "In direct contrast to German philosophy which descends from heaven to earth, here we ascend from earth to heaven."[21]

Although many are familiar enough with the Marx who "turned Hegel on his head," there appears to have been a parallel confusion over the actual result of this philosophical reworking. For the "earth" from whence Marx ascended was not a static, mechanical, "material world" in which economic forms dictated thought processes. What seems forgotten is that, while Marx's epistemological project represented a critique of the idealism of Hegel, it just as significantly represented a critique of the static materialism of Feuerbach. Marx addressed both sides of the philosophical dichotomy in which, on the one hand, the material world is an expression of a metaphysical "spirit" and, on the other, consciousness is a mere

reflection of a material world. He also went beyond both by inter-
jecting the mediational role of *conscious human activity*. Thus he
transcended the traditional dispute between classical idealism and
classical materialism by recognizing the primacy of "sensuous human activity."[22] "Subject" and "object" were not conceived of as
dichotomous, but as dialectically interwoven through human activity consciously undertaken; in other words, in praxis, a new form of
consciousness that neither reflects nor is reflected by the material
world. Praxis is purposive activity that changes the world and is
changed by it at the same moment. From this perspective, human
labor in capitalist society takes place within an exploitative context
that generates opposition. The activities of workers against capital
contain in themselves transformative potential, for in the course of
struggling to liberate their "social being," they are simultaneously
liberating their "subjectivity": "their association itself creates a new
need . . . the need for society . . . and what appeared to be a
means has become an end."[23]

Thus Marx's assessment of the revolutionary potential of the
working class rested on the character of its revolutionary praxis
rather than on ideology in the abstract. The extent and development of collective activity embodied a collective subjectivity:

> To Marx, that workers associate means that they create new bonds
> and links among themselves, that they come out of the isolation and
> loneliness imposed on them by capitalist society. . . . The associa-
> tion of workers in their meetings and groups is by itself a most
> revolutionary act, for it changes both reality and the workers them-
> selves. This association creates other directedness and mutual-
> ity. . . . The act and process of association, by changing the worker
> and his world, offer a glimpse into future society.[24]

It was precisely this conception of consciousness-in-association that
later informed Rosa Luxemburg's promotion of independent, collective self-organization of workers in the general strike and that
prompted Antonio Gramsci to stress participation in workers' councils as vehicles of revolutionary consciousness.[25]

By focusing exclusively on the attitudinal and verbal responses of
individual workers, sociology has been generally blinded to class
sentiments expressed in the collective activities of workers, which
themselves may represent attitudes and values and may create a

context for the transformation of ideation. Solidarity is created *and* expressed by the process of mutual association. Whether or not a future society is consciously envisioned, whether or not a "correct" image of the class structure is maintained, the building of solidarity in the form, and in the process, of mutual association can represent a practical attempt to restructure, or reorder, human relations. Thus, as I will demonstrate empirically, in the United States the formation of unions and the maintenance of strikes and rank-and-file insurgent groups within unions can be transformative activities that create and express solidarity simultaneously, embodying consciousness in a process largely impervious to the standard sociological survey.

I do not suggest that such activities are "revolutionary" in the sense that they are designed to overthrow the social order or are capable of doing so in any simple or direct way. But although workers may not be poised to make revolution, they may in certain activities express a consciousness that, though short of the will or capability to make revolution, represents a transformative associational bonding that can shape class relations in significant ways. The point is that analyses of class consciousness should be based on actions, organizational capabilities, institutional arrangements, and the values that arise within them, rather than on attitudes abstracted from the context of social action.

Indeed, such an approach seems consonant with the most persuasive recent historical studies of class consciousness.[26] For example, Ronald Aminzade has studied the growth of class solidarities in nineteenth-century Toulouse, France, focusing on the breakdown of certain associational forms, such as the highly ritualistic, exclusive, and rigidly hierarchical brotherhoods of bachelor journeymen, called *compagnonages,* and the emergence of new forms of association revealing the sensibilities of a wider solidarity. In contrast to the *compagnonage,* the "mutual benefit society" included unskilled workers, organized strikes, and served both as a "cover" for the collection of strike funds and as a means of surveillance of employers after strikes. For Aminzade, changing social solidarities are reflected in the changing character of associations.

Mary Ann Clawson has similarly compared fraternal orders in Europe and the United States in the nineteenth century. On both continents these played an important cultural role. In Europe fra-

ternal orders were largely class-exclusive, promoting and nourishing class sympathies and traditions, whereas in the United States
they were from the outset cross-class organizations, and as such
inhibited comparable associational bonds.

John Foster's study of the Industrial Revolution in three English
towns represents an attempt both to understand class consciousness by relating its appearance or absence to the social structure
and to characterize the variety of responses by the working class to
the rise of capitalism. For Foster, "class consciousness" represents
a working-class response (at one end of a spectrum of responses)
that is ideologically crystalized as a critique of capitalism as a system. But Foster argues that if such class consciousness has meaning
beyond the rhetoric of working-class leaders, it will have a structural expression in the movement that advances it. Such a movement will be acting to overcome ethnic and occupational divisions
that divide the working class and prevent a sense of total class
identification.

Foster views "status systems" (at the other end of the spectrum)
as the chief mechanism of labor fragmentation. But his focus is on
the historical process of people constructing status systems (or
subgroups) in order to protect themselves from inequality and
lack of control over their lives, as well as to preserve and defend
certain lifestyles and privileges. Class consciousness and status are
not treated as passive attributes, possessed or not by isolated individuals, but as active social processes of people structuring their
lives.

Foster approaches residence and marriage as two important indi-
cators of social distance among sectors of the working class. For
example, he reasons that if marriages were more common between
craftsmen and laborers, or Irish and English, in one town or another, we can assume a breakdown of traditional hierarchies of
occupational and ethnic status and an increasing identification as
part of a common class. Foster also studied the breakdown of the
"employer household," which yielded to emergent cultural institutions in the shape of the pub and the friendly society. Of particular
value here is that he stresses the potential of the latter either to
become politically and culturally tied to "bourgeois authority"
(through licensing practices, and so on) or to become autonomous
institutions of working-class solidarity.

Persuasively employed in these historical accounts, the notion of status grouping as an active process of exclusion, and solidarity as a means by which the subordinate usurp the power of the dominant, has also been raised articulately in sociological theory, though this has not been reflected widely in empirical research.[27] Part of the difficulty, I think, is that a "gradational" conception of class predominates in American sociology rather than a notion of class as a "relation" that structures or shapes social action.[28]

The notion of "social class" as it is typically employed in American sociology differs in important respects from "class" as it is understood by most Marxists. Not surprisingly, this has led to a good deal of misunderstanding, with each side frequently talking past the other. Within the field of "social stratification," classes are generally conceived of as collections of individuals with shared social characteristics, or in possession of similar amounts of a scarce resource (education, income, occupational prestige). Distinctions are made on the basis of the quantity of resources each individual receives, or the nature of the independent variables associated with one recipient group or the other. This approach may be useful for answering important questions about the degree of inequality embedded in a society's distribution network, but it is often unwittingly confused with Marxist notions of class, which hinge on the dynamics of the relations of production in society.

The Marxist emphasis on class analysis is linked to a general theory of historical change. It seeks to answer questions about the historical genesis and transcendence of exploitation of one social class by another. Class is seen as an exploitative social relationship between those who own and control the means of production in society and those whose labor power is necessary to set the means of production into motion. It is this "coercive relation" that "compels the working class to do more work than the narrow round of its own life-wants prescribes"[29] and that provides the social relations of production in capitalist society with what is viewed as an inherently antagonistic tension. Thus, as Duncan Gallie notes, "the key to understanding workers' attitudes and objectives must be sought in their everyday experience of social relations with their fellow workers and with their employers in industry. . . . The critical element in Marx's theory of the emergence of an awareness of the exploitative character of class relations lay in the experience of collective social conflict."[30] There are innumerable social relations that may be antagonistic (ethnic, racial, familial, status, religious, sexual), but for Marxists it has been the coercive nature of the class relationship, manifested in class struggles, that has had primacy in the general theory of systemic change.

As opposed to a static notion of class as a stratified structure, the conception that informs this project recommends a view of class as a dynamic phenomenon in which particular classes have no independent being, but are functions of their relationships to other classes. Thus the collective activity and mobilization of both workers and employers take place within a conflictual context and should not be considered apart from it. As such, class consciousness essentially represents the cultural expression of the lived experience of class, an experience shaped by the process of interaction of these collectivities in opposition to one another. I would argue that an inquiry into the forms this expression might take must not bear the burden of apriorism too heavily, for as E. P. Thompson has emphasized: "We can see a *logic* in the response of similar occupational groups undergoing similar experiences, but we cannot predicate any *law*. Consciousness of class arises in the same way in different times and places, but never in just the same way."[31]

When conceived of as cultural expression, class consciousness seems less a matter of disembodied mental attitude than a broader set of practices and repertoires available for empirical investigation. On one level, this approach treats culture as the "peculiar and distinctive way of life of the group or class, the meanings, values and ideas embodied in institutions, in social relations, in systems of beliefs, in mores and customs, in the uses of objects and material life."[32] Such "maps of meaning" are not simply ideational, but are objectivated in social relations, institutions, and practices.

Although this seems a reasonable starting point for a "culturalist" approach to class consciousness, the focus in this project will be on those moments when the customary practices of daily life are suspended and crisis requires a new repertoire of behavior, associational ties, and valuations. All too often, culture has been treated as an integrated whole, as a solid, cohesive patterning of life that tends to minimize or disregard discontinuity and rupture.[33] Positivist sociology, like anthropology in its dominant forms, suffers from this seamless conception of culture:

Culture has had an admittedly rough deal from sociology. When not whittled down to a "branch name" for what used to be traditionally considered the domain of the high brow (belles lettres, refined music and arts, leisure activities) or stretched to embrace the totality of human and/or social existence, it is, at best, handled in a way which infallibly renders it redundant. . . . Like the notions of social system, the term culture responds to the need to express the vague idea of the interlocking, dovetailing elements of human life, or an intrinsic congruence of human individual biography as well as of consistency within the individuals' interaction; it stands for the hope of the essential predictability of the human responses to standard contingencies, the hope built on the assumption of the basically determined nature of human life activity.[34]

Not only has a cultural status quo been upheld by proponents of a conservative view, but also some of the most progressive critics of American cultural life tend to sustain the hegemonic myth of culture. Individualism, narcissism, and class subordination read as personal failure are often seen as dominant values absorbed and reproduced by the powerless with little recognition of problematic, indeed counterhegemonic, cultural practices and impulses.[35]

In recent years, a rich body of work has appeared that moves away from simple notions of passivity and cultural absorption, recognizing the complex structuring of working-class culture. For example, Michael Burawoy's study of the culture of shop-floor life shows how the labor process itself is structured to manufacture consent rather than rebellion at the "point of production," and Paul Willis has documented the masculine ethos among male industrial workers that inhibits protest against difficult and dangerous tasks on the job.[36] Ira Katznelson's *City Trenches* shows how class consciousness has been dichotomized in American society, with politics in the community expressed through a language of ethnicity and territory, while politics in the workplace maintains a language of class division. Similarly, David Halle illustrates the varying identities of male workers at work, at home in their communities, and as "Americans" in relation to a wider political culture.[37] Moreover, the importance of divided spheres of cultural life in the expression of class consciousness is represented firmly within the dominant paradigm of feminist scholarship, which regards the public/private, work/home dichotomy as crucial in the study of class consciousness.[38]

Taken together, this literature recommends a view of class consciousness as structured, fractured, or limited in one way or another by the cultural processes that organize and reproduce daily
life. To focus on the praxis of the daily life of the working class
rather than simply on the attitudes and ideas of individual members is to radically shift attention away from what can be measured
by standard survey research.[39]

At the same time, as Victor Turner notes, "social life . . . even
its apparently quietest moments, is characteristically 'pregnant'
with social dramas."[40] I want to pursue a theoretical approach that
offers a view into the interstices of dominant cultural patterns,
however fractured, structured, or divided, for although it is crucial
to understand the customary practices of everyday life, as B. Babcock argues, "what is socially peripheral is often symbolically central," and those periodic ruptures in cultural life may sometimes
tell us more about the consistencies than the consistencies themselves.[41] Such a perspective informed the study of the strike in
Lloyd Warner's most important volume of the Yankee City series,
The Social System of the Modern Factory:

> The best of all possible moments to achieve insight into the life of a
> human being is during a fundamental crisis when he is faced with
> grave decisions which can mean ruin and despair or success and
> happiness for him. In such crises men reveal what they are and often
> betray their innermost secrets in a way they never do and never can
> when life moves placidly and easily. If this is true for the study of
> men as individuals it applies even more forcefully to the study of
> men in groups. It is when all hell breaks loose that the powerful
> forces which organize and control human society are revealed.[42]

"Moments of crisis" can indeed be illuminating, but Warner's
implication seems to be that a "truth" or "essence" can be revealed
in them. If so, then those Vauxhall workers who militantly rebelled
after Goldthorpe's survey had found them acquiescent were expressing their true collective selves in that action, and the accom-
modating attitudes expressed in the survey were somehow less
real. I want rather to recognize the varying, contextual nature of
working-class responses and would agree with Sartre that ultimately the working class ought to be understood in its varying
expressions—its daily life activities (Sartre's "seriality"), institu-

tional existence (trade unions, political parties), and periods of social struggle ("fused groups," in Sartre), for as he noted: "The working class is neither pure combativity, nor pure passive dispersal, nor pure institutionalized apparatus. It is a complex, moving relation between different practical forms."[43]

Whereas the study of class as "pure passive dispersal" has been virtually the exclusive focus of "stratificationism" and has figured prominently in what R. W. Connell has termed "categorical Marxism," this book focuses on the "group fusion" and collective actions that workers frequently manifest, yet that have been almost completely ignored in the consideration of American working-class consciousness.[44]

Because I want to begin to free the notion of class consciousness from the purely ideational, attitudinal bonds by which it has been shackled, I will largely dispense with the term "class consciousness" so that we may be able to consider a wider range of cultural practices generated in social struggle. The concept I employ instead is that of "cultures of solidarity"—a notion whose elements allow for a fluidity not easily available in the traditional conception of class consciousness.

By "cultures of solidarity" I do not mean subcultures in the shape of "sub-sets—smaller, more localized and differentiated structures, within one or other of the larger cultural networks" or cultural formations existing happily amidst the folds of the "parent culture."[45] Rather, I mean a cultural expression that arises within the wider culture, yet which is emergent in its embodiment of oppositional practices and meanings. This notion of emergent culture is drawn from the work of Raymond Williams, who variously terms it "counter-cultural," "counter-hegemonic," or "oppositional" culture. Such expressions arise within the hegemonic culture and can represent something original and independent. As Williams emphasizes: "Cultural process must not be assumed to be merely adaptive, extensive, and incorporative. Authentic breaks within and beyond it, in specific conditions which can vary from extreme isolation to pre-revolutionary breakdowns and actual revolutionary activity, have often in fact occurred."[46]

The use of the plural, "cultures," in my formulation is meant to afford analysis of discrete case studies of collective actions of workers and their cultural expression, rather than beginning from the a priori, generalized sense of class against class implied in common usage of terms such as "class solidarity" and "class consciousness." I will demonstrate how these case studies have been structured and shaped by class relations at a more generalized (national, societal) level, as well as by the limits and possibilities of their more generalized manifestation, but my empirical focus will be on action and interaction at a local (shop-floor, workplace, community) level. That is, rather than taking the generalized sense of class consciousness and attempting to cut the empirical fabric to fit a fully specified design, I will examine case studies of local cultures of solidarity—of the lived experience of workers in collective action—to provide a basis for understanding class capacities at a more generalized level. This seems to be a basic point in doing cultural analysis. As Clifford Geertz states: "To an ethnographer, sorting through the machinery of distant ideas, the shapes of knowledge are always ineluctably local, indivisible from their instruments and encasements. One may veil this fact with ecumenical rhetoric or blur it with strenuous theory, but one cannot really make it go away."[47]

Some may be troubled that I do not provide a more fully developed conception of class at the outset and that most of the workers studied do not express a more fully developed language of class themselves. But as Louise and Charles Tilly note:

> We dare to speak of "class conflict" because so many of the struggles portrayed in this book pitted sets of people who occupied similar positions with respect to the means of production—social classes, that is, or fragments of them—against others who occupied different positions. That usage opens us to the objection that the people involved did not cast their action in terms of class, were not truly aware of their class interests, or defined their enemies inaccurately. To these hypothetical objections we can only reply that such demanding standards for class conflict nearly banishes class conflict from history; however engaging the vision of workers speaking articulately in class terms and acting decisively on the basis of an accurate assessment of their interests and enemies, the event itself has been rare indeed. We settle for a less demanding and wider ranging conception of class conflict.[48]

Similarly, in the studies offered below, I will settle for a less demanding and a wider-ranging conception of class conflict. In each case, I attempt to ground consciousness in the dynamics of collective action and organization against employers—to study the cultures of solidarity that emerge in industrial action. My subject is not class conflict, if one's conceptual requirement is class "writ large," but class action as it is expressed in specific industrial conflicts and framed by institutionalized trade unionism and the industrial relations system in which it operates. As A. R. Luria found in his research on social change in Soviet Central Asia in the 1920s (according to John Foster):

> Even the lowest level of trade union involvement demands a social practice that challenges, as nothing else, the assumptions of individualism and creates a quite new context for the formulation of concepts and attitudes. . . . The collectivism inherent in trade union activity is seen as indispensable for the creation of a basic class consciousness that can, in the course of struggle and sometimes with surprising speed, be transformed into a consciousness of a much higher political level.[49]

Although I believe that this view is basically correct, as I indicate in chapter 2 and seek to demonstrate in the case studies that follow it, industrial action embodies a transformative potential when it can achieve a degree of independence from the institutional structures designed to contain it. That is, in the United States a routinized, bureaucratic system has been imposed to channel conflict and sharply limit worker solidarity, and "cultures of solidarity" will thus tend to emerge only when workers or employers circumvent routine channels and workers seek, or are forced, to rely on their mutual solidarity as the basis for their power.

Because institutionalized trade unionism has largely become a party to the overall structure, my "cultures of solidarity" are not coterminous with unions. Cultures of solidarity are more or less bounded groupings that may or may not develop a clear organizational identity and structure, but represent the active expression of worker solidarity within an industrial system and a society hostile to it. They are neither ideas of solidarity in the abstract nor bureaucratic trade union activity, but cultural formations that arise in conflict, creating and sustaining solidarity in opposition to the dominant structure. Forged in crisis, cultures of solidarity can represent, sometimes merely in germinal form, "micro-societies in which the laws of macro-society are not only suspended but replaced by a new regime of direct action," as Henri Desroche has characterized the millenarian and revolutionary drama.[50] A brief look back at class conflict in the 1930s may help illustrate.

The 1930s saw massive mobilization within the working class to meet the challenge of sustained, repressive corporate anti-unionism. The dramatic collective actions of workers were a necessary response to the intensive countermobilization of employers expressed in the wholesale hiring of strikebreakers, virulent police repression of strikers, and the thuggery of men such as Harry Bennett, head of the infamous "Ford Service Department." In such a context, the notion that mutual solidarity was the only reliable source of working-class strength was a generally persuasive one, actualized in extraordinary solidarity strikes in 1934 and the sit-down movement of 1937.

Thus it was neither fine theoretical distinctions in party line nor a particularly firm ideological commitment that led many workers to support radical leaders during this period. Rather, the "Musteites" in Toledo during the Auto-Lite strike, the Trotskyists of the Minneapolis uprising, and the Communist Party cadre in the San Francisco general strike and the sit-down strikes were all granted acceptance and exercised strong leadership to the extent that they cultivated, nourished, organized, and defended the untrammeled expression of class solidarity. Corporate praxis during the period continually served to remind rank-and-file workers that the basis of their strength as a collectivity lay in their ability to act in solidarity. Radicals gained influence in the labor movement largely because, in contrast to the conservatism of much of the AFL leadership, they were willing to rely on and cultivate mutual solidarity to win the decisive battles.

During the course of these struggles, "cultures of solidarity" were constructed by workers. That is, tactical activities, organizational forms, and institutional arrangements were employed that represented the expression of solidarity and its creation simultaneously in the process of their development. These cultures of solidarity took myriad forms in response to the specific features and demands of particular struggles.

For example, in Minneapolis, a city ruled by the "Citizens' Alliance" (an anti-union employer association), coalyard workers and truck drivers of Teamsters Local 574 struck for union recognition in 1934.[51] In sharp contrast to the president of the international union, who refused to back the strike and once it was under way publicly "red-baited" strike leaders to divide them from the rank and file, the Trotskyist strike leaders worked to garner support from the whole of the city's working class.

The culture of solidarity that emerged included a range of components and practices. In an effort to minimize the availability of strikebreakers, unemployed workers were mobilized to support the strike. Fifty roads into the city were guarded by well-organized pickets, who turned non-union trucks away. For the first time, "flying squadrons" were organized to provide a "mobile guard" of pickets that could be sent anywhere in the city at a moment's notice. Jeremy Brecher notes that more than five hundred strikers massed at union headquarters day and night throughout the strike, waiting to be dispatched.

Mass meetings were conducted nightly, and elaborate communication networks were established to keep strikers and supporters aware of developments. A "women's auxiliary" was formed and put out leaflets, walked the picket lines, and staffed a huge strike kitchen that served thousands of strikers and sympathizers. In addition, a strike hospital was organized (with two doctors and three nurses); and fifteen auto mechanics set up a machine shop to service the cars and trucks of the flying squadrons.[52] Through it all, an entire labor community was awakened and mobilized to support the strike. Thirty-five thousand building trades workers declared a sympathy strike, the Central Labor Union Council voted its support, and thousands of union and non-union workers alike joined street battles against strikebreakers and police. In addition, small shopkeepers and farmers donated food and other provisions. After a month of open warfare, in which demonstrations involving tens of thousands took place (including a funeral cortege of forty thousand for a slain striker) and street combat occurred almost daily, the strike was victorious.

For our purposes, the victory is a secondary consideration, for the importance of this example of class conflict lies in the *processes* of solidarity. The organization and maintenance of flying squadrons, food distribution centers, clinics, and communications networks,

and the mobilization of family members, union and non-union workers, and farmers in support of the Teamsters were all emergent
institutions, practices, and organizational forms that at once created
and expressed solidarity. A "counterhegemony" emerged to replace
the social institutions and cultural practices that dominated working-
class life in Minneapolis in 1934. The culture of solidarity that developed had not existed previously, and though episodic in the sense
that it may not have been maintained in the same form at the same
level of intensity afterwards, its impact on class relations in Minneapolis and on labor history nationally was not negligible. As Eric Leif
Davin and Staughton Lynd have shown, "Every major center of
industrial unrest in 1934 witnessed the rise of labor party activity the
following year."[53]

The leaders of the Minneapolis strike were radicals, but their
leadership capacity was based on the promotion of working-class
solidarity, rather than on an exposition of socialist ideology per se.
Art Preis notes: "The Local 574 leaders warned the membership
over and over to place no reliance or hope in any government agent
or agencies. . . . They preached reliance only on the mass picket-
lines and militant struggle against the employers."[54] The cultures of
solidarity formed to accomplish these tasks and objectives represented *in practice* a clear opposition to existing class relations, a
struggle that prefigured its objective. This suggests that militant
activity created the context in which class consciousness emerged.
Revolutionary society may not have been envisioned by workers
beforehand, but in the course of the struggle, they in effect created
a new "society." The demands of the conflict necessitated new
social arrangements, which in the process of their creation reveal
the richness of the class consciousness of the period.

The political character of this class consciousness was embodied
in the act of association itself, as the revolutionaries of the period
were well aware. As Sam Darcy, a Communist Party member, later
wrote of the San Francisco general strike, "the very fact that it was
a sympathy strike gives it its political character, a declaration of
class consciousness on the part of the San Francisco workers and,
secondly, an act of unified class action."[55]

Obviously, the expression of worker solidarity in a general strike
is a good deal nearer the model of class consciousness found in

classical socialist literature than any practical expression we are likely to find in the contemporary United States. However, just because the model does not exist, it does not mean that there is no class consciousness whatsoever. This book rejects the view that either a classical model exists or nothing at all (the common assessment), and thus argues that there are expressions of worker solidarity in collective action that have been largely ignored in social analysis because they do not meet the standard or classical model of what class consciousness *ought* to look like.

Those who approach the issue of working-class consciousness with a priori expectations—whether optimists or pessimists—are likely to be disappointed by what they will find here. The optimists may be pleased by the often extraordinary expressions of militant solidarity documented below, but they will doubtless be disheartened by the failure of these expressions to sustain themselves and bring clear, unambiguous victories. Conversely, pessimists will be quick to deny or minimize working-class solidarity, while finding the failures or weaknesses more deeply rooted than I have found them to be. Whether one draws hope and inspiration or a cynical sense of futility from the collective actions analyzed is less important to me than that the factors that frustrate or sustain them be considered in the light of the real context in which they operate. This work proceeds, then, in a necessary tension between the important and underestimated expressions of class solidarity and militancy in local conflicts and their often fragile, fragmentary, and defensive character.

The differences between solidarity and collective action in the 1930s and in the contemporary period are substantial. But although there have been well-known internal divisions that have been significant in limiting working-class action historically, what has been consistently minimized or ignored is the structuring of the terrain on which conflict takes place. Ultimately, my focus will be on the dynamics of solidarity and the practical instruments of worker mobilization in the contemporary period. Such mobilization is extremely problematic, considering the actions of employers that are designed to derail it.

In chapter 2, the enormous scope and the varying forms of corporate activity against solidarity throughout the twentieth century will be examined. As I will show, militancy was manifested in the context of extreme opposition in the 1930s, and opposition has continued to shape its expression since then. The location of, and the possibilities for, worker mobilization and collective action today have been profoundly shaped by previous struggles, processes, and initiatives, and it is by understanding this changing terrain that contemporary cultures of solidarity can be properly situated.

Chapter Two

Corporate Action and the Bounds of Solidarity

Chapter 1 introduced the concept of "cultures of solidarity" as a social encasement for the expression of working-class solidarity, an emergent cultural form embodying the values, practices, and institutional manifestations of mutuality. I described certain elements of a mass strike during the 1930s in Minneapolis in order to outline the contours of such solidarity, not because that decade represents the exclusive historical domain of solidarity, but because its depth and scope then were of such proportions as to exemplify class consciousness in an almost ideal-typical way. Although the task of illustration is thus made simpler, and the "compelling myth" has sometimes served as a useful guide to action (as in the syndicalism of Sorel),[1] there is a danger in extracting events from their proper context. For many, the 1930s have served as a vantage point from which to view subsequent labor relations, but often with little recognition of the real processes out of which the events of the 1930s unfolded. This has led a generation of scholars to lament and ponder "what went wrong" with the American working class after that tumultuous era, without seriously considering the formidable constraints imposed on workers in their attempts to act in concert.

The aim of this book is to investigate recent expressions of solidarity and collective action among American workers through analyses of three case studies, focusing on the dynamics of mobilization and the complex processes of their formation. But within this inquiry it is crucial to recognize that "class struggle" is a two-sided affair. "Labor history" as a chronicle of events and processes must also be informed by a "management history" of counterprocesses and events in order to make sense of the actions of each in relation to the other.

This chapter will trace the expression of solidarity historically in the context of its opposition, from the turn of the century to the present. Instead of heralding heroic actions and extraordinary displays of worker solidarity as others have done elsewhere, however, I focus here on the breadth of opposition placed in the path of emergent solidarity, opposition that has permeated the industrial landscape throughout the twentieth century. The diversity of strategies employed, the level of organization and cooperation achieved, and the massive resources devoted by employers to weakening and breaking solidarity are, in part, testimony to the historical potency of working-class loyalties. But rather than simply chronicling the strategies of employers, I will attempt to show how those strategies have progressively narrowed the scope of industrial action for workers since World War II, resulting in an increasingly limited range of possibilities for working-class activism today. That is to say, in order to chart the terrain that contemporary cultures of solidarity must negotiate, I will trace employer strategies and document the weight of the opposition encountered by workers as one way of examining how contemporary manifestations of working-class solidarity have been shaped and conditioned by previous corporate initiatives.

I will begin by describing the context of corporate activity out of which the CIO breakthrough was achieved in 1937. In important ways, the character of employer activity, both coercive and paternalistic, helped dictate the complexion of unionism as well as the workers' repertoire of collective action in the early CIO period. In turn, capital responded by embarking on a sustained, and largely successful, attempt to weaken the labor movement by severely narrowing the scope and the potential for collective action. The strict limitations imposed during the war years, and later codified by the Taft-Hartley Act, resulted in the postwar labor movement being institutionalized in its present enfeebled condition. More important for the case studies that follow, the form and content of contemporary expressions of collective action and consciousness continue to be shaped by this historical legacy and can only be understood in the light of it.

Overall, the effort to break solidarity has as rich a history as the attempts to forge it. Much of this history involves struggles over unionization (both the destruction of existing unions and the suppression of nascent ones), but the locus of solidarity has often been pushed beyond the union-as-institution. Although solidarity has always been part of the ethos and practice of the labor movement, the centrality and primacy of mutual solidarity as the basis of social power has sometimes been diluted, deflected, or bartered away to varying degrees among different segments of the movement. In recognizing that unions themselves have not always embodied the highest expressions of solidarity, it should not be overlooked that efforts to organize unions, however limited and uneven, from the nineteenth century to the present have had to rely on, or have at least been informed by, the values and practices of mutual solidarity.

Concomitantly, corporate action has been largely designed to delimit or destroy labor's solidarity, with the open shop as an important focus of activity. Though complete freedom from unionism has not always been necessary to guarantee largely unbridled management power (as we will see from the 1940s and beyond), anti-unionism has represented a "first line of defense" against the expression of class loyalties among workers.

"Family Factory Relations" and the Open Shop

The process of molding an ethos of work discipline, obedience, and time-thrift out of agrarian sensibilities and practices during the Industrial Revolution in England took place over many generations and met with a good deal of resistance.[2] The American counterpart to this process—employers seeking to shape an industrious factory workforce from an immigrant population of largely rural heritage— took place throughout the latter half of the nineteenth century, gathering impetus at the turn of the century. At the time when Frederick W. Taylor's theories of "scientific management" were gaining currency among industrial planners, the need for a pliant, docile, and disciplined workforce was more apparent than ever.[3] As

David Montgomery notes, paternalistic corporate welfare programs were initiated to "hasten the cultural transformation of the
immigrants by promoting the attitudes of 'thrift, sobriety, adapta-
bility, [and] initiative' that would allow employers to assign them
easily to industrial tasks."[4] Professionalization of corporate personnel managers coincided with this process to control general worker
discontent more effectively and further facilitate the "Americaniza-
tion of Aliens."[5]

The classic example of this effort was the Ford Motor Company's
"sociological department," a cadre of forty men, each equipped
with a car, an interpreter, and a driver, who visited auto workers to
determine their "eligibility" for Ford's unprecedented daily wage
of five dollars. In an officially commissioned biography of Henry
Ford, Allan Nevins and Frank Hill describe these investigations.[6]
Each worker was to furnish detailed information on his marital
status, the number and ages of his dependents, his nationality, his
religion, home ownership status, amount of mortgage or rent, level
of debt (and to whom), whether money was sent home, whether
boarders were kept, amount of savings and life insurance, family
diet, health, recreation, and so forth. In addition, each investigator
made a general assessment of the worker's "habits," "home condition," and "neighborhood."

Henry Ford's own testimony to congressional investigators reveals a combination of compassion, self-righteousness, and a pro-
found paternalism:

> The company maintains a corps of 40 men, good judges of human
> nature, who explain opportunity, teach American ways and customs,
> English language, duties of citizenship, who counsel and help the
> unsophisticated employees to obtain and maintain comfortable, con-
> genial, and sanitary living conditions, and who also exercise the
> necessary vigilance to prevent, as far as possible, human frailty from
> falling into habits or practices detrimental to substantial progress in
> life. The whole effect of this corps is to point men to life and make
> them discontented with a mere living.

Subsequent testimony revealed the limits his compassion reached.
Ford went to great lengths to explain that the "profit-sharing plan"
(his term for the five-dollar daily wage) was a completely voluntary
affair: "No man is influenced to change his mode of living, his

habits, or character in order to qualify under the profit-sharing plan if he does not willingly so elect." However, the consequences of noncompliance were made quite clear: "No coercion is laid upon any employee, but if he is not living a sober life, or is neglecting his duties as a father or husband, and he persists in such course he cannot be an associate of our business." Ford insisted that no thought was given to the economic well-being of the company when the program was initiated, that the object was "simply to better the financial and moral status of the men." But he also noted that productivity under the plan had increased by 15 to 20 percent and that absenteeism had decreased from 10 percent to .3 percent. Hence, he conceded: "Our experience leads us to conclude beyond doubt that the interest taken in employees as to their individual welfare is most desirable from every standpoint, not only that of the employee and his family but of the business itself." Clearly, this was not a bad "sidelight" for an industrial relations program created with "no thought of betterment in this direction."[7]

It is important to remember that while corporate "social work" was busy molding an industrial culture to meet the requirements of employers, skilled, seasoned craftsmen were countering these efforts by teaching immigrant proletarians their own version of shop-floor customs and practices.[8] Moreover, programs such as Ford's profit-sharing plan did not necessarily have to produce direct benefits to employers in terms of productivity and output to be considered successful. Their success could be measured less tangibly by the extent to which they deflected an impetus toward unionism. In fact, many reforms provided important benefits to workers. For example, International Harvester hired Gertrude Beeks specifically to attend to the "social welfare" of Harvester employees.[9] Embarking on a program to improve sanitary conditions in the factory, Beeks had the company drill wells to supply clean drinking water to the workers (not a minor improvement, as water impurities had been a major cause of illness); she brought in fans to clear the air; she had toilets installed and lunch rooms built; and so on. In addition, Beeks organized a choral group among the workers, solicited contributions for a library, and set up a summer camp for the families of Harvester workers. But lest workers develop too keen a taste for reform, companies that undertook social welfare programs often simultaneously engaged in more coercive and repressive anti-union campaigns, as the history of labor relations at both Ford and International Harvester indicate (see below).

A more sophisticated and more widely employed manifestation of corporate "welfarism" was the "employee representation plan," or "company union," originally developed in a programmatic form by John D. Rockefeller. The events surrounding its genesis highlight factors that sometimes influenced labor relations policy. The "Colorado Industrial Plan" or "Rockefeller Plan" was developed in the wake of the Ludlow Massacre of 1914. In 1913, the United Mine Workers Union had successfully organized the Rockefeller-dominated Colorado Fuel and Iron Company and had presented a list of demands including a 10 percent wage increase, observance of the state mining laws, discharge of armed guards, free choice of boardinghouses and doctors, and, most important, union recognition.[10] After the local management refused to bargain with the union, the men walked off their jobs and were summarily evicted from their company-owned homes along with their wives and children. A virtual civil war brewed as a union organizer was murdered, strikers armed themselves, and the governor ordered the entire National Guard to the scene. The strikers were out for over eight months, residing in a tent colony with their families until the infamous night of Easter 1914 when "company-employed gunmen and members of the National Guard drenched the strikers' tents with oil. They ignited them after the miners and their families were asleep. When the miners, their wives and children ran from the burning tents they were machine-gunned."[11] Nineteen strikers and kin were killed, thirteen of them children. The public outcry that followed coincided with a series of muckraking articles aimed at Rockefeller's Standard Oil Company. In the aftermath of these events the "Rockefeller Plan" to establish a board representing both management and employees as a forum for discussion of working conditions and grievances was unveiled, amid a fanfare of publicity. Rockefeller himself spent two weeks in Colorado conducting inspections and talking with miners, their families, and mine superintendents. Newspaper readers throughout the country read how John D. had attended a local social function and danced with nearly every woman on the floor. But Irving Bernstein records a brief interchange with one William Hood that reveals as much about the dogged class instinct of a coal miner as it does about the "new" image of a once-aloof industrialist:

> *Hood:*   Is dat you, Mistah Rockefeller? . . . Now is dat so! An' you-all heah shakin' hands wid a black boy like me! . . . I'se a most faithful employee for you-all, suh. An' I wants to known, suh, when I'se goin' tuh git on de pension-list? . . .
>
> *Rockefeller:*   Well, I'm not on the pension-list myself, yet, William.
>
> *Hood:*   Yes, but you-all ain't doin' no laborious labor.[12]

In October 1915, 2,846 workers (out of 4,411 eligible) voted on the plan, and 2,404 voted in favor of it. The plan was instituted, and although there is no conclusive evidence that the establishment of similar programs in other companies was a response to such violent class conflict, it is clear that at least one group of industrialists felt threatened by the Rockefeller war at Ludlow and adopted very similar strategies. During the events at Ludlow, Cyrus H. McCormick, on business in New York, wrote to his son of the activities in front of the Standard Oil Company offices, "where excited agitators were making violent speeches against Mr. Rockefeller and his son."[13] Shortly thereafter, the McCormicks unveiled their own plan. The account offered by Robert Ozanne of the cooperation between the two families, connected by both marriage and class interest, provides a glimpse into the practice of corporate solidarity:

> In 1914 and 1915 the McCormicks had loaned industrial relations know-how and personnel, in the form of Clarence Hicks, to the Rockefellers, hard pressed by the tragic dispute at Ludlow. But the war brought a resumption of labor troubles at International Harvester, and it was now Rockefeller who in 1918 came to the aid of the McCormicks by releasing Arthur H. Young of the Colorado Fuel and Iron Co. to head a newly established industrial relations department at International Harvester. . . . .
>
> . . . As early as October 1918 he called in his mentor at Colorado Fuel, the internationally famous labor relations consultant McKenzie King, whose novel and ingenious "company union" plan had succeeded in rescuing the Rockefellers from the United Mine Workers. Together they drew up for International Harvester a slightly modified version of the Colorado Fuel plan . . . to protect the company from advancing unions.[14]

The "employee representation plan" was the organizational expression of the corporate welfare ideology that flourished in the Progressive Era. Supporters heralded the concept as the preeminent form of industrial democracy, in which the floodgates of "open communication" would be opened, creating a new epoch of consensual industrial relations. In an address before the American Management Association, one corporate proponent of company unions extolled their advantages: "The quickened sense of freedom and responsibility blossoms into loyalty. Perhaps this is the finest flower of employee representation—loyalty. . . . It is loyalty such as no wage system can buy, enlisting their wills in jointly working out the democratization of industrial operation."[15]

Despite such enthusiasm for democracy, most employers introduced company unions as a method of undermining organizations that might be controlled by the workers themselves. The company union provided workers with a semblance of organization, while management could exercise its dominion by retaining controlling power. It was a caricature of a trade union, in which workers were involved in deciding the most innocuous of issues; decisions on important issues were made by a board that allowed the company to retain controlling votes, forestalling real organization by the workers while maintaining open-shop conditions for the company. Although the company union took different forms, its essential advantage was that it could replace *working-class* solidarity with *company* solidarity, *shop* solidarity, or "family factory relations." As one industrial relations advisor candidly put it: "After all, what difference does it make whether one plant has a 'shop committee,' a 'works council,' . . . or whatever else it may be called? . . . They can all be called 'company unions' and they all mean the one big fundamental point—*the open shop*."[16]

The company union afforded management a great deal of leeway in a range of "problem" areas, as a group of workers would now aid management "in making employees see the necessity and wisdom of a decision that would otherwise become disagreeable and troublesome." It was particularly effective in engineering wage reductions. One company boasted of developing "a carefully worked-out plan of reducing wages during a period of depression without the usual resentment from the workers."[17] The officials of the Bridgeport Brass Company described the ease with which wage cuts were facilitated with the help of company union "representatives": "The representatives of the workers got together and drew up plans that were so eminently fair that we not only accepted them but thanked the workers. They unanimously agreed that there should be a horizontal wage reduction of 10 percent, to revise all preferential classifications and abolish overtime pay."[18] There is no indication of whether the workers at Bridgeport Brass felt their "representatives" to be as generous as management found them, but the point is that, for the time being, the concept worked successfully in fulfilling management wishes and preventing effective worker organization.

Robert Ozanne's extensive documentation of the "industrial council plan" at International Harvester Company sheds some light on the operation of "family factory relations." The company rationale for establishing the industrial council plan, a program that lasted for twenty-two years, is not easy to pin down.[19] The employees were informed that management was taking the initiative "to establish closer relations between employees and management" and that its implementation would "make for the greater contentment and well-being of us all." Another explanation, more global in scope, yet actually an elaboration of the first, was a response made by Cyrus McCormick III to the 1919 AFL convention, which had denounced company unionism as a thinly veiled union-busting tactic. McCormick emphasized the value of the works council as an "ally" of organized labor and an effective form of collective bargaining. He characterized his program as one that would democratize industrial relations, in contradistinction to "Eastern European syndicalism," which could not, according to McCormick, grasp "the fundamental solidarity of the American people."

However, a third and conflicting rationale is revealed in a letter from the head of industrial relations at Harvester, Arthur H. Young, to Cyrus McCormick II as the plan was being developed. It represents Young's recommendation in the midst of a discussion of the most opportune moment to initiate the plan:

> It may be true that, six months from now, labor will be more plentiful, but on the other hand it may also be true that conditions will be less unsettled in that period and that a condition of unemployment will possibly bring with it greater anarchical and "bolshevik" activities than has before attended similar periods. I feel certain that the activities of the labor organizers will be much more radical in char-

acter, now that the war is over, than they have been heretofore. Furthermore, there is a greater need for the adoption of clearer statements of fair and democratic principles by leading industrialists, because such pronouncements will serve as beacons on the very turbulent sea of industrial relations existing just now. If we withhold action and make no move to combat the efforts of labor agitators and anarchistic workers, it is certain that some of our employees will be influenced by their propaganda. And I think that the general condition of society is such that there is a distinct danger, because of the worldwide unrest of what we popularly term the "working classes."[20]

This internal company communication is particularly illuminating. First, it indicates that although the company was to have the workers vote on whether or not to institute the plan, one influential position was that by waiting six months, the vote would take place in the context of a period of high labor supply, and consequently the company would enjoy a certain advantage based on the workers' fear of unemployment. More important, although "democratic principles" played a role in offering the plan, they were clearly subordinate to corporate fears of open rebellion. In International Harvester's highest echelons, the notion that there existed a "fundamental solidarity of the American people" competed with the equally compelling (though not openly stated) view of the primacy of class struggle in industrial affairs.

The whole operation of the works council at Harvester appears to have reflected this latter position. The council was made up of an equal number of employer and employee representatives, but the scope of council activities was largely determined by management. Management was given the right to veto any employee proposals and the company president reserved the right to cast tie-breaking votes in the event of an impasse.[21] According to Ozanne, the plan was carefully designed to ensure the isolation of workers from one another. There was no provision for any employee meetings, and employee representatives, though elected by departments, had no agreed-upon right to call a meeting in their constituent departments. Even the nominating process took place without a meeting.

Employee votes were frequently split on most issues, whereas management representatives consistently voted as a bloc, ensuring management prerogatives and preventing the company president from having to exercise his (potentially embarrassing) tie-breaking power. Although the existence of the works council protected International Harvester from successful union organizing campaigns for many years, demands for wage increases were repeatedly raised by workers on the council. These demands were mostly unsuccessful, but wage cuts were frequently enacted, forcing the employee representatives to spend most of their energy fighting to restore cut wages rather than obtaining real wage increases.

It is important to understand how such cuts were facilitated to understand some of the constraints imposed on working-class action in general. Wage cuts at Harvester were preceded by well-orchestrated (and sometimes prolonged) "softening-up" periods.[22] During these periods, management would meet with employee representatives to point out the low rate of plant operations and cite wage cuts at other plants, with the implication that the only way to keep the men working was for them to accept such a cut. Ozanne explains that at one such meeting, Arthur H. Young insisted that although a 20 percent cut would be necessary he would understand if the representatives attempted to amend this proposal to 15 percent so that they could "save face" with their constituents; subsequently they would be overridden by management and then would be able to accept the original 20 percent cut the company wanted.

Shortly after this cut was imposed in May 1921, the company began a new softening-up process in an effort to cut wages yet again. This time, the employees thought they could appeal to the constitution of the works council, which prohibited wage readjustments within six months of each other. However, as management conveniently interpreted the constitution, the employees could waive the prohibition by a vote of their representatives. After a prolonged period of meetings, in which management called for a 27 percent cut for day workers and a 32 percent cut for shift workers (two or three representatives openly protested, but most were "tongue-tied in the presence of management"), it seemed as though management would have its way again.[23] But when the secret vote was counted, employee representatives had voted eleven to three against, with management voting unanimously for the cuts. When the plant superintendent wanted to know why the workers had voted the way they had, one representative replied: "The men come to me and say 'Mr. Joe, better to starve without working than to starve and work too.'"

Management responded: "Looks to me as though [top management will] be forced to close down the plant . . . if the plant is shut down, you can feel pretty sure that it was your action that caused it."[24] These workers, who could not meet with their constituents, much less their fellow representatives, without management representatives present, were intimidated by the threat and called for another vote, in which they accepted the 27 percent and 32 percent wage cuts by a voting margin of ten to four.

But while this series of actions shows the workers to be completely submissive in the operation of the company union, the rank and file at Harvester readily "tossed out" representatives who were so easily intimidated, even though there was little that a more militant group of representatives could have accomplished within this structure. Attempts to organize *real* trade unions would most certainly have been met by discharge. Defeats such as the one described above did provide valuable lessons later on, as workers at Harvester and elsewhere were given a taste of what real organization might provide.

The promotion of company unionism was only one weapon in a larger arsenal of corporate anti-union activity in the pre–World War II period, but it was a popular management strategy. Robert Dunn's estimates, based largely on data from the National Industrial Conference Board, found the number of companies adopting company union tactics to have grown from 145 in 1919 to 430 in 1926.[25] The passage of the National Industry Recovery Act in 1933 saw a precipitous jump in the number of company unions as employers interpreted Section 7a's ambiguous "right of labor to representatives of its own choosing" as sanction for company unionism.[26] By the spring of 1934, 25 percent of all industrial workers were employed in plants with company unions, with two-thirds of these organized under NRA auspices.[27]

Data from the iron and steel industry show a particularly vigorous promotion of company unionism in response to the NRA. Of the seventy-one company unions reporting in 1935, fifty had been established under the NRA, and this was considered a very conservative figure, as not all companies reported (see table 1).

The company union strategy, widely employed throughout the twenties and thirties, reduced Progressive Era social welfarism to a system that, while paternalistic and sometimes benevolent in form,

TABLE 1. *Company Unions Existing in the Iron and Steel Industry in April 1935, by Time of Establishment*

	Establishments	Workers Involved	
		Number	Percentage
Before National Recovery Act	17	15,680	25.2
During National Recovery Act	50	41,146	66.2
Not reported	4	5,348	8.6
Total reporting	71	62,174	100.0

Source: U.S. Department of Labor, Bureau of Labor Statistics, "Characteristics of Company Unions, 1935," Bulletin 634 (1936), table 9, p. 54.

Note: These figures are biased on the conservative side because one of the larger steel companies with an estimated 52,000 workers participating in company unions refused to answer the Bureau of Labor Statistics questionnaire.

was essentially coercive. The structure of employee representation plans did allow for at least a semblance of worker participation in decisions affecting shop-floor life, but these programs were carefully constructed to keep managerial control intact. In times of economic expansion workers no doubt received some material benefits, certainly more than workers in plants with no representation at all. For management, however, the real strength of this type of program lay in its ability to facilitate management control in periods of economic contraction—that is, when there were losses to be absorbed, it was possible to get labor to accept them under the imprimatur of a "democratic" procedure. Company unions would not have worked smoothly if they had given workers an opportunity to meet collectively to discuss problems. A company union could survive with worker participation only if workers saw it as their sole source of power, and a mass meeting of workers in this context would no doubt have brought the workers' real source of strength into sharper relief.

In promoting company unionism, employers ironically, yet naturally, pursued a policy that attempted to obtain a 100 percent "closed shop" for their unions as part of their strategy of maintaining "open-shop" status in relation to actual trade union organization. But company unions in the twenties and thirties frequently

provided the organizational and structural basis for the establishment of genuine unions in the electrical, steel, and other industries.[28] In fact, at International Harvester, George Fielde, employee representative of the docile works council, later went on to
lead the radical Farm Equipment Workers Union, CIO, in numerous militant strikes.[29]

Although it is generally assumed that corporations employed
either the relatively benign methods associated with Progressive
Era welfare ideology *or* the more repressive tactics of force and
intimidation to keep workers from organizing, a more accurate
interpretation may be that companies employed both tactics simultaneously, or at least were able to shift from one to the other with
little ideological difficulty. The view that some corporations had an
enlightened approach to labor relations while others stubbornly
clung to antiquated feudal notions may appear compelling when
one views the Rockefeller decision to allow his employees some
representation in the aftermath of the Ludlow Massacre. However,
one commentator notes that corporations that adopted company
unions frequently at the same time supported (financially or otherwise) the efforts of employer associations such as the U.S. Chamber
of Commerce and the National Association of Manufacturers to
undermine unionism on a national scale.[30]

And at International Harvester, an economic downturn just
months after the resignation of Gertrude Beeks (the personification
of welfare reform) caused the general manager of manufacturing to
request what appears to have been a clear and sudden shift in labor
relations strategy. The recommendation begins as a virtual call to
arms: "I know of no case where the employers have taken a firm
stand with their help and a strike has resulted, in which the employers have not won. . . . We are in a more favorable position today to
have a fight with labor, if necessary, than we have been for some
time past or are likely to be for a long time." It goes on to anticipate
the costs to the company of a violent, prolonged strike, and concludes "that by taking a firm stand on this question and putting it
through, we shall end up by having our men in better control, that
they will respect us more, and that we will have less labor troubles . . . for several years to come than we would in adopting any
compromise stance."[31] Indeed, well-organized, sometimes brutally

coercive, tactics were utilized by employers, often alongside more benign methods. Concerted campaigns conducted by large corporations or well-financed employer associations were embraced on a wide scale throughout the period preceding the formation of the CIO and represented a threat to emergent labor solidarity as great or greater than the "family factory relations" embodied in company unionism or welfare reform.

Corporate Repression and the CIO Breakthrough

American labor history is known throughout much of the world for its particularly violent character. The attempts by employers to break unions with the assistance of federal troops, the National Guard, Pinkertons, private militias, and hired thugs made such little-known places as Coeur d'Alene, Cripple Creek, Everett, Homestead, and Flint into watchwords of American history. But the use of military and paramilitary force to secure the will of capital, though not infrequent, has been only the most blatant means of breaking workers' associations. Although perhaps less dramatic, corporate espionage, organized strikebreaking, and open-shop propaganda campaigns have probably been significantly more costly to corporate treasuries, as well as to working-class solidarity.

Before 1900, employers generally handled their labor affairs without the strategic assistance of nationally organized employer associations. Thus, while the owners of the shoe factories in Lynn, Massachusetts, the mine owners of Johnstown, Pennsylvania, and employers elsewhere frequently united in common cause against the stirrings of their workers, these were local events and not part of any nationally coordinated effort. In 1903, however, the convention of the National Association of Manufacturers declared that it was necessary to approach labor relations in a collective manner.[32] The solidarity of workers, expressed in sympathy strikes, boycotts, and mass picket lines and marches, would thereafter be met by the combined efforts of an organized employer class. Trade associations, once a forum for the promotion of commerce, became a source of expertise and organization for corporations intent on meeting the challenge of working-class solidarity. David Montgomery's case study of the machinists shows that they drew the attention of just such an offensive in the first decade of the twentieth century. As the International Association of Machinists registered some successes in Chicago, intransigent employers raised the costs of that success in Chicago and elsewhere by attacking the machinists' prime weapon, the ability to halt production. The National Metal Trades Association spearheaded the offensive by providing legal, financial, strategic, and security assistance to struck employers. The NMTA organized strike-breaking outfits such as the "Independent Labor League of America, made up of workers . . . who were ready to go anyplace in the land to replace strikers." It also helped form an elaborate espionage network to infiltrate the labor movement. Montgomery cites an exposé published in 1904, which identified spies "on the AFL Executive Council, among national officers of several unions, federation field organizers, city trades assemblies, and union convention delegates." Employers acted through the American Anti-Boycott Association to engage in legal action against boycotts and sympathy strikes, "successfully establishing judicial precedents for the issuance of injunctions and the collection of damages against unions in such cases."[33]

The early open-shop campaigns consisted of a range of approaches. Reinhard Bendix has listed the variety of methods used by employers to maintain non-union status. In addition to the creation of counterorganizations (company unions), employers selectively hired "cooperative" workers (and fired the "uncooperative"). They consciously sought to buy off trade union leaders in an effort to siphon off labor's most effective spokesmen. Leaders who could not be bought were red-baited, accused publicly of serious crimes, or blacklisted, the point being to drive a wedge between the leadership and the rank and file or to eliminate the leadership altogether. Spies were employed liberally as a way of ensuring that management was cognizant of union strategy and had some hand in formulating it. According to a slogan printed on a bulletin advertising espionage services to employers, "Forewarned is forearmed." Espionage also served to maintain fear and paranoia in the union ranks, rendering communication and solidarity a costly and dangerous affair. Strikebreakers were to be called on to break picket lines and undermine work stoppages. Consequently, such programs demanded that good relations be forged between the company and the local police and militia. The political and financial clout wielded by employer associations was to be used to pressure the courts, the press, and local politicians to attack the trade unions and defend the corporations publicly. According to Bendix, all of these efforts were supported cooperatively by financial donations to employers engaged in battles with the unions. Any faint-hearted employers were pressured by their peers to support the cause of the open shop. Education was an important element of the early open-shop drive, with plans calling for the establishment of "trade schools" designed to teach "management philosophy." Internal education was partly facilitated by an anti-union organ, *The Review,* a monthly journal published by the National Metal Trades Association, which was later retitled *The Open Shop Review.*[34]

Although this sort of anti-union activity was used by employers throughout the first two decades of the century, it played its most prominent role in the aftermath of World War I, at the tail end of a militant strike wave of four million workers that left the "captains of industry" visibly shaken.[35] Through the war years the Industrial Workers of the World (the Wobblies), with over 100,000 members and a spirit that touched many times that number, had borne the brunt of repressive action in scores of communities. Wobblies were jailed, beaten, and lynched for their labor agitation and their opposition to the war.[36] Invoked repeatedly during the postwar strike wave, the cry of "Red" against strikers in the Boston Police strike, the Seattle general strike, and elsewhere served to kindle middle-class passions and cloud the issues over which millions were struggling. As Richard Boyer and Herbert Morais point out, ideology was hardly a sufficient explanation for the fierce postwar militancy among industrial workers:

> Communists were but one tenth of one percent of the country's population but milk had jumped since 1914 from nine to fifteen cents a quart, eggs from thirty-seven to sixty-two cents a dozen, butter from thirty-two to sixty-one cents a pound, and sirloin steak from twenty-seven to forty-two cents a pound. This fact and not Bolshevism was the cause of a strike wave involving 4,000,000 American workers but the open-shop drive of the National Association of Manufacturers, using the red scare as its main weapon, convinced millions of the middle-class that every strike was the beginning of revolution.[37]

Even the AFL resorted to attacking the IWW (and its call for "one big union") with fierce red-baiting and the mobilization of scabs to break Wobbly strikes, partly to add legitimacy to "responsible" trade unionism and increase its own membership and partly to forestall the organization of unskilled workers.[38]

From 1918 to 1920 the struggles of many American workers were notable for their ferocity, but so was the official repression mounted against them, and the organization of the mass-production industries (and millions of unskilled workers) was thus delayed for a generation.[39] This period saw the red scare develop into a powerfully effective weapon as the Wobblies, the immigrant victims of the Palmer Raids, and the many workers (the losers of the 1919 steel strike, for example) whose strikes were broken after being labeled "Bolshevik-inspired" could attest.[40]

The most dramatic attacks on the emergence of solidarity were leveled by the government in the midst of postwar anti-red hysteria, but the employers and their organizations continued to make important open-shop gains throughout the 1920s. An atmosphere of fear and anxiety spread through the working class during the depression of 1921, with an unemployment rate of 19.5 percent providing fertile ground for an intensification of this offensive. It was an opportune moment for the U.S. Chamber of Commerce and other employer groups to launch "the American Plan," which merged the ongoing open-shop drive (and its accompanying tactics) with racist, nativist sentiments and movements. Employer associations forged links with the American Legion, the National Security League, and the Ku Klux Klan in a formidable combination in the service of open-shop "Americanism."

In the face of the offensive, the working class revealed a vulnerability that was to be its Achilles' heel in later employer attacks. Although many unions opposed the Klan for carrying the banner of the open shop, white workers (Catholic as well as Protestant) offered little opposition to the racist and nativist thrust of the movement. The KKK "afforded an outlet for many of the constant frustrations of life, including economic tension as well as social insecurity, by providing a wealth of scapegoats against whom wrath might be vented."[41] Confronted by powerful nativist reaction fueled by the employers and their allies, "the 'new' immigrants retreated into the sanctuaries of ethnic community," weakening the prospects for solidarity across skill levels and across ethnic and racial barriers for many years to come.[42]

The combination of forces in the "American Plan" movement gave an added boost to anti-union initiatives. Within a year, four states (New York, Illinois, Michigan, and Connecticut) had a combined total of 137 organizations dedicated to proselytizing for open-shop ideology, and nationwide 540 organizations were actively promoting the cause of anti-unionism.[43] The income of the National Metal Trades Association had risen from $127,696 in 1918 to $541,236 in 1921 as more and more employers "eagerly sought the blacklisting, spy, and strike-breaking services offered by the association." Apparently its money was wisely spent, as Thomas R. Brooks notes that the machinists union (IAM), the chief union in the industry, saw its membership decline from 330,800 in 1920 to 77,900 in 1924. Union membership in general declined steadily from a peak of 5 million in 1920 to 2.9 million in 1933.[44]

Such concerted assaults on union activity were used successfully throughout the twenties and well into the thirties. The breadth of anti-union propaganda that was disseminated during these times is partially revealed in the 1936 report of the National Association of Manufacturers:

PRESS: Industrial Press Service . . . reaches 5,300 weekly newspapers every week.
Weekly cartoon service . . . sent to 2,000 weekly newspapers.
"Uncle Abner Says" . . . comic cartoon appearing in 309 daily papers with total circulation of 2,000,000 readers.
You and Your Nation's Affairs . . . daily articles by well-known economists appearing in 260 newspapers with a total circulation of over 4,500,000.
Factual Bulletin . . . monthly exposition of industry's viewpoint sent to every newspaper editor in the country.
For Foreign-Born Citizens . . . weekly press service, translated into German, Hungarian, Polish, and Italian, printed in newspapers with a total circulation of almost 2,500,000.
Nationwide Advertising . . . 6 full page ads about the "American System" of which 500 newspapers have carried one or more.

RADIO: "The American Family Robinson" . . . program heard from coast to coast over 222 radio stations once a week, and over 176 stations twice a week.

Foreign Language . . . 1,188 programs in 61 languages over 79 radio stations.

MOVIES: Two 10-minute films for general distribution, seen by over 2,000,000 people.

PUBLIC MEETINGS: 70 meetings featuring 8 professional speakers.

EMPLOYEE INFORMATION SERVICE: A series of 25 leaflets distributed to over 11,000,000 workers.

POSTERS: Over 300,000 for a series of 24 for bulletin boards in plants throughout the country.

FILMS: 10 sound slide films for showing in plants.

OUTDOOR ADVERTISING: 60,000 billboard ads scheduled for 1937.

PAMPHLETS: "You and Your Industry Library" . . . over 1,000,000 copies of a series of seven pamphlets distributed to libraries, colleges, businessmen, lawyers and educators.[45]

The U.S. Chamber of Commerce, with a membership of 700,000 employers, sponsored similar anti-union propaganda efforts at least as wide as the above. But union-busting and prevention were not confined to dissemination of propaganda. In the La Follette Senate committee hearings of 1938, it was revealed that employers were spending $80 million a year for espionage services. Boyer and Morais have reported on the extraordinary scope of labor espionage in this period: "230 detective agencies furnished the largest American corporations with 100,000 spies, who were thought to have penetrated every one of the country's 48,000 local trade unions."[46] And while the National Association of Manufacturers was distributing thousands of copies of a booklet endorsing the strikebreaking "Mohawk Valley Formula," corporations were busily putting this theory into practice.

The "Mohawk Valley Formula" gained popularity among employers after it was successfully used by the "Little Steel" companies to destroy the Steel Workers Organizing Committee in a conflict leading to the infamous Memorial Day Massacre in which ten peaceful marchers were killed and eighty-eight injured outside the gates of the Republic Steel plant in South Chicago.[47] The program was developed by James R. Rand of the Remington Rand Corporation to combat union organizing drives, but its components were far from original: "It provided for the systematic denunciation of all labor organizers and leaders as dangerous radicals, use of local police to break up labor meetings, propaganda campaigns to align the citizenry behind law and order, organization of vigilante committees to protect plants which hired strikebreakers, back-to-back movements and threats to remove the industry from the community if labor were not put in its place."[48] The garnering of community support on the side of employers and threats to cripple an area economically through plant closings had been used by employers earlier to break strikes, but it appears that such strategies appeared in codified form for the first time in the "Mohawk Valley Formula." Other elements of the plan, the attempts to isolate the leadership from the rank and file and reliance on local police to aid strikebreaking, were well-tested tactics by the latter part of the 1930s.

Against such a sustained offensive by employers, the weaknesses of the National Recovery Act appeared in ever sharper relief. The mass solidarity strikes of 1934, with their accompanying violence and disruption, were easily seen as a portent of things to come, particularly as they were occurring within an atmosphere of mounting hostility and militance on the part of the employing class. From the perspective of President Roosevelt, something had to be done to "cool out" the growing conflict. General discontent was increasingly focusing on the anti-labor policies of Roosevelt's New Deal policies, and after some trepidation he decided to support a more equitable labor reform program.[49] Subsequent to Senate approval, Roosevelt gave his support to the Wagner Act, creating the National Labor Relations Board, which would conduct union elections and regulate labor practices in general. But although the law was signed in the summer of 1935, it was immediately challenged in the courts, where it was tied up for the next two years. Many expected that the law would eventually be declared unconstitutional, and outside the courtroom the battle raged on. Employers had apparently decided to break the law unless forced by the power of unions to recognize it.[50] Earl Read, chairman of a committee of lawyers brought together by the American Liberty League to fight the law, stated the employers' position succinctly when he declared, "I feel perfectly free to advise a client not to be bound by a law that I consider unconstitutional."[51] So while the Wagner Act seemed to signal an advance for the union movement, only the force of worker mobilization would cause it to be obeyed.

The particular mechanism workers used to enforce their right to organize collectively was the dramatic and widely employed sit-down strike. As demonstrated over and over in 1936 and 1937, the sit-down represented a potent weapon in defeating strikebreaking strategies and provided the key to the unionization of the mass-production industries. The tactic served to successfully undermine many of the open-shop practices directed at union campaigns. With such an extensive spy network in place, employers could identify and discharge union organizers and supporters with little possibility of mass action being mobilized to defend these workers. The sit-down helped lift such constraints on mass mobilization. As Bert Cochran points out: "With the sitdown, a determined, disciplined minority could close down an entire plant and, because of the integrated nature of the industry, cripple thereby an entire line of manufacture, at the same time blocking attempts to start a back-to-work movement with scabs and strikebreakers."[52] With workers peacefully occupying the factories, management was reluctant to bring in strikebreakers for fear of damage to the machinery; and besides, the strikers on the inside enjoyed a clear tactical advantage in that they possessed intimate details of the plant interior.[53]

Company officials were also reluctant to call in the police to evict strikers, as extensive property damage and violence would have been likely, and a police charge on peaceful sit-down strikers could potentially turn public sympathy against the employer and the police department. In addition, as Jeremy Brecher notes, "The initiative, conduct, and control of the sitdown came directly from the men involved." Hence, attempts to isolate union organizers from potential supporters (as had been done many times previously) would have been strategically misdirected.[54] Again, these advantages addressed a whole history of corporate open-shop activity, a fact quickly recognized by workers and union organizers in scores of industries. In March 1937 alone, 167,210 people engaged in 170 occupations of employers' property; and within a year, 400,000 had contracted the "sit-down fever."[55] According to one historical account of the period, CIO offices were being deluged with phone calls from excited workers shouting: "We've sat down! Send someone over to organize us!"[56] By the end of 1937, the old AFL had grown by a million new members, and the fledgling CIO's membership jumped fourfold to 400,000. Industrial unionism was expanding not because of federal legislation, but as a result of the successful expression of solidarity and militance by the workers themselves. In fact, Green makes the point that "the CIO's biggest gains came when the Wagner Act was being challenged in the courts and 'virtually ignored' by employers."[57] It was not the law that proved decisive in labor's greatest victory to date, but a culture of solidarity that could freely negotiate a set of tactics and methods to meet the employers (with *their* tactics and methods) head-on and carry the workers through.

The year 1937 had clearly been a watershed for mass industrial unionism. Yet employers, though momentarily dazed by these events, continued to struggle bitterly against both union workers and those who sought collective organization. A renewal of corporate terrorism began in 1938 in the midst of high unemployment and lasted until the beginning of U.S. involvement in the war. Strikes during that year showed that the "Mohawk Valley Formula" was alive, well, and still capable of registering successes. For example, long strikes in union factories in Philadelphia and Iowa, caused by management attempts to cut wages, were broken after prolonged red-baiting campaigns. A report on the latter recommends itself as a textbook example of Remington Rand, Jr.'s theory in practice. Sixteen of the strike leaders were arrested, whereupon

> they were described as "Red Revolutionaries" as the State Militia was ordered into the little Iowa town where martial law was declared and where union men "were hunted like partridges on the mountainside." . . . For ninety-eight days the strikers fought on against vigilantes and citizens committees, against back-to-work movements and charges of Moscow plot, against wholesale arrests by the military, and injunctions and contempt citations by the courts.[58]

Not only did the militant industrial union movement face a determined open-shop barrage from employers and their agents throughout the thirties, but it also had to contend with an increasingly conservative AFL, which prospered in 1937 partially as a result of employers signing contracts with the AFL as a means of undercutting the more militant and unpredictable CIO. A memo was sent from the president of the International Association of Machinists to all officers instructing them to contact employers to emphasize the union's ability "to prevent sitdowns, sporadic disturbances, slowdowns and other communistic CIO tactics of disruption and disorganization."[59] One union official whose job it was to bring auto workers into the AFL (in the midst of the surge of industrial unionism) boasted to the auto manufacturers: "I never voted for a strike in my life."[60]

Thus far, I have traced the formidable obstacles placed in the path of worker solidarity throughout the pre–World War II period. In each of its manifestations (welfarism, repression, or a combination of both), corporate activity consisted of an unremitting assault on emergent unity. This unity was also partly limited from within the union movement itself, as the opportunism of some unions undercut the potential gains of others, even as the open-shop knives of capital were being sharpened against all.[61] Yet with all the treachery, the propaganda, and the power of the corporations and their allies, it was a reliance on mutual solidarity and forceful, yet thoughtful, militancy that paved the way toward, and eventually achieved, a unionism that reached across skill levels, embodying a class solidarity equal to that of its adversary. The massive displays of working-class struggle during 1934, led by those whose visions stretched well beyond bread and butter, formed a culture of solidarity in which industrial unionism could be cultivated. The fact that sit-down strikers occupying the workshops of America, ringed by tens of thousands of their peers protecting them, could win industrial unions in spite of the decades of intense anti-union propaganda and violence to which they had been subjected is testimony to the potency of the culture of solidarity in the 1930s. However, the 1940s saw changes in the character of labor relations that transformed the terrain on which previous battles had been waged and affected the expression of working-class solidarity in important ways for many decades to come.

Limiting the Terrain of Solidarity

The outbreak of World War II generated great changes in American society generally and in the nature of industrial life in particular. It is widely held that the tripartite unity of "business," "labor," and "government" forged in the context of extreme national emergency consolidated organized labor as a respectable, if not an equal, "junior partner" in American society.[62] But the consolidation of organized labor during the war was not without cost to the expression of working-class solidarity, and the new structures and relationships that were formed have had an enduring impact on the substance and scope of working-class action down to the present.

Trade unions *did* emerge from the war commanding considerably more social authority than before. Union membership had grown from 10.5 million in December 1941 to 14.7 million at the close of the conflict, industrial unions were firmly established in the mass-production industries, craft unions had extended to new areas of the workforce, and the union leadership enjoyed an enhanced prestige and status among the powerful.[63] Indeed, by 1944 the president of the U.S. Chamber of Commerce, an organization whose anti-union credentials had been well established, conceded that "measured in numbers, political influence, economic weight, or by any other yardstick, . . . labor is a power in our land."[64]

Ironically, labor's respectability emerged within a political environment that had become decidedly pro-business. The Roosevelt administration, which before the war had appeared to distance itself from the industrialists and show some sympathy for the growth of organized labor, fell fully in line behind management initiative during the war. One prominent New Dealer, Rexford Tugwell, lamented the rush of corporate executives who took charge of defense agencies and procurement boards:

> Washington had become a kind of madhouse. . . . There had descended on the capital flocks of businessmen and their various satellites in pursuit of profitable war contracts, or of escape from regulations, or in search of favors of other sorts. . . . It became more and more difficult to keep the economic expansion orderly, to avoid flagrant profiteering. . . . Cynicism spread out from this vortex. . . . It was in these circumstances that [Roosevelt] succumbed to the pressures exerted by the conservatives for a more sympathetic White House attitude toward business.[65]

The political changes brought about by such pressures were acknowledged candidly by FDR himself in his announcement that "Dr. New Deal had been replaced by Dr. Win the War."[66] Yet it was precisely this pro-business, pro-war orientation that led the Roosevelt administration to secure a modicum of security for the expansion of unions. A modified union-shop arrangement was established in exchange for considerable concessions from unions.

Throughout the war years, unions relinquished the right to strike, accepting compulsory arbitration of all grievances, and agreed to a wage freeze.[67]

The ubiquitous exhortations for "national unity" in the face of the Axis threat were received as enthusiastically by the labor movement as they were by most sectors of society. Virtually all problems, questions, and directions taken up by the unions were posed in terms of the war effort. Thus President Phillip Murray greeted delegates to the 1944 CIO convention with the following words: "This convention will . . . give prime consideration to . . . programs designed to expedite the winning of the war. . . . If our nation needs our production and our production must be had, it shall be the firm purpose of the members . . . to provide all of the materials essential to the successful conclusion of the war."[68]

During the war, government intervened in labor relations on an unprecedented scale. In 1940 and 1941 the War Department under Henry Stimson expanded its labor subdivision by hiring corporate lawyers to deal with labor-management disputes, by consistently pressuring Roosevelt to support stronger legislation to control labor, and by inciting Congress and the public against strikes. Molding public opinion to view strikes as "unpatriotic" was a relatively simple task in the context of such feverish times, and the AFL joined in by denouncing strikes, particularly those that could be deemed "communist-led."[69]

A steady process of cooptation began as labor leaders took places on the National Defense Mediation Board, and later on the War Labor Board. Although this added new legitimacy to the labor movement in America, it also served as a brake on any labor activity that might have disrupted war production. Stan Weir notes the allure these prestigious appointments held for many labor leaders: "Many of the leaders of labor at that time were still of a generation whose parents (or themselves) had come to America 'below deck' in steerage. To be 'called to Washington' was by itself a tremendous status payoff."[70]

Exulting in their newly acquired acceptance into the ranks of the decision makers and prodded by the severity of the national emergency, the labor leadership undertook to end all strike activity for the duration of the war effort. By the time the War Labor Board was established in December 1941 to facilitate the settlement of "all disputes by peaceful means," a hundred leaders of AFL unions and the AFL's entire Executive Council had already voted to uphold a no-strike policy for its membership.[71] The CIO followed suit, issuing no-strike pledges each year at its conventions. The pledges were also supported by the then-influential Communist Party, which, following the Nazi assault on the Soviet Union, had shifted its line dramatically by adopting a vigorously patriotic stance. The slogan "The Yanks are not coming," aimed at an American society deemed imperialistic, had been quickly scuttled in favor of "Defend America by giving full aid to the Soviet Union, Great Britain, and all nations who fight against Hitler." Harry Bridges, the militant head of the West Coast longshoremen and a well-known communist, went so far as to advise his fellow laborers that "your unions today must become instruments of speedup of the working class of America."[72] Indeed, American industry had become nothing more than a source of war material in the eyes of many. Uninterrupted production would be the working-class contribution to the war effort.

The CIO leadership could morally maintain its no-strike pledge by consistently emphasizing its resolve to maintain the pledge in the face of the pressures of management provocation and the weakness of government agencies. Sacrifices by the workers were held to be particularly honorable in relation to corporate leaders considered "soft" on fascism: "We recognize that the enemies of our war effort would constantly seek to provoke labor into engaging in strikes and that there are employers who, for their own personal profit, would endeavor to take advantage of our war situation and attempt to exploit labor regardless of the impact of their policies upon the war effort."[73]

In other words, the no-strike pledge was sold to the membership as an *expression* of the class struggle, rather than as an abandonment of it. Corporate leaders, although uneasy about the notion of national unity (with their workers), were induced to join in by the staggering profits to be had from huge government war contracts and tax-free war plants. The taxpayers contributed $117 billion in war contracts to the largest one hundred corporations, with profits reaching an all-time high, growing 250 percent above prewar profit levels.[74]

While the bureaucratization of the union leadership increased

steadily as CIO leaders entered into partnership with government and industry, rank-and-file restlessness continued unabated
through the war years. Despite union members' strong support of
the war against fascism, wildcat strikes raged throughout American
industry in direct opposition to labor's no-strike concession.[75]
Although the wildcat strike was not a new phenomenon,[76] it became an increasingly important tactic in the hands of workers
whose leadership was becoming all too willing to subordinate the
workers' interests to the demands of war production and to the
preservation of their new-found friendship with government and
industrial leaders.

The wave of wildcat strikes during the war seemed to "set a new
pattern of industrial unrest," according to Jerome Scott and George
Homans, as 14,000 *officially* recorded strikes involving almost
seven million workers occurred, virtually all of them among workers whose union leadership had taken the no-strike pledge.[77] In
1944 alone, 4,956 wildcat strikes erupted, many of them in Detroit,
which had converted much of the auto industry to the production of
war material.[78]

Most unions never polled their membership on the no-strike
issue. If they had, most would have found the rank and file solidly
behind the war effort. Most workers would have probably endorsed
the no-strike pledge in principle. In practice, however, a very
different picture would have emerged, as it did in the United Auto
Workers, one union that *did* poll its membership. In the UAW poll
(taken in the winter and spring of 1944), 65 percent of those voting
upheld the pledge, while *during the same period* a majority of auto
workers were conducting wildcat strikes.[79] This apparent contradiction between belief and action was actually an accurate response to
a contradictory set of conditions: whereas their leadership stood
firmly united with both industrialists and the government in the
name of patriotism, conditions on the shop floor were anything but
unified. Workers were faced with a hostile management, which
they saw reaping enormous profits, while they were being expected to sacrifice in the form of speedup (through harassment) and
a wage freeze (while the cost of living skyrocketed), without any
guarantee that they would even have a job when the war ended.
(Many expected a postwar reconversion depression.)[80] Under such
conditions, and with their leadership now much closer to manage-

ment than to the shop floor, workers took action that circumvented a hostile bureaucratic apparatus.

As such, most of the strikes, with the exception of the mass strike of Akron rubber workers in 1943 and the strike at six Chrysler plants in 1944, were conducted in opposition to the national and local union leadership.[81] But these were not anti-union battles. Even though the upper leadership of the unions usually fought vigorously against them, in general the most intense struggles took place in plants "where union traditions had their deepest roots." Nelson Lichtenstein emphasizes that although industrial neophytes brought a fresh militancy to war production plants, "a dense shop steward system, a history of local activism and a radical milieu gave organizational and social coherence to the inchoate rebelliousness of workers new and old"; and that "even the numerous departmental 'quickie' stoppages took place under the informal leadership of union-conscious militants, who were unwilling to let the UAW's national commitment to the no-strike pledge stand in the way of what they considered the effective and traditional defense of rank and file interests."[82]

The rank and file knew that relinquishing the right to strike removed any "incentive" the company had to settle grievances, and this, combined with unreliable and time-consuming government arbitration boards, left workers to their own devices to settle problems. As one Buick worker put it:

> When we found that there was no other solution except a wildcat strike, we found ourselves striking not only against the corporation but against practically the government, at least public opinion, and our own union and its pledge. . . . The corporations were showing no sense of patriotism or loyalty and were contributing nothing. All the sacrifices were on the part of the workers.[83]

The wildcat strike movement during the war represented a "practical critique" of "national unity" and the notion that the interests of labor and capital were one. Union officialdom may have subscribed to this view, but many workers did not, and they undermined the attempt (signified by the no-strike pledge) to disarm them. As the war came to a close, the division between the workers on the shop floor and the forces of "labor peace" were outlined sharply as workers unleashed a massive strike wave that must have shaken the hope that the partnerships developed during the war would endure in its aftermath. According to James R. Green, "The dam broke":

> Strikers simply ignored labor leaders who wanted to maintain the wartime no-strike, maintenance-of-membership pact with the government and industry. By the end of 1945, 3.5 million workers had engaged in 4,750 work stoppages, costing employers 38 million workdays. In January, 1946, 174,000 United Electrical Workers and 800,000 Steelworkers joined the 225,000 GM auto workers already on strike, creating the greatest work stoppage in United States history. More was to come. In total, four industries experienced general strikes and a total of 4.6 million people engaged in nearly 5,000 work stoppages, costing employers a staggering 116 million workdays.[84]

But strikes were only the most visible form of working-class struggle during the war and its immediate aftermath. A steady erosion of managerial rights to control the labor process was taking place on the factory floors of America, representing a threat to capital as great as, or greater than, the work stoppages. Rank-and-file activism and militance "commonly elevated the shop steward to co-equal status" with shop-floor management, whose authority was being increasingly challenged and superseded.[85] A study of six major industries found virtually all corporations worried about the erosion of their authority in their plants, with one auto company representative making this succinct point: "If any manager in this industry tells you he has control of his plant he is a damn liar."[86]

Some basic changes had been wrought in labor-management relations during the war years. The most lasting was in the relationship of unions to government and industry. The bitter, adversarial role of unions was tempered in the tripartite governance of U.S. industry, a "partnership" entered into by labor leaders in exchange for a measure of union security and a new social legitimacy. The leadership of labor was made legitimate during the war and by the conclusion of the conflict had become a recognized segment of the nation's power elite. Presidential advisory boards, foreign policy councils, and congressional staffs were opened to "respectable" labor leaders, and legislative lobbying became an important (and sometimes effective) focus of union activity. But although leadership reached new heights of legitimacy, the "spirit of truculent independence"[87] expressed by rank-and-file workers during the war was to trouble American industry well beyond it. Whereas the bureaucratization of labor allowed managements to begin to separate the leadership from the rank and file (as prewar strategies had largely failed to do), control over an often restive workforce became increasingly difficult as a culture of solidarity was maintained below the surface of American industry. Yet this culture of solidarity did not exist underground because of a bureaucratized leadership alone but was confined there by the power of law and the state in the form of the Taft-Hartley Act, a law designed to provide management with a host of measures to ensure the impotence of labor and maintain managerial control of industrial life.

Duly impressed by the process of "de-Taylorization" under way in American industry at the close of the war, employers moved to quash it posthaste. By 1946 corporate America was in a prime position to launch a new offensive against labor. Roosevelt, a potentially untrustworthy ally of industry (and commanding wide popular appeal), was gone, foreign competition had all but been eliminated by the war's devastation, and the heavy debts incurred during the war by foreign governments had created a useful dependency on American bankers and industrialists. Yet two problems remained to be addressed, summarized by Charles E. Wilson, head of the General Electric Corporation, upon his entry into the Truman administration: "Russia abroad, Labor at home."[88] The first was based on the considerable influence and respect enjoyed by the Soviet Union, particularly in southern and eastern Europe after the defeat of Hitler, and the obvious long-term threat this represented to American capital, which was anxious to dominate international markets. The latter problem reflected the general breakdown of shop-floor control, highlighted by the wildcat strikes throughout the war and brought into sharp relief by the massive strike wave and shop-floor chaos that engulfed American industry subsequent to it.

The Cold War barrage of anticommunism was to provide a key to the solution of both problems. Although directed at all segments of society, from military and government functionaries to academics and artists, nowhere was the Cold War more disruptive than in the labor movement under the Taft-Hartley Act. The act represented a direct assault on the traditional expressions of working-class solidarity and action. Passed in June 1947, it was fashioned by a battery of corporate lawyers as a giant step toward repeal of the Wagner Act

of a decade before. According to Congressman Donald O'Toole of
New York: "The bill was written sentence by sentence, paragraph
by paragraph, page by page, by the National Association of Manufacturers."[89]

The act had a broad scope. It weakened union security by outlawing the closed shop and making the union shop and maintenance-
of-membership subject to an NLRB election. States could proceed
to restrict union security even further (the basis for "right-to-work"
legislation). Not only were union security provisions now subject to
a bureaucratic election (rather than to the force of collective
strength), but also union representation would now be determined
by a percentage of votes of the *workforce as a whole* rather than as
a percentage of those voting (hence failure to vote would count
against the unions).[90] Foremen were prevented from joining or
forming unions, halting further erosion of management control
over the shop floor.[91] The use of the strike was limited considerably
by Taft-Hartley, as it outlawed sympathy strikes and secondary
boycotts, both potent and proven weapons of class solidarity. Essentially, unions could no longer help one another in the most benefi-
cial ways. The president of the United States would now have the
power to temporarily halt strikes by imposing a sixty-day "cooling
off" period. In addition, the law greatly strengthened the hand of
employers *during* strikes by stipulating that strikebreakers could
vote in union representation elections, and it held that employers
could bring strikebreakers into a union plant and "decertify" the
existing union through a legally sanctioned petition for an election.
Furthermore, the law opened the way for injunctions against mass
picketing that would later make the running of scabs into a struck
plant a much easier affair. Essentially, the Taft-Hartley Act rendered illegal those forms of solidarity that had previously proven
themselves effective. Manifestations of independent working-class
solidarity would now be deemed illegal in most cases, and severely
constrained in others.

Moreover, the shop steward system, which had generated formidable militance and resistance earlier, was enfeebled by the law,
which encouraged bypassing it in the grievance system.[92] The growing distance between the labor leadership and the rank and file was
codified and institutionalized by the strength of law, as union leaders were to be held liable for not acting as disciplinarians of the

membership.[93] Strikes during the term of a contract were union leaders' legal responsibility, which meant that they were forced to oppose the rank and file in wildcat strikes. Union leaders were now subject to fines and arrest for failing to try to break wildcat strikes. The intent was to give increased control to leaders considered "less radical" than an unrestrained rank and file by strengthening the institutional power of bureaucratic unions.[94] Indeed, writing in the *Harvard Business Review*, Phillip Taft (no relation to Senator Robert Taft of Taft-Hartley) criticized the United Auto Workers of America in 1946 for not having a sufficiently bureaucratic hierarchy "which almost automatically claims the offices as a right." He argued that the existence of a democratic union environment

> sometimes paralyzes decisive action against violations of contractual obligations, since officers fear that stern steps against breaches of discipline or extreme demands may have a harmful effect upon their political future. . . . Instead of judging issues on the basis of their merits, the union officer who fears the wrath of his members is not likely to offer unpopular advice, and he may, in fact, encourage his followers to expect economic improvements the industry cannot afford.[95]

He went on to warn that "employers who clamor for more democratic unions ought to realize what they are likely to get." Essentially, the Taft-Hartley Act offered an implicit, unintended critique of the notion of an "iron law" of trade union oligarchy, as it sought to forge labor peace by outlawing traditionally successful forms of rank-and-file solidarity, while creating a stratum of labor bureaucrats to enforce the bureaucratic regime.

Many labor leaders first responded by urging noncompliance with the law. The CIO Executive Board unanimously pledged to let the Taft-Hartley affidavit "wither on the vine."[96] Mass demonstrations were held in protest, and both the miners under John L. Lewis and the communist-led United Electrical Workers pushed to oppose Taft-Hartley with a general strike.[97] Lewis lashed out with vehemence at Taft-Hartley, calling it "the first ugly, savage thrust of Fascism in America" and "the ugly recrudescence of government by injunction." He summed up the merits of the act for labor in congressional testimony: "There is no virtue in the Taft-Hartley bill. . . . There are 2 or 3 lines in the exordium that say that labor has the right to organize. There are 70 pages of a pamphlet that will follow that dares you to try it."[98]

Yet the opposition to Taft-Hartley never gained the steam required to mobilize effectively against it, and what did emerge dissipated rapidly amid fierce factional struggles within the union movement itself.[99] Factions and blocs within unions found they could rely on the anticommunist provisions of the act to purge radicals who posed a challenge to the union leadership, and communist-led unions were now more vulnerable than ever to raids by other unions trying to increase their membership.[100] Such fratricidal warfare dissolved any possibility of united opposition to Taft-Hartley and had a significant impact on future labor relations as well by placing labor radicalism on the defensive.

The anticommunist provisions of the law represented a formidable assault on the radicalism that had played such an important role in earlier working-class struggles. Although many CIO leaders had pledged not to sign the anticommunist loyalty oaths when they were first enacted, they soon found that failure to sign meant the virtual destruction of their unions, as NLRB protection could be withheld, leaving the union totally vulnerable to corporate anti-union practices. Furthermore, failure to sign prohibited the non-compliant union from appearing on any labor board ballot, ensuring that the union's membership rolls would rapidly wither away to nothing.[101] As it was, employers were using the refusals of some leaders to sign the oath as an excuse to bargain with other, less militant, unions.[102]

These pressures, combined with a willingness to engage in internecine warfare, led many CIO unions to support and embrace the anticommunist provisions in order to raid the "red unions." The breakup of the communist-led United Electrical Workers represented one very revealing case: "By 1953, after five years of raids and the chartering of a rival international, some *eighty* different unions had parceled the UE's jurisdiction and were bargaining for a membership only half the size of the 1948 UE rank and file." Equally ominous were the effects of this sort of cannibalism on the militant shop-floor leadership. As Mike Davis notes, "On one day in Chicago alone . . . three electrical companies fired more than five hundred UE officials and stewards (and were later upheld by the NLRB under provisions of Taft-Hartley)."[103] In all, eleven unions were expelled from the CIO.[104] Taft-Hartley had chartered the long-standing goal of employers to "de-radicalize" the union movement, making it extremely difficult for labor to operate with any significant independence from capital. As Harry Bridges testified:

> The basic principle of the Taft-Hartley law is to protect the so-called rights of the individual, to be an informer, to be a scab, a strike-breaker, an anti-union, internal union wrecker . . . a real job is being done on trade unions, a real job is being done to wreck them from within, to split them and weaken them in any way.[105]

The Taft-Hartley Act and the anticommunist purges associated with it produced setbacks for individual unions and for labor as a whole. The electrical and textile industries were especially hard hit in terms of membership. "Operation Dixie," the CIO's master plan for organizing the South, collapsed, and new organizing attempts in other areas folded as well.[106] All told, 900,000 union members were lost to the CIO as a direct result of the anticommunist purge.[107] Moreover, the general aims of corporate anti-unionism were advanced and given legal sanction, with collaboration by a vast cadre of top labor leaders. By 1950 the possibility of the labor movement as a whole embodying a broad culture of solidarity had narrowed significantly. Industrial class conflict would continue, but on a very different field of battle.

Below the Surface of the Social Contract

Meanwhile, in the academy, sociological analysis in the postwar period was dominated by the "end of ideology" thesis and its variants.[108] Clark Kerr and his associates applied this thesis directly to industrial relations, where they found that "mature industrialization, with its well-developed institutions and web of rules . . . its greater consensus" was "a different phenomenon" from "early industrialization," which had been characterized by violent and frequent class conflict.[109] What had once taken the form of open revolt had given way to a "bureaucratic contest," with precedents, arguments, and statistics representing the new class warfare.

Completely ignoring the fact that Taft-Hartley had signaled a powerful escalation in the battle against labor, social analysts from a wide range of perspectives suddenly discovered a "new consensus" between labor and capital in the midst of postwar prosperity. Barrington Moore viewed the reduction of economic inequality as sufficient to eliminate traditional sources of contrast and discontent; Herbert Marcuse lamented the end of class struggle, resulting from a confluence of interests in the "preservation and improvement of the institutional status quo"; and Robert Blauner found the decline in class consciousness and militancy among industrial workers to be a direct reflection of the "growing consensus between employees and employers."[110]

Missing the conflictual roots of this new "social contract," analysts of the workplace in "post-industrial" society focused on a bureaucratization and routinization held to be characteristic of a "mature" system of collective bargaining. It was generally argued that such routinization had supplanted the industrial conflict of an earlier era, and that theories resting on the importance of class conflict had consequently become outmoded. But because these social scientists generally looked only at the formal representations of industrial behavior, they reported only on a limited sphere of social relations. Although routinization had indeed taken place (more the result of Taft-Hartley than of an inexorable process of bureaucratization), the failure to recognize significant countercurrents to this apparent orderliness yielded an unbalanced and distorted picture. In fact, wildcat strikes (as well as rank-and-file dissident movements) were becoming a significant phenomenon in American industry just as industrial relations and the American labor movement were being routinized in the post–Taft-Hartley collective bargaining climate.

The strike as a form of worker protest went through a significant transfiguration, according to the "end of ideology" prognosis. For Daniel Bell, there had been a "secular decline" in the number of strikes; for Harold Wilensky, the strike had been "blunted" as a weapon; and for Arthur Ross and Paul Hartmann, it had simply "withered away."[111] Actually, analyses of postwar trends in strike activity contradict the view of a quantitative decline in strike rates, and official government data, while showing periodic hills and valleys, show no sustained decline in the number of work stoppages throughout most of the century (see table 2).[112]

But what do the official data on strike rates actually tell us about

TABLE 2.   *Number of Work Stoppages in the United States, 1927–79*

Year	Stoppages (thousands)	Year	Stoppages (thousands)	Year	Stoppages (thousands)
1927	.7	1945	4.8	1963	3.4
1928	.6	1946	5.0	1964	3.7
1929	.9	1947	3.7	1965	4.0
1930	.6	1948	3.4	1966	4.4
1931	.8	1949	3.6	1967	4.5
1932	.8	1950	4.8	1968	5.0
1933	1.7	1951	4.7	1969	5.7
1934	1.9	1952	5.1	1970	5.7
1935	2.0	1953	5.1	1971	5.1
1936	2.2	1954	3.5	1972	5.0
1937	4.8	1955	4.3	1973	5.3
1938	2.8	1956	3.8	1974	6.1
1939	2.6	1957	3.7	1975	5.0
1940	2.5	1958	3.7	1976	5.6
1941	4.3	1959	3.7	1977	5.5
1942	3.0	1960	3.3	1978	4.2
1943	3.8	1961	3.4	1979	4.8
1944	5.0	1962	3.6		

Sources: U.S. Department of Labor, Bureau of Labor Statistics, "Analysis of Work Stoppages, 1974," Bulletin 1902 (1976); and *Handbook of Labor Statistics*, Bulletin 2070 (December 1980), table 167.

industrial conflict? Figures on the number of strikes, their duration, the number of participants, and the "man-days" involved are generally taken as a measure of strike "intensity."[113] However, if we are concerned with the substance of a strike and the development of industrial relations, where the solidarity exhibited in a strike might be an important element, equating the length of a strike with its "intensity" can be quite deceptive. For example, a two-hour wildcat strike that harnesses the solidarity of the workers in a plant and wins their demands immediately can be more "intense" and contribute more to laying the groundwork for future collective action than a hard-fought six-month strike that costs the workers dearly, both materially and spiritually. Because strike rates are not sensitive to the dynamics of human relations, the researcher must be.

Although strikes may not have declined in number, the nature of the strike did indeed change in important ways. The official union-sanctioned strike became more of a "pressure tactic" than a weapon of "class war." Charles Tilly notes that such routinization meant that strikes "settled down to a few standard formats, acquired their own jurisprudence, became objects of official statistics."[114] When we combine the bureaucratization of the strike with the establishment of rule-governed systems for the settlement of grievances on the shop floor (as Kerr and Wilensky noted), then industrial relations seem to have become thoroughly tranquilized. The fact that almost all labor-management contracts contain a no-strike provision, or an agreement that there will be no strikes during the term of the contract, means that company commitments and deliveries can be made on the assumption that production will continue uninterrupted throughout the contract period. As it is generally illegal in most union-management agreements to strike while the agreement is in effect, the periods when a strike might be expected are known well in advance, eliminating the element of surprise and allowing ample time for preparation, finishing important jobs, and stockpiling and shipping manufactured goods. Yet, despite the existence of rule-governed procedures for maintaining a stable and orderly system of collective bargaining, the evidence indicates that the practice was not reflective of the theory in the postwar period, and that although Taft-Hartley may have succeeded in containing many traditional expressions of worker militancy, others simply relocated elsewhere.

Both management and labor sources alike indicate that grievance systems have not provided an effective means of settling disputes during the life of a contract. For example, it was reported that the rebellion in the early 1970s at the Lordstown, Ohio, General Motors plant, which received a good deal of attention, was fueled by the fact that *twenty thousand* grievances had piled up and were waiting to be heard at the time.[115] A similar situation has existed in the steel industry.[116] A book published by the American Management Association indicates the depth of the problem:

> In the past ten years, the number of written grievances has nearly doubled from 138,000 in 1963 to 264,000 in 1972. . . . A high percentage of these grievances are concentrated in a growing group of plants where literally thousands of grievances are written and allowed to pile up with little effort made to resolve them promptly on

their merits. Instead, they are accumulated, a crisis situation is precipitated, and then a demand is made to settle them on a wholesale basis with little or no regard to the facts or merits.[117]

In the mining industry, stalled grievance procedures led to literally hundreds of wildcat strikes each year between 1950 and 1975, because it often proved to be more profitable for management to stall on the settlement of a grievance than to resolve it promptly.[118] Instead of the rule-governance signaling an end to industrial conflict, as many sociologists had supposed, the contract itself has been used to delay, postpone, and nullify resolution of the issues. A contract signifies acceptance of its terms by management and union, but the workers themselves often demonstrate their dissatisfaction with bureaucratization by adopting forms of protest and struggle that circumvent and actually confront these established procedures. The failure of the union leadership to deal aggressively with grievances has been shown to be an important factor in precipitating wildcat strikes.[119] Moreover, because the union leaders are bound to the terms of the agreement they have signed, they often become the disciplinarians of the rank-and-file membership.[120] In response to this routinization, the wildcat strike has played a prominent role in postwar industrial relations, providing an important extra-institutional mechanism for the maintenance and pursuit of workers' rights. Essentially the wildcat strike has represented a critique by action of the postwar social contract, a sporadically employed, but nevertheless clearly stated, opposition by workers to the controlled contract unionism of their leaders and employers.[121]

Despite almost insurmountable problems with the official sources of data, we have some indication that wildcat strikes have taken place frequently and, in some industries, on a regular basis, outside of the established collective bargaining process.[122] A Brookings Institution study in the late 1950s found the number of such strikes to be extensive.[123] The study included a survey of 108 corporations, and although collective bargaining was its specific subject, Garth L. Mangum reports that 62 of the companies listed wildcat strikes as an important management problem.[124] Mangum offers an extensive case study of wildcat strikes and slowdowns at a single steel plant, "Westdale," in his doctoral thesis. In that plant, he found 77 wildcat strikes and slowdowns in a fourteen-year period (1944–58), with 71 of these taking place between 1951 and 1958. Other industries experienced even more wildcat strikes. Mangum found auto companies where over 700 wildcat strikes took place in the three-year period of his study, and he contends that the rubber and electrical industries experienced a similar rate of these strikes. Access to such a detailed case study affords us some insight into the staggering number of wildcat strikes "missed" by official strike statistics. According to the supervisor of labor relations at Westdale, "two stoppages were taking place for every one recorded" in company records.[125] Moreover, at Westdale, there were 17 wildcat strikes that were shorter than a full eight-hour shift, which would thus not have been picked up in the Bureau of Labor Statistics (BLS) data for that period, as only strikes whose duration exceeds an eight-hour shift are recorded.

To my knowledge there have been no comparable quantitative studies of wildcat strikes since the Mangum study, and thus all the estimates of the numbers of such strikes are at best informed guesses. Bureau of Labor Statistics data indicate that roughly one out of every three strikes is a wildcat. But because the BLS data only include strikes of six workers or more that last for a minimum of a full shift, there is a disproportionate undercounting of wildcat strikes, as successful ones frequently last less than a full shift. If the proportions found in the Mangum study are even roughly accurate for the general situation, then the majority of all strikes throughout the postwar period have been wildcats. That is, there have been more illegal, unplanned wildcat strikes than well-planned, routinized, union-approved strikes. Problems of data collection inhere in the character of wildcat strikes because management and labor officials alike are reluctant to divulge concrete information, precisely inasmuch as such strikes fall outside the regular collective bargaining channels these officials subscribe to and attempt to maintain.[126]

Whether or not we have an accurate measure of the number of these strikes in the postwar period, it seems clear that the wildcat strike became prominent as a reaction to the outlawing of traditional forms of collective action and the bureaucratization of trade union practices and institutions. But though the form of the wildcat strike is suggestive of ways social contract unionism has limited the expression of worker solidarity to guerrilla-type actions, analysis of the dynamics of such strikes (see chapter 3) illustrates the possibilities, as well as the limits, of mobilization under a heavily routinized industrial regime. Although the militance and solidarity characteristic of American workers in the 1930s did not die, it certainly was forced underground. As I will argue later, in many ways its manifestation represents an implicit critique of the postwar social contract and the inability of workers to realize their power on the shop floor through it. But it is important first to show how corporations have increasingly been engaged in their own practical critique, inasmuch as their most recent offensive threatens to destroy the very unionism whose character they sought to confine with the Taft-Hartley measures.

Corporate Union-Busting and the "New" Industrial Relations

In November 1981 *Fortune,* a bellwether of corporate thinking, published an article entitled "The Decline of Strikes," celebrating "the new, increasingly militant tactics of management." It detailed the steady decline in official and unofficial strikes since 1976 and observed triumphantly that the percentage of representation elections won by unions was down to 45 percent (from a peak of 94 percent in 1937, and 61 percent in 1966), as well as noting other indices of a weakened labor movement. The article concluded with what can only be interpreted as a trenchant call to arms: "Managers are discovering that strikes can be broken, that the cost of breaking them is often lower than the cost of taking them, and that strike-breaking (assuming it to be legal and nonviolent) doesn't have to be a dirty word. In the long run, this new perception by business could turn out to be big news, not only about labor relations but about the health of the U.S. economy."[127]

In articulating what had increasingly characterized the labor relations climate for a decade or more, the article was declaring publicly that the social contract with American labor was over. The unofficial "truce" that had stabilized collective bargaining (if not all of shop-floor life) through three decades—a period in which union members could expect a steadily rising standard of living in an expanding corporate economy—was now ended. By the late 1970s, though the official spokesmen for the labor movement stubbornly clung to the rhetoric of partnership, much of corporate America was pursuing a strategy that hinged on the crippling of labor as a social force. [128]

Perhaps the most evocative expressions of the climate are found in the attempts to break the official strikes that had represented an apparent routinization of conflict through three postwar decades. As unions are increasingly learning, the object of strikebreaking is not simply to enhance corporate bargaining power at the negotiating table, but to dispense with a bargaining table altogether by creating what has been termed "a union-free environment." [129] The management approach in such strikes inevitably shapes the ways in which workers mobilize to sustain them (see chapter 5), creating conditions of conflict not unlike those in periods before Taft-Hartley.

However, unlike earlier offensives, the current efforts are being accomplished with the aid of a burgeoning billion-dollar industry, consisting of more than a thousand legal and consulting firms that specialize in the destruction of existing unions and the suppression of nascent ones. [130] One survey of eight hundred representation elections found such consultants involved in virtually every union defeat, and union decertifications (formal procedures introduced under the Taft-Hartley Act to eliminate an established union) have increased sixfold since 1968, largely with the help of the consultants. In the 1980s, close to a thousand local unions are being challenged each year by decertification elections, with managements and their consultants successful in 70 percent of all cases. [131]

Moreover, for each successful union-busting campaign, there are many more unions that have preferred to settle contracts quickly on the employers' terms rather than risk the prospect of decertification. "Concession" bargaining was first conducted in the 1970s as a way of restoring profitability to high-wage industries facing foreign competition, and it soon became clear that many more unions would face corporate demands for wage, benefit, and work-rule concessions in other industries eager to take advantage of the "new industrial relations." [132]

This general climate is altering the atmosphere of the workplace, particularly in terms of the legitimacy and standing of the trade union. The "push-button" unionism that represented a corporate trade-off to union leaders in exchange for acceptance of the social contract, and that maintained a fairly steady growth in membership rolls, has given way to an increasingly hazardous terrain for union activity and organization. As the experience of workers who contemplate unionism shows (see chapter 4), fearfulness, which can hover closely about union activity in the most receptive workplace, is deliberately cultivated by management consultants in organizing drives. In more cases than not in the 1980s, the formation of a trade union is treated as a dangerously subversive affair.

Some of the most repressive strategies employed against unions in the prewar era have been renewed in the current period and may prove to be more effective because of their increased level of sophistication. In the 1980s the union proclivities of workers are increasingly monitored in elaborate pre- and post-employment screening and data collection. Employers commonly rely on psychological examinations, polygraph tests, and (in a return to more traditional methods), direct surveillance of the shop floor.[133] In congressional testimony collected in 1980, an agent of a West Coast detective firm was revealed to have been just one of twenty-five operatives employed by a large engineering company in the late 1970s to spy on fellow workers during their break periods, as well as on the job. At the congressional hearings on "Pressures in Today's Workplace," the agent explained some of his activities:

> Anybody we overheard talking pro-union we would write their names down. If their names appeared in more than one agent's report, we would find ways to set them up, get them fired, or subsequently arrested by the Monrovia Police Department. . . . I was instrumental in having forty-six employees terminated that were pro-union and another sixteen, I was in on setting them up and they were subsequently arrested by the Monrovia Police Department, one [of] which was arrested and deported.

Although it is impossible to accurately gauge the scope of anti-union espionage activity, congressional testimony revealed at least ten other workplaces in southern California alone where similar operations were under way, suggesting that it may be extremely widespread.[134]

Such evidence indicates a clear break with the postwar social contract between business and labor, but anti-union employers rely heavily upon the very bureaucratic mechanisms earlier constructed to maintain the social contract. For example, in a study of 130,000 National Labor Relations Board elections between 1962 and 1977, it was found that the union success rate was reduced by 2.5 percent for each month of delay between the time an election was filed for and the actual conducting of the election during the first six months of delay.[135] Not surprisingly, anti-union consultants have taken advantage of this situation. In one anti-union seminar for corporate executives (organized by a consulting firm), the lecturer emphasized the value of delaying tactics in disrupting union campaigns.

> Delay is crucial to your strategy. Delay in setting up a first conference. Dig up issues on appropriate units, supervisors, confidential employees, part-time workers. Don't consent to an election until all issues are resolved. Then delay hearings. Delay briefs with excuses.
>
> Stall and delay wherever possible. When 30 percent of the employees have signed cards the union can file for an election. Can you stack the election? Yes—hire new people. Time is on the side of the employer.[136]

It is during the period of delay that managements can move to exert their coercive powers through threats, promises, surveillance, and the discharge of employees. Perhaps the most frequent and damaging tactic used in the period preceding an election is the discharge of pro-union workers. It has been estimated that as many as fifty thousand union activists are involved in illegal discharge cases each year, with the number of workers indirectly affected multiplied many times over.[137] It seems that NLRB sanctions are so weak that it becomes profitable for employers to violate the law on illegal discharge. As a consultant advised: "Remember, if you commit an unfair labor practice the union could have the election set aside. However, if an election is scheduled and it doesn't look good for the company, pull out all the stops, take the risk."[138]

Although there are important differences in labor's ability to respond, the ferocity of the current employer drive to prevent and eliminate unions recalls the period prior to World War II reviewed earlier, in which espionage and strikebreaking figured as prominent corporate tactics. However, just as worker solidarity was derailed then by the imposition of company unions as well as by repression, today's union-busting proceeds hand-in-hand with similar "participation" schemes. In some cases unions have been broken by corporations in order to lay the groundwork for a more "cooperative" approach later. As one commentator noted in a recent article in the *Harvard Business Review*, "Some companies, as they move from control to commitment, seek to decertify their unions and, at the same time, strengthen their employees' bond to the company."[139] Again, as during the earlier era, managements can pursue repressive strategies as they simultaneously attempt to forge "family factory relations." As Thomas Kochan and Michael Piore point out: "Many companies that experienced significant diversification and growth in the 1960–1980 time period find themselves following a very aggressive and sophisticated strategy of union avoidance both at the corporate level and in new plants while at the same time in older plants negotiating concessions from unions and encouraging the development of labor-management cooperation and worker participation."[140]

Kochan and Piore pose these strategies as if they were contradictory, but it has been argued that many "worker participation" schemes serve the same function company unions did over fifty years ago—to create a semblance of worker power without the ability to realize it. Moreover, there is evidence that the formation of joint worker-manager "Quality of Work Life" programs can serve to pit workers against one another. As one Ford worker and union activist noted:

> Of course, when QWL programs are initiated, they begin by emphasizing that you must be competitive with Japan. As you get more involved you discover that you must also be competitive with Chrysler and General Motors. Finally, you face the worst possible situation. The Dearborn Stamping Plant must be competitive with the Cleveland Stamping Plant or the company will close down the Dearborn operation and transfer the work to the Cleveland plant. Now you have union members being pitted against other union members to decide whose plant gets shut down first.[141]

It is no accident that union leaders in the auto industry and elsewhere, skeptical of "participation" in the past, are warming to the idea more and more, for they preside over unions whose membership ranks have been decimated by massive lay-offs and plant closures. In the context of widespread job insecurity, corporate attempts to forge "a less adversarial relationship" on the shop floor are suddenly treated quite seriously by union leaders whose only alternative is a militance they have spent thirty years avoiding. Unfortunately, such workplace "innovations" do not seem to have stemmed job loss and are likely to further weaken the union movement.[142] Drawing the parallel between prewar company unions and current labor-management cooperation, Sar Levitan and Clifford Johnson argue:

> In many ways, participative management schemes represent the latest reincarnation of traditional attempts to secure the voluntary cooperation of workers and to encourage their identification with profit-maximization goals. . . . Typically labor's priorities are ignored when they conflict with profit-maximization efforts and workers are allowed to participate in corporate decision making only insofar as they do not infringe upon management prerogatives. Contemporary initiatives to motivate workers may be dressed in new packages and delivered with fanfare, but they leave corporate power structures unchanged and give workers no alternative to confrontational methods in protecting and advancing their interests.[143]

Taken together, the obstacles to worker solidarity and militance in the recent period have been formidable. But as I have emphasized, the militant solidarity of the 1930s, expressed in mass strikes and factory occupations, took place in a similarly inhospitable climate. By drawing on their own collective resources, employers mounted paternalistic campaigns to replace class loyalties with "family factory relations." They inculcated values and established facades of "representation" to deflect and channel worker mobilization. In conjunction with, or in place of, a praxis of "social welfare," employers also invoked severely repressive measures to combat solidarity. They eliminated, coopted, and isolated those ideological currents (and their proponents) whose main unifying thread was class solidarity, while employing labor spies and strikebreakers to undermine working-class organization. In the prewar period public opinion was molded and remolded to oppose unionism by an almost constant barrage of anti-union, open-shop propaganda. Yet, despite the massive resources directed against it, labor solidarity was a power that won significant gains for many workers in the 1930s. Industrial unions were built that linked together workers in whole industries, across skill levels and ethnic groupings, into powerful organizations that have had a substantial impact on twentieth-century American social and economic history.

In the recent period, corporations have resurrected strategies and tactics that recall the earlier period of corporate mobilization. The burgeoning industry of anti-union consultants and the hiring of strikebreakers and detective agencies, as well as the establishment of various "cooperative" schemes to undercut worker solidarity, are representative of a return to practices workers once countered in mass collective actions. For contemporary American workers to act in concert, however, they must address not only the demobilizing tactics of their employers but also a whole new set of obstacles constructed since the 1930s. The role of the state in industrial relations is considerably greater than it was before the war. Largely owing to Taft-Hartley, workers today must contend with elaborate mechanisms designed to defuse collective mobilization through the routinization of their grievances, as well as the formation and maintenance of their union security. Traditional (and traditionally successful) forms of mass mobilization and collective action have been outlawed. For forty years ideologies of worker solidarity against capital have been banned and discredited, and their proponents have largely been eliminated or frightened into submission. Workers must also contend with a rigidly hierarchical, bureaucratic union leadership, schooled in the pragmatic ethos of the social contract, for whom independent activity and shop-floor solidarity are an anathema. In the postwar period, collective rank-and-file initiative has often been treated as a threat to a leadership bound to the ordered, bureaucratic machinery of the grievance process and the labor board, as well as to the general goals of American capitalism.

The wall of opposition placed in the path of worker solidarity and collective action is indeed a formidable one, but in part this is testimony to the threat it poses to capital, the state, and labor bureaucrats whose careers depend on maintaining firm obstacles to it. Arguments about the inherently acquiescent, individualistic character of American workers seem facile in the light of the massive structures and resources devoted to controlling collective impulses. Though less evident in recent years, romantic prognostications of general strikes and "revolutionary situations" do not fare very well either. Both sorts of perspectives sustain a preconceived model of class-conscious behavior that bears little relation to the ways in which conflict is actually structured in American industry.

Because the overall system is designed to channel and derail worker solidarity, independent activity and initiative will not likely appear on the surface of that system, nor will it likely appear in recognizable forms. To understand the dynamics of worker mobilization and collective action, it is necessary to peer into the interstices of the routinized collective bargaining system, where, in order to realize their collective power against a wall of opposition, workers are often forced to act independently of that system.

The case studies of collective action that follow represent attempts to understand the capacities of worker solidarity in the sorts of collective actions that frequently develop in this oppositional climate. Although shaped by the industrial relations system from which they arise, the "cultures of solidarity" formed in conflict also embody challenges to it.

How workers act and interact in relation to a union and management that subscribe to that system is examined in chapter 3. The focus will be on the micro-process of worker solidarity and its impact on a work-group of foundry workers, highlighting the extra-institutional dimensions of shop-floor life as well as the organizational dynamics represented by the continuing "gap in expectation between union leaders and the rank and file."[144]

In the second case study (chapter 4), I trace the process of a union organizing campaign by women hospital workers. Here the scope of collective action is wider, enveloping an entire institution in the face of an aggressive anti-union campaign mounted to demobilize worker solidarity in the process of its organization.

The third study (chapter 5) outlines the processes of worker mobilization beyond the workplace in a surrounding community in the midst of a sustained management-provoked strike. It offers a glimpse of worker solidarity developing a broader cultural expression.

The studies concentrate on various experiences of collective action among different groups of workers on different levels and aim to provide the basis for a preliminary assessment of the dynamics, limits, and possibilities of solidarity and collective action among contemporary American workers. Each takes place within the dominant system of industrial social relations I have outlined here, and, though extra-institutional elements figure prominently, their form inevitably springs from the logic of that system.

Part Two

Contemporary Expressions of Consciousness and Action

The Internal Dynamics of
Wildcat Strikes:
Routinization and Its Discontents

In the previous chapter, I indicated in a general sense how the Taft-Hartley Act and the postwar social contract have molded the bureaucratic character of contemporary American unionism, limiting the open expression of militancy and solidarity. In this case study, I will examine the impact of this legacy on grievance resolution in a steel-casting factory, showing how rank-and-file union members sometimes circumvent the bureaucratic channels established to curtail open conflict by engaging in wildcat strikes that represent an implicit break in the social contract. An examination of the anatomy of two wildcat strikes raises significant questions about spontaneity, rationality, and the dynamics of solidarity in collective action. Moreover, the processes of these actions highlight the paradox of the post–Taft-Hartley union leader, forced to oppose rank-and-file initiative while enforcing an often ineffectual bureaucratic unionism.

Built in the early part of the century as a small iron foundry, Taylor Casting Company is located in the highly industrialized region of northern New Jersey. By the mid 1970s Taylor had grown into a medium-sized company engaged in the production of alloy castings especially treated for resistance to industrial wear, corrosion, heat, and abrasion. For more than sixty years Taylor had been a family-owned and -operated firm; the two co-owners of the company were the sons of the founder.

Aside from the New Jersey plant, which manufactured the bulk of the company's products and housed the corporate headquarters, the Taylors had built a smaller, more modern plant in the rural South during the 1960s. The Southern plant was non-union and less labor-intensive, but the New Jersey plant represented the heart of the company's manufacturing operations when this study was undertaken.

Taylor Casting Company had a workforce of more than three hundred employees on two eight-hour shifts at the New Jersey complex. About fifteen were non-union lab technicians who worked in a small laboratory building about a hundred yards from the main plant. The company headquarters were located in a larger office building on a hill overlooking the plant, beyond the factory gates. About twenty-five non-union clerical workers and fifteen to twenty executives and salesmen worked there. The rest of the employees were unionized production workers, who worked throughout the main plant.

Steel castings were manufactured on a job or order basis, with certain contracts calling for hundreds of small castings the size of a softball, others calling for dozens of castings that resembled fire hydrants, and others calling for immense two- or three-ton castings the size of a large automobile, each taking a whole shift or more to complete.

The various processes of production were divided by departments throughout the plant. Preparation of mold patterns and the blending of raw materials took place in departments near the foundry. The main production area was the foundry itself, in which various metals were melted in large furnaces, molds were constructed, and the molten material was poured from huge ladles into the finished molds to cool. After cooling, castings were taken to the finishing department for refinement before being shipped out as pump and machine casings and other industrial parts.

The workforce was fairly heterogeneous in a number of respects. The average age was about forty, with a good deal of variability both across and within departments. In terms of formal job classifications, there were generally an equally distributed number of workers who could be considered "skilled" and "unskilled" in most departments. The ethnic and racial character of the workforce was quite mixed, with the plant fairly evenly divided into black, white, and Hispanic. These categories do little justice, however, to the real cultural diversity at Taylor. "Whites" included Poles, Italians, Irish, Portuguese, and white Southerners; "Hispanics" consisted of Argentinian, Puerto Rican, and Dominican workers; "blacks" included Haitians and Jamaicans as well as native-born Americans from both the South and the North. Certain groups were concentrated more in some departments than in others, but virtually all departments were integrated to some degree. Although such racial and ethnic diversity, combined with status distinctions and age differentiation, could have been a source of wide social distance and discord among workers at Taylor, the actual activities and requirements of work, combined with certain patterns of social interaction, served to minimize these divisions.

Procedures for job bidding were based on departmentwide, rather than plantwide, seniority. In important ways, this benefited the company and watered down the possible benefits of high seniority for workers. With departmental seniority, management did not have to contend with a high degree of mobility across departments or with attendant costs in productivity for training workers unfamiliar with work processes in new departments. For the union, this seniority system often meant that a neophyte might bid into an attractive job in his department before workers with high seniority in other departments could do so. This condition served to strengthen the bonds between workers *within* departments to a considerable degree. The amount of interdepartmental transfer was minimized, so consequently in a given department many of the workers had worked closely together for a longer time than they would have if job bidding across departments had been easier. When the company hired new workers, there was an incentive to orient them to workgroup cultural life, because the odds were that they would probably stay in that department for the duration of their employment at Taylor. Thus departmental cohesion was probably stronger than if plantwide seniority had been in effect.

Status distinctions between "skilled" and "unskilled" workers conceivably might have been a source of tension between workers within departments, but there were countervailing processes and mechanisms that neutralized or minimized this danger. First, although there were certain jobs that required mostly "muscle" (the "bull gang" and the "pouring crew") and others that required advanced skills (pattern maker, molder, skilled maintenance worker), there were also many jobs that demanded a considerable degree of knowledge and skill even though they were not typically considered "skilled trades" (furnace operators, finishing department welders and grinders, inspectors, machine operatives). Second, relative "occupational prestige" in an ideological sense tended to have less status importance for workers than did the actual conditions of work, which were determined as much by one's department and the stage of production one was engaged in as by the actual job title held. For example, while skilled pattern makers and maintenance men (electricians, pipefitters, carpenters) enjoyed relative freedom from constant supervision and a higher pay scale than most, their "unskilled" helpers received benefits that, although not quite as high, were better than the conditions of some skilled workers in other departments. Thus, both pattern makers *and* their unskilled helpers could work at a relatively leisurely pace (owing partly to favorable production quotas and partly to the relative geographic remoteness of their department), and both received the fruits of a favorable bonus arrangement above their base pay. Similarly, skilled maintenance men and their unskilled helpers were free of constant supervision because they worked throughout the plant rather than in one designated area (making supervision difficult). Moreover, the nature of the job was such that they could create almost unlimited overtime, allowing "unskilled" maintenance helpers to take home paychecks that were the envy of more skilled workers elsewhere. In other departments, supervision could be relatively constant, the tempo of production steady, bonuses more difficult to achieve, and overtime virtually impossible, regardless of skill level. Although such departmentally based benefits and liabilities might have promoted interdepartmental jealousies, these were eclipsed by other sources of dissonance, as we will see later on.

The expression of cultural differences among the workers at Taylor was mostly confined to good-natured joking, which provided a medium for diffusing tensions. Often, comedic "arguments" over such matters as the proper way to cook collard greens or the relative merits of "arroz con pollo" and "chicken cacciatore" took place during lunch breaks. But there was a real sharing of culture that frequently went on as well. Informal breaktime "mini lectures" were conducted on topics from "raccoon-hunting in South Carolina and New Jersey" to the "beauty of the Puerto Rican mountains and coastline." After one relatively new worker was discovered bringing homemade Portuguese wine in his thermos bottle for lunch, some kidding took place, laced with jealous undertones: "Hell, if I was caught hittin' on the brew, they'd boot my black ass out of here quick!" And: "I hope you don't think you're gonna drink all that wine by yourself. . . . Let me get a taste!"

After the kidding, however, came a discussion about the role of wine in Portuguese and Italian culture, where, from childhood, people regularly drink wine with meals. Workers usually treated discussion of this sort fairly seriously, and almost everyone in the break room offered at least one observation on the topic. When the whistle blew signaling the end of the break, the gathering almost invariably broke up on a light note, such as this comment by a native of South Carolina: "Well, if that's the way they eat lunch over there, I guess I'm as Italian as these other guys."

Racial and ethnic animosity rarely surfaced in groups of more than two or three workers, but it was not uncommon when working in a small group of white workers to hear racial epithets. Comments such as "The colored have their paycheck spent before it's even cashed!" and "Who are they to complain? I don't make any more than they do, but you don't hear me bitchin' about shit that happened three hundred years ago!" were heard from workers who had worked closely with, been on friendly terms with, and even staunchly defended black workers in the plant. The phenomenon of racial prejudice among workers seemed more complex than can be summed up here; the same workers could express very contradictory feelings at different times and in different settings, and simple characterizations are neither easy nor likely to be fruitful.

What I want to emphasize is the widespread use of humor as a mechanism to minimize the potential for intragroup conflict. Kidding and joking about racial, ethnic, and cultural matters provided a safe outlet for the expression of prejudices and differences. It served to mediate (and punctuate) many of the shop-floor interactions among workers: the frequent banter of sexual innuendo and entendre; the operation of the weekly "football pool"; water fights

in the summer and snowball fights in the winter. Certainly the all-
male character of the workforce provided a wider range of things to
be immediately shared than if it had been a workforce of mixed
gender. Within this context, however, the processes of male bonding represented a general social bonding of the factory workforce,
and thus essentially a class cohesion within the plant.[1] The sharing,
affability, and social intercourse among workers provided a collective means of overcoming the sheer drudgery, boredom, and intense "sameness" of much of the work performed in the factory.

At Taylor, social interaction tended to create an underlying harmony (or at least minimized potential disharmony) among a relatively heterogeneous group of workers. However, harmony seems
to have been maintained by what workers did *not* talk and laugh
about as much as it was by the things they shared. Potentially
divisive social, political, and religious issues were rarely discussed.
When they were, they were either dropped fairly quickly or were
treated to rhetorical one-line clichés that served to neutralize the
controversial impact of the issue: "It's all just politics," "The more
things change, the more they stay the same," and "It's a free country." Workers rarely expressed religious beliefs except for occasional benign references to a group of three Baptists in the department. These workers met during the last fifteen minutes of the
lunch break every day to read the Bible together, and others always
spoke of them with obvious respect. In general, the limits on what
could be discussed were informally, yet consistently, enforced by
the work-group as a mechanism to minimize discord.[2]

The bonus system provided an occasional exception to this general rule. Base wages at Taylor were about half the wages in the
auto industry or the basic steel industry, and the union was a small,
relatively unknown foundry workers union. The bonus system was
largely tied to weekly departmental production quotas in which
workers had to achieve a certain "weight" in order to command a
bonus for that week. Sometimes the bonus system was the cause of
friction between workers and management, either because of disputes over the proper "weight" of castings or the failure of management to weigh castings on Friday (even though they were ready for
shipment), thus withholding Friday's production from the week's
quota. Occasionally, workers expressed jealousy over the relative

ease of "making weight" in some departments. Usually, these workers were in a department where bonuses were either too complicated to figure out consistently or too difficult to achieve. Such jealousies were usually expressed through horseplay and joking of one sort or another.

This was not true of relations between the pattern-making department and other departments. The two primary officials of the union local (president and secretary-treasurer) were skilled pattern makers, and as such received a substantial daily bonus, regardless of output. While other departments (the foundry, for example) also received high bonuses, dissatisfaction with the bonus system in general was often directed at the union officials, because workers felt that they had "taken care of" their department to the exclusion of others. Rumors and innuendoes about the union officials' relationship to management abounded, with comments such as: "Vic sold us to the company at the last contract for a new Cadillac." And: "Where'd Vic get the money to buy all that real estate he owns? Not out of his paycheck, that's for sure!" Such charges were never formally brought or supported, but when made among a group of workers, they were rarely challenged.

Union meetings were held every two months at the Polish-American Hall near the plant. They took place on weekday evenings, which prevented second-shift workers from attending, but they were not well attended by day-shift workers, either. A small group of administration loyalists attended meetings regularly, as did a few other active members, but usually attendance was low, varying with the issues. At times, members who attended registered isolated and particular complaints about aspects of the bonus system, the resolution of specific grievances, certain shop conditions, or the adequacy of union representation. The few criticisms made to the union leadership were largely ineffectual, as the meetings were conducted under tight control of the union president. He would use the union constitution, procedures of order, and the agenda to ward off and quash criticism before it could develop too far and become generalized. The deftness with which he could blunt, channel, and deflect criticism suggests that he had been castigated many times before throughout the ten years or so of his tenure.

The First Wildcat Strike

The first wildcat strike took place in late October 1975.[3] The only previous strikes that anyone remembered were over renegotiation of contracts, the last one having occurred four years earlier. An hour after the day shift started work, word began circulating that the company had fired Richie, a maintenance worker, for sleeping on the job. Because maintenance men worked throughout the plant, Richie was fairly well known as a likable co-worker, but one who occasionally drank more than most; no one doubted that he had indeed fallen asleep on the job. But he was a co-worker who had been at Taylor for six or seven years, and his dismissal caused men in and out of his department to be visibly upset. As workers learned the details of the firing, they began to stir. It turned out that the dismissal stemmed from the testimony of a security guard who had discovered Richie asleep while making his rounds. Because the firing took place without any negotiation or reliance on the formal grievance "step" system, workers felt the union had been undercut, adding fuel to the dissatisfaction over the affair. A group of men from the maintenance department went to the union president to seek remedial action. Within two hours the president, the chief steward, and company representatives had convened in the company office, where they met for almost an hour. When the union officials came through the plant after the meeting, they were asked what had happened. The president replied: "Nothing yet; but we'll take this directly to arbitration if we have to."

The break-room atmosphere was noticeably sullen during lunch in the finishing department, where I worked. Very little mention was made of the fired worker, and there seemed to be a general feeling of resignation. But during the lunch break the maintenance department workers apparently had discussed the possibility of a walkout, for within twenty minutes of the return-to-work whistle, a finishing department welder whose work station was adjacent to the maintenance department was moving from work station to work station, motioning and shouting, "Shut it down . . . maintenance is walking out and we're gonna shut the whole place down!"

Men started moving from their work stations toward the center of the finishing department. But contrary to romanticized images of workers acting in forceful unison, there was definite hesitation on the part of many at this initial stage of the action. A walkout was clearly "illegal" according to the union contract, and the workers faced certain dismissal if they were unsuccessful. Action that would jeopardize one's livelihood was not to be taken lightly and would not occur without a certain amount of careful deliberation and negotiation. I would designate three phases of development of the collective action, generally manifested in the physical movement and positioning of the workers.

The first phase lasted about ten to fifteen minutes and began with the workers in the finishing department positioning them-selves to evaluate the situation. Five or six workers moved swiftly and directly to the mouth of the exit leading to the loading dock and courtyard area, where they were confronted by the departmental foreman (see diagram 1). Another group of about six to nine work-ers, not as tightly knit a body of men and not as vocal, formed a semicircular ring behind the first group. The third group, which consisted of four to five workers, stayed closer to their work stations in separate areas of the department, "hanging back" and individu-ally observing and listening. Some of these apprehensive workers were actually touching their machines, but not working them, as if their proximity to their work stations was a way of staying uncom-mitted, yet observing the work stoppage halfheartedly.

The foreman planted himself firmly near the doorway leading to the exit and ordered the men back to work, repeating himself slowly but emphatically a few times in different ways and asking, "Why are you men not working? The shift isn't over yet." At one point he loudly read off the names of the most prominent strikers (those in the forefront), writing down names as he read them off and charging, "You men are fired for engaging in an illegal work stoppage," and louder still to those in the background, "If you other men don't start working immediately, you'll be fired right along with these men." He was dealing with different groups differently at this point in an effort to dissuade the more hesitant, isolate the more committed, and prevent unity.

The workers seemed to be very conscious of the spatial relation-ships between them, with Group I workers coaxing and motioning Group II workers to pull in closer to them, and Group II workers calling back and occasionally going over to Group III workers try-ing to bring them closer. In effect, workers were negotiating over

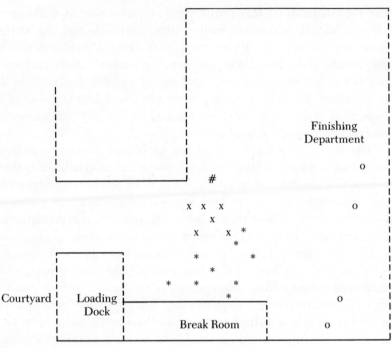

KEY
\# = Foreman (workers' focus)
x = First group (committed)
* = Second group (not fully committed yet)
o = Third group (no commitment to strike yet)

DIAGRAM 1. Phase 1 of Wildcat Strike

the level of commitment to be displayed at this very crucial stage of
mobilization. There was a sense of extreme tension at this point,
because the level of activity and participation was uneven; and
there was a sense (expressed increasingly adamantly by the more
committed workers) that this must be a *group* action to be successful, that as long as workers were at different levels of commitment,
the whole group was vulnerable.[4] This was expressed in two ways
by Group I workers: first, in almost desperate coaxing and pleading
to Group II workers, as well as heated explanations of the issues
involved (which were also going on, although less adamantly, between Group II and Group III workers); and second, by increasingly "standing up to" the foreman verbally. This verbal duel
seemed to have two purposes: (1) to show those who were "hanging

back" that they could challenge the company and that the group was strong enough to express its defiance, and (2) to create an appearance of unanimity by loudly and adamantly addressing the foreman, convincing him that attempts to divide the group were futile. These "keynotes" represented attempts on the part of some to resolve the ambiguity of the situation for others.[5] They were seen both in the defiant statements to the foreman and in the prominent spatial positioning of Group I workers in relation to him (the personification of the company). This posturing played an important role at this stage, because the workers in Group I were (in general) the more active and articulate workers in the department, and their influence and forcefulness would seem to have carried "more weight" than the Group III workers in influencing the direction of the momentum.

The Group III workers were spatially isolated, but it is not clear that they actually opposed the strike. More likely, they agreed in principle with the group sentiment as it became defined yet did not want to "step over the line" until it became reasonably certain that their jobs would be protected by the force of numbers. As a group jells, its vulnerability to company action decreases, as a mass firing of all workers is unlikely.

Phase 2 of the strike began when virtually all the workers in the department had come together, and the group began to move through the exit toward the outside courtyard by the loading platform (see diagram 2). The group moved slowly and deliberately, in an almost amoeba-like fashion, with no one moving too fast (to avoid being isolated and singled out), and no one "hanging back" too far, for the same reason. The foreman attempted to reassert his authority in the alleyway leading to the courtyard, and his tactics reflected the changing character of the group. It was clear that all workers now had at least a surface level of common commitment, and his threats were thus directed toward the group as a whole, whereas earlier threats were made to take advantage of disunity. Loudly, yet calmly, the foreman spoke up:

You men better think twice before going through with this illegal action. I'll have every one of your time cards pulled. . . . Let your union representatives take care of whatever grievances you have. . . . Is this action worth your job to you?

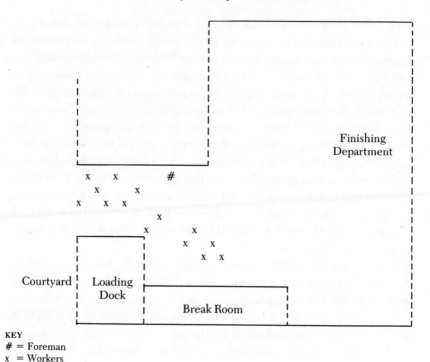

KEY
# = Foreman
x = Workers

DIAGRAM 2. Phase 2 of Wildcat Strike

At this point the atmosphere still remained tense among the workers. They were a relatively small group, and it was hard to see into the courtyard from this vantage point to assess how many other workers from other departments were already in the courtyard area. No one spoke, but their spatial positioning reflected the changed circumstances. The workers were standing much closer together than before and were staring directly at the foreman, many with their arms folded in front of them or their hands on their hips, adopting a more confident stance. This phase lasted only three or four minutes before a new phase began.

There was no sharp demarcation point between phase 2 and phase 3. I observed the transition in only one department—the finishing department—but mobilization in other departments probably went through similar processes of grouping and regroupment, with workers moving toward the courtyard area until what I have termed phase 3 was under way. At this point, workers converging on the courtyard found themselves among a larger group of workers from other departments (see diagram 3), giving rise to a clear change in the mood of the strikers. The tension of the previous twenty minutes or so, caused by a real fear of losing one's job, dissolved into near jubilation as workers enthusiastically greeted co-workers from other departments. The joy was most probably based on the shared understanding that with much of the workforce on strike together, they could defy the company with the strength of numbers as well as with the power derived from a united stance. Their expressions almost resembled those of school children as they rush out the doors of a grade school on a warm spring day, laughing and jostling good-

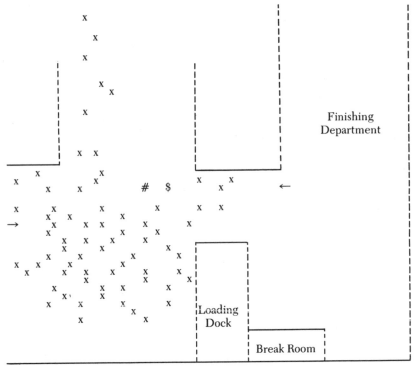

KEY
x   = Workers
= Foreman
$ = Plant manager
→   = Directional flow of workers into courtyard area

DIAGRAM 3. Phase 3 of Wildcat Strike

naturedly. The workers sensed that they were past the difficult part, that there was little doubt now who would have the upper hand.

Again, the company response changed in recognition of the new circumstances. The foreman was joined by the plant manager in the courtyard area; they both had worried-looking expressions and whispered to each other incessantly. Other company personnel walked hurriedly from the company office back and forth through the crowd every few minutes, apparently reporting on the work stoppage and its effects on production, and taking a good deal of heckling from the crowd in the process. After about fifteen or twenty minutes, the foreman (with the plant manager still beside him) finally addressed the large group of strikers: "You men have taken an illegal action. . . . Since you don't appear ready to return to work, you must leave the property immediately." The workers stood their ground, with a few shouting that work would resume when the fired worker was rehired. But for the most part, they stood silently, waiting to see what the company would do next. At that point, the plant manager, who except for the owners represented the highest company authority, stated: "If you men don't leave the plant immediately, we will not hesitate to call the police and have you escorted out." After a moment of nervous shuffling and quick glances by workers to others, a statement came from within the crowd: "Go ahead and call the cops . . . if you think they can move us all out of here." A chorus of voices shouted agreement, and a chant erupted from one section of the crowd, "Call the cops, call the cops, call the cops . . ." There is little doubt that with the collective power that was felt throughout the ranks at this point, many of the workers would indeed have accepted this challenge.

At this stage the workers had defied company authority at its highest levels and a strong sense of solidarity had emerged, growing stronger at each phase of the action. Solidarity among the workers was not an a priori "fact," but grew out of this interactive process of negotiation between workers in their confrontations with authority.

But what about the authority within the ranks of the workers? The union officials were noticeably absent from the scene until about twenty minutes after the confrontation with the plant manager.

When one worker loudly asked, "Where's our union president now?" he was informed that the leaders were meeting with the company officials in the pattern-making department. Shortly thereafter, Vic, the president, emerged from the plant and stood up on the loading dock platform to address the crowd. He began: "First, I want to say that I respect you men for caring so much about one of our own. But this is no way to show your concern." At this point the crowd interrupted him with loud boos and jeers, which continued for about a minute. When they subsided, he went on:

> I know how you're feeling, but the contract, which *we* agreed to, should not be broken, even if the company does so first. The company has told me that they won't negotiate over Richie's firing until you go back to work. But they *will* talk about it when you do. I feel confident that we can win this thing, so if you want Richie to get back, you should go back to work and let your union take care of it. This kind of action can only bring us trouble. If the plant shuts down for good, we'll only have ourselves to blame.

This brought a sustained expression of anger from the men. Jeering and yelling continued for a few minutes; cries of "Sellout!" and "Company man!" were heard from various locations in the crowd. At that point, "Gage," a young black worker whom others considered a radical activist and a "fighter" jumped up on the loading platform.[6] He spoke for about five minutes, detailing a list of company abuses—the unequal incentive system, the problems with departmentwide seniority, the high levels of dust and other safety hazards throughout the plant, the firing that had precipitated the current situation. He tied each abuse to both the company's sole concern for higher productivity and profit and the inaction on the part of the union leadership. He concluded:

> The union's more worried about the company's profits than our working conditions. But remember . . . *we're* the union; black and white united, right here. . . . *This* is the union [motioning over the crowd], and we can't let them forget that!

Loud applause and cheers followed from the ranks. His statement had articulated what appeared to be a common view held by the workers—that "union" in principle is an expression of the rank and file's interests and is best articulated through their collective action, and that the union leadership here was more concerned with "managing" the workers than with pursuing their interests effectively.

A scenario that evolved during the course of the strike provides strong evidence that the workers were very conscious of defending "the union" even as they were conducting a walkout against the wishes of the union leadership. In the early stages of phase 3 of the action, strikers asked a furnace operator why he was "hanging back" near his department. He replied that he had a "heat" in and could not totally abandon his work station, that he would have to keep watch on the gauges and finish the "heat" before fully joining the others. A young and fairly inexperienced worker began to get upset and essentially accused him of breaking the strike. At this point, a few older and more experienced workers explained to him that if a "heat" cooled down before it was ready, it would be ruined and the union would become liable for the loss because it had resulted from an illegal job action (an amount in the tens of thousands of dollars). Such a liability could have virtually destroyed the union's meager resources. These workers, as well as others standing in the vicinity, understood this and agreed that there was no need to sabotage the "heat" in order to win the strike. They would treat this worker as an exception. This concern, both for the production process and for the union, reveals a very conscious and rational definition of the situation. Some had been berated earlier for "hanging back" in the early moments of the strike, but here an exception was made that proved acceptable to the group as a whole. An action that appeared to be "out of hand," as evidenced by the company threat to have the police remove the strikers (probably for fear of possible destruction of property), seems to have been generally "in hand" at all times.

The workers milled around in the courtyard area for about two hours before any new developments took place. The company must have been concerned about the prospects of a picket line keeping out the second-shift workers, for about half an hour before the day shift ended, the union president came out of the foreman's office, where he had been since his earlier address. From the top of the loading platform he announced: "The problem hasn't been solved yet, but I guarantee that if you men go back to work, Richie will have his job back tomorrow." And in response to the anticipated boos and jeers, he quickly continued: "If he's not back in the morning, you can set up a picket line and keep the place closed down. All I ask is that you return to work now and if we're not successful, you can continue your action tomorrow."

This met with some derision at first, but then some questions were raised from the crowd as to the feasibility of successful negotiations. They spent a few minutes discussing the proposal in groups of four and five. A member of the crowd proposed that "we return to work for now, but that we continue the job action tomorrow . . . that we don't punch in in the morning unless we have proof that Richie's been rehired." A vote was taken, which carried by a small majority. Many were skeptical, but most workers felt that the decision to continue the job action would be in the hands of the rank and file the next day and so little would be lost by finishing out the shift. The following morning Richie was waiting at the plant gates as workers gathered before punching in. Apparently he had been called by the company and told to report back for work.

Break-room discussion centered on the wildcat strike throughout the next week or so. Tales of bravado abounded, with each worker trying to outdo the other about how he had "stood up" to the company and won. Despite the fact that the union president had actually negotiated the rehiring, it was almost unanimously held that Richie would never have been rehired had it not been for the walkout. Workers felt that without militant collective action, the negotiations either would never have been held or, if held, would have been ineffectual.

Although management might have viewed the wildcat strike at Taylor as an irrational outburst, it actually had an orderly, deliberate, and "rational" character. As the action developed, unity and solidarity were created in the process of interaction with the company and among participants. Workers, divided by their level of commitment and participation in the early stages of the action, coalesced into a unified group when circumstances appeared to favor success. Those who were more committed needed to raise the level of commitment of the others in order to protect themselves from isolation and company reprisal, as well as to ensure victory. They did so by actively encouraging solidarity among the group and creating the appearance of a formidable force in response to company threats. This "keynoting" minimized the different degrees of participation by the workers, demonstrating that they not only *could* resist company power but *were* resisting it. It also served to communicate to management that efforts to demoralize the workers and dissipate their mood were futile.

The solidarity the strike achieved and expressed was not inherent in the workforce, as some might romantically contend, but was to a significant degree a product of the collective action itself. But although solidarity was not an a priori "fact," neither was it without a social basis. For the conditions of work and the day-to-day social interaction they shaped created at least a surface level of mutuality, a foundation of trust among the workers.

The wildcat strike brought into sharp focus the day-to-day relationship between rank-and-file workers and the union leadership. The workers refused to heed the return-to-work request voiced by the union president and generally considered him a "company man," a "sellout," and a bureaucrat for attempting to control the workers' anger and for trying to keep the dispute within the prescribed collective bargaining channels. Although the union leadership was criticized, the workers did not display an overall anti-union sentiment. To the contrary, they protected the union from a possible lawsuit by not sabotaging or allowing others to sabotage a key part of the production process, and they generally attempted to enforce their definition of "union" in opposition to that of the union leadership. In effect, during the course of this strike, they defined "union " beyond the formal organizational context in which it operated on a day-to-day basis. Because they had little faith that leadership could, or would, win reinstatement of the fired worker using routine channels, they created a new medium for the redress of grievances, one that was not limited by contractual constraints, with their contrasting interpretations. They circumvented—indeed, for an instant, they broke—the "social contract" established between labor and capital in American industry by their violation of codified order and formal authority. They did not create a wholly new authority per se, but enforced an authority based on their perception of how a union should fight for its members, as opposed to how their leadership would pursue the issue.

We should not underestimate the risks of relying on solidarity rather than on established collective bargaining arrangements. All the workers knew that a wildcat strike was a very serious offense. If the strike had been unsuccessful (i.e., if only some workers in one department had participated), the company would have fired most, if not all, of the participants, and the union would not have been able (nor would the union president have been inclined) to protect the jobs of the wildcatters. In an industrial setting, discharge is the equivalent of "capital punishment."

The wildcat strike was an extraordinary example of collective action and solidarity as it was unfolding, but day-to-day life in the plant soon returned to normal. Relations between the rank-and-file workers and the union leadership were not noticeably different, nor were relations between workers and management.[7] Moreover, beyond the heightened bravado and boasting in the week following the action, one would not have been able to discern a "higher level" of ideological class consciousness among the workers after the action than before it. For the next few months, shop-floor life continued as usual. Although on a day-to-day basis the residue of the strike appeared to have been negligible, analysis of the next wildcat strike suggests something else.

The January Wildcat Strike

Taylor Casting Company's New Jersey plant was an old one, a fact increasingly evident in the finishing department as the winter cold intensified. The department was extremely drafty, because the large doors of two of the entrances were left open much of the time to facilitate the frequent movement of steel to the outdoor "heat-treatment" furnaces at one end of the department and through to the shipping department in another section. The doors were heavy, garage-type doors, which took some effort to open and close, and most workers in the finishing department wore insulated vests and jackets over their work uniforms and insulated underwear beneath to withstand the chill in the plant during the winter months, rather than having to open and shut the doors completely.

Although the workers chose to acclimate themselves to the cold of the workroom area, the extreme chill of the break room was a constant and increasing focus of grumbling and complaining as winter approached. The break room was divided into three sections: a small dining area with two heavy picnic tables and benches around the outer walls; a locker room where workers stored their belongings and changed their clothes; and a washing and toilet area. The three sections of the break room were divided by walls with doorless entranceways. A rickety door that would not close all the way was all that separated the dining area from the outside, letting a constant draft of cold air sweep through the length of the break room. The only heat came from an ancient radiator, whose force was barely enough to warm the dining area, but not the other sections of the break room.

The men complained frequently about the cold in the morning as they changed into their work clothes, and less frequently after work, when there was more of an upbeat (and hurried) atmosphere. The grumblings were often lighthearted, but sometimes expressed a good deal of anger toward the company: "You work your ass off for this company and they treat you like you was nothin'." And: "I'd like to see that sonofabitch Taylor gettin' dressed in this ice box just one time." One January morning, when one worker suggested filing a grievance over the lack of heat in the break room, another worker bellowed from across the room: "Man, you know how many grievances we put in on this? They don't give a shit. . . . They don't wanna put out to take care of this place." The finishing department shop steward (a mild, amiable man in his mid fifties) would presumably have been the one to file such a grievance, but he simply nodded his head in agreement, never offering further explanation (nor was he asked for it).

In the days after this particular interchange took place, talk of a strike over the heat issue arose more than once. The initial references to a strike were made by two different workers and were general statements of speculation made in the locker room to no one in particular. At first, such statements elicited light, one-line comments in agreement, but did not seem to be treated very seriously, at least not openly. But over a period of two days, the matter *was* treated seriously by at least four finishing department workers (of which I was one), who raised it among themselves on three separate occasions: twice during breaks, and once in a discussion during working hours (meetings during work were difficult because, although two of the men worked closely together, the other two worked on opposite sides of the department).

Each of the four had been enthusiastic about the first wildcat strike three months earlier, and three of the group had been among the first to commit themselves to it (as part of Group I). I had not been in the forefront of the action but had joined in with zeal once it was under way and had engaged in much of the post-strike recapitulation. As such, all of us were at least potential supporters of similar action and provided one another with a forum for serious consideration of militant activity. The discussions were fleeting ones, but they centered on developing justifications for taking such drastic action. A main point raised was that the company's unresponsiveness to the lack of heat in the break room signified a lack of respect for the health and well-being of the workers more generally; hence, a moral stake should be claimed. Another point raised was that the union president had enough heat where he dressed, and thus he would never present the grievance in an aggressive way; if we were ever to rectify the problem, it would have to be done through militant action. Whether or not this was an accurate assessment of how the union leadership would respond (or fail to respond), together we believed strongly that there was justification enough for strike action.

When and how a strike might begin was never discussed, but as soon as the usual comment about the coldness of the break room was heard after one of these discussions had taken place, one of the group stated forcefully: "Enough of this shit—we gotta take care of ourselves—if there's no heat tomorrow we just don't work—that's it." There was some verbal agreement, some just nodded, others just stood and listened. The same worker asked if everyone would stick together and go through with it. Some committed themselves openly to a strike, but most said nothing. At that point, the four of us who had already been considering the issue began trying to convince the rest to make a commitment for the next day. It was clear that everyone felt strongly about the daily discomfort of undressing in such conditions, but a general consensus of support was reached only after someone suggested that the foreman be clearly notified of the workers' intention to take matters into their own hands if there was no heat the next day. Some seemed to feel that if they struck after clearly warning the company, they were absolved of guilt, and that it was the responsibility of the company to have provided heat all along. That afternoon as workers dressed, two of the activists announced that they had just informed the foreman of their intention to refuse to dress the next day unless there was adequate heat in the break room. Before everyone left for the day, one of the activists took an informal poll to make sure everyone was committed, and it appeared that most were in favor. It would be hard to imagine anyone subjecting himself to the certain peer pressure and even ostracism that would have resulted from having openly opposed the action, but in any case, there was a "public" commitment from most to join in.

As 7:00 A.M. approached, workers gathered in the locker room as usual, but with about half of the department's workforce dressed in their street clothes. The shop steward did not report for work that day, probably because as a union official (however minor) he would be held responsible for getting the men in the department to honor the contract that forbade such action. He had agreed in principle the day before with the sentiment for collective action, and it is likely that he did not want to be placed "in the middle" of a potentially explosive affair. Three or four of the men were fully dressed in their work clothes, appearing ready to go to work, and others just stood around half-dressed. The four activists were busy trying to persuade them to keep their street clothes on. Just as they had been coaxed to display their commitment to the first wildcat strike by their spatial positioning, here the act of not changing into work uniforms seemed to represent a similar visible symbol or display of commitment. We were successful in convincing all but a handful to "show their colors" in this way.

When the whistle blew, workers congregated outside the break room on the work floor waiting for the expected confrontation. One welder immediately walked to his work station, apparently intent on working. He was a veteran worker who was very well respected in the department, and others were surprised that he was not standing with the rest. Activists quickly recognized that because of his stature in the department his abstention might easily exert a negative influence on anyone hesitant about continuing the work stoppage. One of the militants immediately approached him and in an incredulous tone said, "Jesse, you know you've got to stand with us on this . . . everyone walks together . . ." Before the plea was completed, Jesse had dropped his tools and was walking back toward the others (and mumbling the whole way).

Within moments of the work whistle, "Smitty" (the foreman) stormed up to the group and, feigning ignorance, demanded to know what was going on. After a brief but animated exchange over the heat problem in the break room, Smitty announced: "You have a union to take care of these kinds of problems. Whatever your beef, you're here to put in a day's work." He continued on in a clear, mechanical tone of voice: "You are now engaged in an illegal work stoppage. . . . You can either begin working or turn around and head for the gate, but you cannot congregate here like this." As workers shouted at him that the company was at fault, and that they would dress and begin working only with heat, the foreman began reading off the names of some of the more adamant strikers and acting as if he heard nothing.

The participation of finishing department workers was not as divided as it had been in the early stages of the first wildcat strike. While some were more verbally animated than others, most just stood together in a loose grouping outside the break room. Although the threat of discharge was real, Smitty's tone did not seem as threatening as it had in the earlier action, and it seemed as though his statements were meant to get his "official" position "on record." It was as if he had to go through certain motions and was required to say certain things, but it also seemed that his real concern was to get things resolved somehow before the trouble spread to other departments.[8]

One of the four activists suggested that Vic be informed, and within a few minutes the chief steward appeared and announced that Vic had asked him to "see what's going on up here." The chief steward was a large, heavy black man in his forties with a deep, gravelly voice. He did not work in the pattern-making department, and he was not white; consequently, he was not often viewed as being a part of the same circle of union leadership as the president, vice president, and secretary-treasurer.

He spoke with the workers for a few minutes, gathering as many details as he could before approaching the foreman. He openly took the workers' side in the dispute, arguing that the main issue was the heat in the break room and not an "illegal" strike. After a few minutes of angry discussion with the foreman, they both departed toward the foreman's office. This was not interpreted by all workers as a positive sign. Some expressed their unease over what the steward was "up to," and whether a "deal" might be worked out that might undercut the initiative of the workers. Some suggested that the steward's open support for the workers might be no more than playacting and that a sellout might be in the works. Others disagreed with this interpretation, citing the chief steward's general reputation as a responsible and basically honest man, but for some an uneasiness and tension had suddenly been created.

Although it was clear that the steward was obligated to negotiate the demand for heat, there were questions about what the results of such negotiations might be. Because the job action involved the workers in only one department, there was a possibility that isolation would make them vulnerable to punishment.

Some of the workers who had played a role in mobilizing the strike (and who had been singled out by the foreman) talked openly of spreading it to other departments, or at least preparing to do so. One of them walked over to the other end of the finishing department to explain the situation to a group of foundry workers standing at the entrance to the department and watching from a distance. When he returned, he announced that they seemed confident that they could mobilize the foundry if necessary, and this was greeted with some relief by the strikers. Within minutes workers had broken up an old workbench, gathered some scrap wood, and started a small fire in the center of the department. Most everyone stood around it, joking about how cold it was and about how they could create their own heat if the company would not supply it. Even when the foreman emerged a little while later, they kept the fire (and the humor) going. After initially ordering the men to douse the fire, the foreman seemed to ignore it. Although he refused to discuss the heat issue or explain what had transpired with the chief steward (who was nowhere to be seen), he seemed surprisingly tolerant, almost conciliatory.

The company responded to the work stoppage in a curious way. It had not yet produced a higher company authority to intimidate the strikers, as it had during the first wildcat strike; and though the constant threat of discharge was implicit in the overall dynamic of the situation, the foreman resorted to the threat only sparingly and without a great deal of emphasis. As noted earlier, it appeared that the company was primarily concerned with containing the walkout within the finishing department and did not want to provoke a wider strike by hasty repressive actions. Thus although the wildcatters (and particularly the leaders) viewed their isolation as a weakness that had to be overcome, it may actually have served to strengthen their hand by acting as an implicit threat that a wider, more destructive strike was possible.

This threat was given further substance when, after an hour or so, a worker from the maintenance department joined the group of wildcatters as the foreman looked on. A few gathered around him to report what was happening, and a few reminded him in no uncertain terms that solidarity from the maintenance department was expected, indeed demanded. He did not need a reminder that the finishing department had acted in solidarity when the maintenance worker was fired three months earlier, and he made it very clear that support would be forthcoming "from our guys" if necessary. Although the foreman was too far away to overhear the message, it was clear from the heightened enthusiasm of the strikers that sufficient solidarity could be garnered at that point.

In a short while the chief steward returned and summoned the workers to join him in the break room. Everyone filed in with some concern until he stated that the company had agreed to provide heat shortly. He then suggested that everyone get to work and that all would be taken care of. Virtually everyone balked at this suggestion, preferring to wait until the company's actions could be verified.

Most of the finishing department workers stayed in the break room after putting on their work clothes, waiting the half hour until the foreman and two delivery men brought in and assembled a huge, bazooka-like space heater. The workers were clearly pleased with themselves and nudged and joked with one another as the heater was installed. Once it was turned on, providing a blast of warm air, the workers cheerfully filtered out of the break room to begin work for the day.

Some important patterns and differences between the two wildcat strikes are immediately apparent. In both instances, solidarity was not "automatic," but had to be created through a process of interaction among the participants and in relation to the company. In the first action, statements of defiance and prominent spatial positioning in relation to the foreman served to create an appearance of solidarity that quickly became an actual manifestation of it. These keynotes communicated the possibilities of solidarity to workers at different stages of commitment, as well as communicating collective solidarity to company authority. The dynamic shifted as workers came together and as company tactics changed in the light of emergent (and expanded) expressions of solidarity.

During the January strike, certain actions served a similar purpose. Getting workers to commit themselves the day before to the action, mobilizing people *not* to don work clothes, burning wood on the shop floor, and getting tentative displays of solidarity from the foundry and maintenance workers were all symbolic gestures designed to *communicate and create* solidarity to potential participants and company authorities.

But the two strikes were not just distinct "moments" of solidarity with similar patterns of development. The character of the second action was partly a function of the process manifested in the first. It appeared as though the union officials and the company were acting more cautiously in response to the second strike because of the success of the first. The strikers had already demonstrated that a strike could spread rapidly and broadly. The union president (who by virtue of the seriousness of the dispute would have been the union official most likely to intercede) sent a lesser official, who was better able to keep things calm and contained. Similarly, the foreman was the only company official on the scene, and he acted with a noticeable degree of calm. Essentially, it seems that solidarity and successful collective action in the later strike were made easier by what the men had learned from the success (and drama) of the first.

Perhaps a more important link between the two actions was that an incipient group of activists who emerged out of (and were "tested" in) the first strike provided an important, though informal, "leadership" network during the second. Four workers who had either played a strong role in the first strike, or had at least made it clear that they enthusiastically supported it, gravitated toward one another when an issue arose to which another strike seemed an appropriate response. Two of them worked closely together on a daily basis (as inspectors), but the other two (a welder and a heat-treatment furnace operator) worked at opposite ends of the department and had previously had little contact with each other, or with the two inspectors, outside of normal social interaction. Race and ethnicity were not binding elements; two of the workers were black, one white, and the other Hispanic. It is likely, however, that as a result of the first strike workers learned who could be counted on to support future strike action and who the potential activists were. This knowledge only became useful months later, when circumstances arose that seemed to favor such activism and an informal network came together to share ideas about the feasibility of another strike.

The Attempt to Consolidate

For the next month or more, the presence of the heater in the break room provided a concrete symbol of resistance to the company and the union bureaucracy. Reference was frequently made to the warmth in the break room and how such comfort had been achieved. To some degree the finishing department had come to see itself, and to be seen by others, as a locus of activism in the plant. The few other militants from other departments began to pay break-time visits to the finishing department, and although the character of group discussions was not dramatically different from before the strikes, militant talk about union affairs was more frequent and more extensive.

The union elections scheduled for April provided a rich source for these discussions. At first there was a good deal of humorous speculation about different people running for union office, with jibes about what some people would do as union president, and so on. But as March approached, the issue was being treated more and more seriously, and discussion frequently centered on the prospect of a challenge to the union leadership.

No one could cite recent electoral challenges to Vic or the other top officers, although there had been a contest when Vic ran for office a decade or so earlier. His opponent, Al, a militant foundry worker, was still working at Taylor, but when someone suggested asking him to run again, he was warned that Al might be too heavy a drinker to handle it and that this made him a pretty unreliable candidate. Jackson, the finishing department welder who had helped lead the January wildcat strike, was strongly encouraged to run by many in the department, but although he seemed very flattered every time this was mentioned, he declined repeatedly. He was viewed as an ideal candidate, as his eight years' seniority

had afforded him an opportunity to get to know workers throughout the plant, and he was well respected for a combination of
militance, seriousness, and good sense. About three weeks before
the union meeting where nominations were to be made, Jackson
(after declining once again) pointedly asked Gage why he didn't
run instead. When others agreed, Gage said he would run against
Vic for the presidency of the union local.

Gage had only worked at Taylor for a year and a half, but much of
this time he had had a job as a forklift driver, which allowed him to
get around the plant and meet a lot of workers. The company had
recently transferred him to the shipping department, and he was
convinced that this was because of his actions during the October
wildcat strike and his reputation as a radical. He believed that
management did not want him in a job that allowed him such
mobility throughout the plant (and the potential for agitation).

Although Gage's political views were probably much farther to
the left than anyone else's, his radicalism does not seem to have been
a major issue for others. Outside of union and plant issues, political
questions were rarely addressed explicitly by Gage, or by anyone
else for that matter. He occasionally would use terms such as "class
struggle" or "ruling class," but these did not represent recognizable
"cues" to most workers. The only clear indication of his radical viewpoint was his outspoken advocacy of militant action. Given the recent history of labor relations at Taylor, this would hardly have been
cause for concern among most of his co-workers. Moreover, Gage
had grown up and lived in the black community of a neighboring
city. Other black workers at Taylor knew him from the neighborhood or had other indirect connections with him through relatives,
friends, and acquaintances. Furthermore, Gage and some other
workers frequently shared rides to and from work. His controversial
political views would appear to have been a relatively minor dimension of a wider pattern of interrelationships.

When word spread throughout the plant that Gage was going to
challenge Vic in the upcoming election, responses varied. Some
responded by suggesting that no matter who was union president,
little would ever change. Other comments noted Gage's lack of
experience in union office, relative to Vic. One older white worker
was most adamant about this. While conceding that Vic's lack of
militance and inability to have grievances resolved promptly were

cause for concern, he asserted: "No matter what, you have to have an experienced man negotiating your contract or they'll chew you up and spit you out in a hundred pieces." In order to leave no misunderstanding of his true position, he emphasized that his point of view was not based on racial prejudice, but rather on his strong feeling that Vic's experience at the bargaining table made him a preferable candidate. But more than a few workers at Taylor were clearly glad that someone was finally challenging the leadership, and in the finishing department at least, the break room buzzed with anticipation and with what appeared to be a certain amount of enthusiasm over the prospects.

In the two weeks before the union meeting where nominations were to be made, a series of minor, but unusual, things happened, indicating that a countermobilization might be under way. One of the group of four finishing department activists was working overtime one evening when the second-shift foreman confronted him by asking whether "rumors" about Gage being a communist were true or not, and whether the worker realized that he was supporting a communist for union president. The "accusation" was made only half seriously, but it was unusual enough for the worker to bring it up the next day among other workers. It was viewed generally as an indication that the company was worried about Gage becoming president of the union and as such was considered a positive sign. There was no evidence that the foreman was expressing anything other than his own anxieties, but workers nevertheless viewed it as evidence of "company sentiment."

When an anticommunist news clipping appeared on the company bulletin board (outside the finishing department) a day or two later, it seemed as though there was indeed some sort of campaign afoot.[9] Because the bulletin board was used for company announcements and policy notices, and because nothing of that nature had ever been posted before, many wondered who had posted it and what it actually meant. No one knew whether the company or union officials (or rank-and-file workers) had put it up, and although no one seemed unduly upset about it, inevitably speculation about the clipping led to the issue of Gage's radical politics. Support for him did not appear to diminish dramatically, but his radicalism was being considered (for the first time) outside the context of union politics and shop issues. By virtue of the justification and rationalization that took place in opposition to the clipping (and the act of posting it), it appeared as though the climate had begun to shift from one of enthusiasm to one tinged by a slight sense of defensiveness.

Gage, Al, and the four finishing department activists in particular sensed that "something was up," and that feelings of enthusiasm had been dampened somewhat by what they suspected were company (or union) initiatives. When (a week before the union meeting was to take place) Gage entered the locker room as workers dressed to go home and announced that he had just been handed a lay-off notice, it was immediately clear to everyone that the company was blatantly interfering in the union's affairs by punishing him for his challenge to the union leadership. Even though Gage had more seniority than others in the plant, he had the least seniority of all the shipping department workers and hence had no recourse through official channels. An angry discussion ensued, and it was widely felt that he had been transferred to shipping so that he would be vulnerable to just such a move. As the gathering broke up, Jackson and the others noted that this would probably backfire on the company; that once the campaign for union office was under way, it would be shown that the company was in league with the incumbent union president; and that the company would be forced to bring Gage back from lay-off as the newly elected union president.

The union meeting was scheduled for 7:00 P.M. on a Thursday evening. That afternoon six of the plant activists met together at a nearby tavern. Gage, who was now unemployed, was there, as were the four finishing department activists (Jackson, George, Horace, and I), and Al from the foundry. It was the first time we had all met as a group outside of work. Over a tableful of drinks (both alcoholic and nonalcoholic), we discussed strategy for the impending meeting.[10] Much of the talk was about the apparent collaboration between the union leaders and the company, and why this represented concrete evidence of the justness of our cause. We joked about how we were being viewed by the union president and management as "a bunch of communists" meeting secretly to "take over the government," and although this was treated as a humorous caricature, we also recalled what a stir had been created by the two previous wildcat strikes. We sat together discussing what had gone on, the strength of the bonds that had been forged between us, and the militancy of the other workers. Gage emphasized the potential for this kind of movement by noting how the "Miners for Democracy" had overthrown the national leadership of the United Mine Workers Union. This example interested everyone, with one worker openly speculating whether such a movement was possible in the foundry workers union. Although this was not treated very seriously, for the first time we were referring to ourselves as an organized entity of some sort.

By the time the impending union meeting came up for discussion, everyone was hungry, and two or three had drunk just enough to somewhat impair their ability to focus on one topic at a time. Before breaking up, leaving enough time so that everyone would be able to eat something before the meeting, we decided that the group would present nominations for vice president and secretary-treasurer, in addition to the presidency. We felt that the election of officers would provide Gage with the support of co-officials when he became president. (It was simply assumed that Gage would win the election with little difficulty.) The group would nominate Al for vice president of the local (in order to ensure strong support from the foundry), and I would be nominated for secretary-treasurer so that it would not be an all-black set of candidates running against white incumbents (hence creating a possible racial affair).

Approximately thirty to forty workers gathered at the union meeting that night: Considering that it was held while the second shift was at work, this was a relatively large turnout for the local. After some minor business was attended to, Vic announced that nominations were open for elected positions. Jackson immediately nominated Gage for president, but Vic shook his head as if to refuse the nomination. He calmly began reading from the union constitution a rule that all candidates for elected office had to be current dues-paying members of the union *and* be employed by a company under agreement with the union. An angry dispute erupted, which at times threatened to break into violence. The group of activists and the others who supported Gage were unprepared for the types of arguments that arose (about the status of a worker who is laid off, but whose union dues are paid up, and so on). After about twenty minutes of heated debate, Vic disposed of the issue by calling for further nominations. When none were offered, he closed nominations by loudly rapping his gavel on the table.

After the announcing that "Eddie D.," the vice president, would be retiring from the company in the coming months, Vic asked for nominations to fill his post. When Al was nominated to run unopposed, Vic did not seem at all displeased, and even said something to the effect of "Welcome aboard." But he quickly moved on to the secretary-treasurer position and, noting that the current office holder would run again, asked for other nominations. When none came right away, he raised his gavel and, in a moment, closed nominations just before someone shouted out my name. Vic went on with the meeting as Jackson protested that he had been entirely too quick to close the nominations, but to no avail. Vic said that there was nothing he could do about it, that once nominations were "officially" ended, he had to enforce closure. The meeting ended with strong dissatisfaction being voiced by the activists as well as others (including at least two administration loyalists). But there was not a very forceful reaction by most workers to the actions of the union president. After the meeting, workers filtered downstairs to the bar to drink along with the union officials, and though there was a certain amount of grumbling by some, there was not the sort of militant reaction that Taylor workers had shown in the wildcat strikes.

The uncontested election did little to change the situation at Taylor in the following months. Because the vice president had little power, except to run meetings in the absence of the president, Al's ascendence to the union hierarchy had little impact on factory life or union politics. Gage was never returned from lay-off and was reportedly hired at an auto plant not far away, and another activist took a job at a paper mill. Although the finishing department remained a center of opposition in the plant, the forces of opposition were somewhat weaker.

Rumors that the plant would close had circulated periodically, but had become more frequent in recent years, and about a year after the first wildcat strike, the company announced that it would end production at the New Jersey plant (reportedly giving one week's notice). They told the workers that the New Jersey plant was no longer profitable and that all production would be moved to the company's other steel-casting plant in the South. Apparently some of the skilled workers were offered jobs in the Southern (non-union) plant to meet expanded production needs there, but there is no indication whether any of them accepted the company's offer and relocated. Rumor had it that Vic, the ex-president of the union local at Taylor, was promoted to the national staff of the foundry workers union when the plant closed down.

Discussion

For some, the case study I have described will seem an unlikely source of data for an analysis of class consciousness. I have not done a survey of the workforce at Taylor Casting Company; in fact, my concern has been primarily with the activities of workers in one department. I have not focused on issues of class identification, occupational prestige, images of society, voting patterns, attitudes, or any of the other typical indices used in studies of class consciousness. Furthermore, I cannot offer a final determination on whether these workers were or were not "class conscious" as this notion is generally understood. In any case, as pointed out in a previous chapter, an unreasonably narrow theoretical framework has been imposed on our conceptualization of class consciousness and the ways in which we usually go about studying it.

I wish to avoid treating class consciousness as a static ideational "attribute" or "possession," subject to a simple verification, and rather to approach it as an active cultural "process" that is complex, shifting, and problematic. This requires an investigation of the interconnections and relations between actions, thoughts, and feelings; an approach closer to the cultural analysis of Clifford Geertz than to the more classic sociology of Richard Centers.[11] I thus employ the concept of "cultures of solidarity" in order to move beyond literal notions of consciousness, so that we may be better able to consider a range of events, behaviors, and processes.

The method of data collection employed in this case study afforded me an opportunity and a framework for observing a complex web of phenomena whose interconnections demand as much interpretive attention as any single strand or element. This method of analysis is informed by the insightful work of Raymond Williams, who suggests that the "fundamental principle" and "basic task" of a sociology of culture is to render intelligible the "complex unity of elements" and the "interrelationships within this complex unity."[12]

Among the workers at Taylor Casting Company, a praxis of solidarity emerged in opposition to prevailing patterns of industrial relations and expressed itself in the dynamics of collective action and a developing organizational network. This "culture of solidarity" was not inherent among the workers. Nor did it miraculously appear out of a vacuum. It was created within the context of a preexisting pattern of active work-group social relationships.

Analysis of the work-group in the literature of industrial sociology provides an important corrective to previous studies that focused on the individual as the key unit of analysis.[13] Much of this work has been primarily concerned with issues of organizational integration and efficiency, but even those whose sentiments and concerns rest firmly with the well-being of workers (from Donald Roy's classic discussion of "Banana Time" to Michael Burawoy's *Manufacturing Consent*) fail to consider the relationship between work-group culture and collective action.[14]

My observations of work-group culture at Taylor suggest that although solidarity was manifested most forcefully during the wildcat strikes, a range of other factors—the frequent use of humor; informal group determination of what should and should not be openly discussed; the nature of the expression of cultural differences; along with particular characteristics of the labor process—combined to minimize the potential for intragroup conflict. Tempering potential discord was an active process of creating and recreating an atmosphere of sociability among a heterogenous group of workers. Although mutual cooperation is necessary to meet the requirements of the labor process, as Burawoy has pointed out, it also provides a foundation for other expressions of "cooperative activity."[15] In the absence of such a climate, it is doubtful whether workers could mobilize activities as risky as wildcat strikes.

Even *with* such a foundation, creating the level of solidarity required to win wildcat strikes was hardly a simple process at Taylor. Collective solidarity was forged through a process of interaction among participants and in response to the company. In the early stages of the first wildcat strike, a group of workers divided by their level of commitment and participation became more unified when the circumstances appeared to favor a successful action. Those who had committed themselves immediately had to raise the level of commitment of the others in order to protect themselves from isolation and reprisal and to ensure that the strike would be victorious. They achieved this by actively encouraging solidarity and by creating an appearance of collective strength in the face of company threats. This appearance demonstrated to the less committed workers the potential power of collective solidarity, thus increasing their commitment to it. It also served to persuade the foreman that efforts to divide the workers were futile, and this, too, helped facilitate mobilization.

This dynamic is crucial in understanding solidarity as an active process. The struggle within the work-group proved to be as important for the success of the strike as the struggle against the company. Had activists not engaged the more hesitant workers, and had the internal struggle not gone on, the "militancy" of just a few activists would have meant little. If the mobilization of the finishing department had come unglued in this way, the strike as a whole would conceivably have been defeated, as mobilization throughout the rest of the plant probably would have begun to unravel as well. Moreover, had the first wildcat strike been defeated, and had some been discharged for their participation, it is doubtful that workers in the finishing department would have been inclined to risk a second strike.

I am not suggesting here that the solidarity achieved in the October strike developed in some incremental, linear fashion (as in an accumulation of "knowledge") toward the second one. The relative calm of labor relations in the period between the strikes is as interesting as the collective outbursts themselves. There was little evidence during this three-month period to suggest that anything extraordinary had taken place, or that anything might. Though we can only speculate, had a survey been taken during this "lull," it is doubtful that the response of workers would have revealed any significant amount of "class consciousness," as that concept is generally treated in sociology. But although answers to questions about class identification, voting preferences, or images of society might not have revealed any remarkable ideological transformation after the first wildcat, an important shift *had* taken place in the ability of workers to engage in further collective action successfully. This was revealed in two processes resulting from the first wildcat that could not have become apparent until the second strike: (a) the formation of a group of activists; and (b) the perception that solidarity was possible and could be maintained.

After demonstrating their activism during the first strike, the network of activists gravitated to one another and played an important role in mobilizing for the second. This loose grouping of workers provided an informal forum in which the possibilities and problems of the second wildcat strike could be considered. When, after some consideration, the idea was raised with the larger group, each of these activists knew that arguments and justifications in favor of a strike could be put forward with an assurance that at least some support would be forthcoming.

With an emergent grouping of activists centered in the finishing department, a locus of oppositional sentiment was created, which remained solidly rooted in the day-to-day culture of the department, yet also began to attract militants from other departments. Thus, a "culture of solidarity," largely germinated during the first wildcat strike and nourished by the second, began to develop an incipient organizational form. Workers with a common identity as activists who were opposed to bureaucratic unionism had developed an internal network. This conforms, in germinal form, to Charles Tilly's conception of organization as "catness" (a category of people sharing a common interest) and "netness" (a network of people linked by a specific kind of interpersonal bond).[16] Although the group of activists was certainly not a firmly developed organization, it did have enough adhesion and sense of purpose to challenge the union bureaucracy for leadership of the local (however feeble the attempt). The inexperience of the activists clearly left them unprepared to resist the company and union demobilization efforts, however, and consequently they failed to mount much more than a token challenge. But had they been afforded another opportunity to repeat the attempt (say two years later), it is at least conceivable that the outcome could have been different.

The development of the two wildcat strikes reveals the evolutionary character of what might seem to be simply "spontaneous" outbursts. To be sure, as a response to the firing of a co-worker, the first strike *was* a relatively spontaneous affair. It was, however, also an action that relied on the mutual trust based on preexisting shop-floor relationships. Moreover, although the participants were faced with spontaneous shifts and decisions at various stages of the strike, their collective negotiations were a crucial element; though perhaps spontaneous in the sense that it was not preplanned, the strike was an action that was structured in certain important ways. In posing a dualism between spontaneity and the planned or rational calculation of collective action, the presence of the structured elements *within* spontaneous action may be missed.[17]

It should be emphasized that the roots of the emergent "culture of solidarity" were in the *praxis* of solidarity, and not in abstract ideas. Although the organizational form lent a certain coherence to this culture, its fulcrum was the two wildcat strikes, each of which *in practice* confronted prevailing notions of unionism and management prerogative. It is worth repeating that Gage, a known radical, was mainly respected in the plant as an "activist" and a "fighter," and much less so as an ideologue. His political views were accepted to the extent that they informed concrete struggles under way, or linked those struggles to similar ones elsewhere.[18]

While the emergence of a rudimentary form of organization suggests that workers had increased their ability to undertake successful collective action, we may note other evidence of this ability as well. The difference in the character of the second strike was, to some degree, a result of the dramatic nature of the first. Both the union leadership and the company reacted to the second strike with a measure of caution, in the hope that it could be contained within the finishing department and settled before the rest of the plant walked out in support. Because workers at Taylor had already demonstrated an ability to shut down the entire plant, the threat of this being repeated seems to have been enough to temper the actions of all parties (including the workers) during the course of the second strike. Although the verbal expressions of support from the foundry and the maintenance department probably could have been transformed into action, this was not in any way guaranteed and would have required a degree of mobilization fraught with danger. But as it developed, the company did not force the workers to "show their hand" a second time, and the workers thus emerged victorious.

Management literature warns of "dangers" to the maintenance of "plant discipline" inherent in successful wildcat strikes. Writing in the *Harvard Business Review*, Leonard R. Sayles cautions: "A clear-cut victory for a group of wildcat strikers may well be demoralizing for the rest of the employees in the plant." And K.G.J.C. Knowles puts it even more succinctly: "There is one thing which can be more damaging to the orderly conduct of industrial relations than an unofficial strike; it is a successful unofficial strike."[19]

This simply underscores the point that if management had immediately crushed the first strike at Taylor, others would have been unlikely for a long time to come. Reliance on solidarity and collective action (rather than on bureaucratic procedures) would probably have been widely discredited among the workers, and the more active proponents of solidarity would have been forced to seek work elsewhere. Had the first action not succeeded, the "culture of solidarity" at Taylor would presumably have been destroyed, and possibly even replaced by an atmosphere permeated by fearfulness and selfishness.

The wildcat strikes described above are probably not dramatically different in form from those that take place every day in American industry. Because each lasted for less than eight hours, they would not have appeared in the Bureau of Labor Statistics's official records for that year, nor would they have caused any significant disruption of the economy outside of this particular plant (or inside it, for that matter). Yet the character of wildcat strikes provides an indication of the willingness and ability of industrial workers to step beyond the bounds of bureaucratic unionism, to circumvent "acceptable" channels of grievance resolution, and to engage in forms of activity expressing mutual solidarity. During a wildcat strike, workers become masters of their own collective destiny by ignoring formal authority and temporarily creating an authority based on collective solidarity. At Taylor Casting Company, the wildcat strikes and their residue represented a temporary fissure in the mode of unionism that has provided much of the substance for the "social contract" between labor and capital for the past four decades.[20] Wildcat strikes represent collective initiatives that are independent of industrial relations structures which have been designed to prevent destabilization through independent rank-and-file action, thus exposing the "Achilles' heel" of the system.[21]

Whether or not workers develop an ideological analysis of the meaning of such activity, in practice they are expressing their dissatisfaction with bureaucratic unionism and their willingness to rely on mutual solidarity. In essence, a wildcat strike is as much against the union leadership as it is against the company, and workers who participate have only their solidarity to rely on to protect them from company (and sometimes union) sanctions.[22] Because there is little legal protection, the risk of losing one's job is considerable. A high level of solidarity and militance must be assured if workers are to undertake such action, let alone see it through to a successful finish. From a managerial perspective, Leonard Sayles has recognized the collective solidarity indicated by wildcat strikes:

> The average worker does not contemplate a walkout lightly, being aware that this is a serious breach of plant discipline and that a stiff penalty—perhaps discharge—may result. . . . Fellow workers may support the walkout of one small group because they recognize that to fail to do so may subject the few who do leave the plant to "capital" punishment, while if they all go out together, management cannot easily discharge the entire department or plant.[23]

The form of the wildcat strike reveals dynamics of solidarity on the shop floor, but the issues over which workers will risk their livelihood are illuminating as well. The literature clearly indicates that such strikes are usually concerned with the rate and amount of production; health and safety conditions; hiring, firing, and disciplining of workers; the amount of personal time and how it is to be used; the hours of work; and compulsory overtime.[24] These issues concern basic aspects of the quality of work life, industrial discipline, and managerial authority, and, as such, they reflect a struggle to shape the labor process not unlike struggles of an earlier era.[25]

Sociological analyses of wildcat strikes have largely failed to acknowledge their relationship to the construction of worker solidarity. For example, in Alvin Gouldner's study of the wildcat strike, he says that he wishes to treat the "collective character" of the strike as a "given" in order to focus on the "relationship between workers and management." However, in his analysis he often focuses on the "collective character" of the strike, if only to dismiss any suggestion that mutual solidarity was involved. He does so in spite of the fact that the strike by "Oscar Center" workers was, by all accounts, a strike in solidarity with workers at a nearby plant owned by the same company. Gouldner refuses to accept that trade union solidarity might be more than simply a "language" used to "couch" attempts on the part of workers to conceal their own selfish interests: "This was certainly not a sentiment born of 'class'-

conscious solidarity with fellow workers in distress. For it would be difficult to imagine these Republican, farm-rooted workers adopting the sentiments of militant class-conscious solidarity." Earlier he suggests that "some of their motives may have been expedient; that is, if they supported the striking Big City workers they could hope for reciprocal help when their own time came."[26]

Gouldner's case study here represents an interesting example of worker solidarity, and though it is not the main focus of his analysis, the analytic points he does make about solidarity reflect a limited conceptual framework. Even though the "Oscar Center" workers engaged in a fairly dramatic wildcat solidarity strike, Gouldner's a priori notions about what "class consciousness" should look like do not conform to his impression of these workers, and he is forced to seek some other motive besides solidarity to explain their actions, such as self-interest. However, it is precisely because it is viewed by workers as a *mutual* affair, and not as an exercise in pure moral altruism (as Gouldner's preconception would seem to require), that he ignores solidarity as a factor. Moreover, by presupposing that "sentiments of militant class-conscious solidarity" are incompatible with "Republican, farm-rooted workers," Gouldner shows how constraining traditional concepts of class consciousness can be.

At Taylor, two of the four militant activists who played an important role in the wildcat strikes, and who formed an important part of the emerging culture of solidarity in the plant, also happened to be a part of the Bible study group that met every day during the lunch break.[27] If one simply presumed "Baptist fundamentalism" to be incompatible with "sentiments of class-conscious solidarity" and failed to examine the activities of these men and their relationship to others in the plant, their role in the struggles at Taylor would be misunderstood.[28]

An important contribution made by Gouldner to our understanding of wildcat strikes, supported in my own analysis of the strikes at Taylor, is that the workers' "refusal to obey" during a wildcat strike represents a "breakdown in the flow of consent . . . the disruption of a social system, particularly in its authority relations."[29] The issue of consent is the subject of a recent study by Michael Burawoy, who has shown how the labor process and the organization of social relations on the shop floor "manufacture" consent. This issue is worth reviewing for a moment in relation to events at

Taylor.[30] As opposed to traditional sociological approaches, which have viewed consensus as a given in American industry, Burawoy treats it as problematic and analyzes the activities organized at the point of production to generate consent. An important component of this process is the "internal state" that coordinates "the interests of union and management through their joint use of grievance machinery and collective bargaining." He shows how the "internal state" obscures class relations by individuating and regulating the concerns of workers through grievance procedures and formal collective bargaining arrangements. Burawoy's is a unique and insightful Marxist contribution to the literature on the labor process and offers a great deal that should be considered, but I will touch only on one element in it, which seems to address the points we have been dealing with.

Burawoy is quite correct in thinking that the routinization of industrial relations is designed to manufacture consent and, in general, does so. This is precisely why the postwar "social contract" has been so acceptable to capital until recently. However, Burawoy's analysis is weakened by his failure to consider the dialectic of this process—namely, that the grievance system in American industry is the source of the collective struggle at the same time as it individuates it. In the previous chapter, I offered evidence that grievance systems are often used by management to delay and derail resolution of grievances; that the inefficiency of grievance mechanisms in many industries leads to large backlogs of unresolved grievances; and that collective reactions (such as wildcat strikes) are often the result of such failures. At Taylor Casting Company workers recognized full well the problems associated with the pursuit of grievances through the system, which is why the wildcat strikes took place. When the union president announced that he would deal with Richie's firing by "taking it all the way to arbitration," workers took another form of action. Rather than accepting the uncertainties and the delay of the grievance process, they collectively took matters into their own hands. The workers in the finishing department knew that the problem might never be rectified if they waited for the grievance system to bring them heat (a *collective* demand). Collective action seemed to offer a more efficient means of resolution. On a day-to-day basis, workers' problems *are* mediated through the mechanisms of the "internal state." Individuation of collective struggle is in fact often the result, and it is here that Burawoy makes an important contribution. The "internal state" is a problematic phenomenon, however, and workers periodically circumvent its mechanisms, revealing the conflict that lies in dialectical relationship to consent.[31]

Thus far I have discussed wildcat strikes and the general "culture of solidarity" that emerged at Taylor as if this culture were a distinctly separate "third force" in the traditional union-management relationship. To the extent that the activities, values, and organizational forms of the "culture of solidarity" were at variance with the union bureaucracy and the company, this is a fairly accurate characterization. But at the same time, in important ways, the metabolic processes of this culture were interwoven with, supportive of, and even dependent on the traditional union structure.

During the first wildcat strike, although the union president was criticized and hounded for attempting to subdue the strike and steer the dispute through "acceptable" channels, the union as a concept and as an institution was never subject to attack. The workers were critical specifically of the limited ways in which unionism had been practiced by the leadership; they viewed their own actions as expressive of its proper form. For many of these workers, the solidarity of the wildcat strikes was what unionism is all about; and the union president was subverting unionism by *his* actions. During this first wildcat, the workers refused to sabotage a key part of the production process so as not to jeopardize the union treasury by provoking a costly lawsuit. This indicates a respect for the production process as well as for the union treasury, both of which were deemed worthy of protection in spite of the defiance directed at company and union officials alike.

Although the militance and solidarity of rank-and-file workers forced the company to concede and resolve the issues at hand in the course of the wildcat strikes at Taylor, it was the union officials who formally negotiated the concessions. The workers used collective action to raise the issues, to halt production in order to provide a powerful bargaining chip, and to persuade union officials that the issues required immediate negotiation. They then expected that the union officials would do the actual negotiating. At no time during these strikes was it suggested or implied that anyone but the union officials ultimately had the formal standing to deal with the issues. The president was expected to negotiate Richie's rehiring in October, and, in January, the same was expected of the chief steward with regard to the heat issue (in fact, union officials were summoned to the scene immediately by the wildcatters). It was recognized by everyone that militant collective action had provided the crucial impetus in settling the grievances favorably, but it was also recognized that the union, rather than some "third force," was responsible for negotiating the workers' interests.

In essence, the fact that there was a union in the plant led members to expect that at the very least they would be defended. This in turn seems to have made it easier to consider militant action (even though a wildcat strike made such a defense legally difficult, and even though the union leadership might not have pursued such a defense). Certainly, the mere presence of a union in the plant gave workers a sense that they had a right to raise grievances and expect serious consideration of them, a sense not necessarily possessed by workers in non-union settings, where complaints are often made at the risk of one's job. The labor historian David Montgomery forcefully makes a similar point:

> The very shop floor militancy which so disturbs corporate executives and union officials alike in the 1970s could not assume the open and chronic form which makes it notorious without the presence of union and legal defenses against arbitrary dismissal. To see the role of unions in this setting as *nothing more* than disciplinary agents for management, therefore, is a facile and dangerous form of myopia.[32]

The relationship between the union at Taylor and the emergent "culture of solidarity" was, in many respects, a contradictory one. The union leadership was severely criticized, yet members also recognized the union as essential to negotiations with the company. The wildcat strikes circumvented the bureaucratic grievance system, yet it is doubtful that without such a system the "right to grieve" would have been asserted at all, much less through a collective work stoppage.

Moreover, although the emergence of an organizational network of activists was an important development at Taylor, centralizing and solidifying opposition to the union leadership, it also reflected a similarly dialectical relationship to the union structure. In its incipient stages, the form and the character of the group were virtually antithetical to the bureaucratic structures and practices of the union hierarchy. Yet despite the open opposition and antagonism activists expressed toward the bureaucracy, they chose to challenge the leadership for control rather than doing away with the union altogether or establishing another one. As far as I know, no other approach was ever suggested or considered. If they *had* been successful in overthrowing the leadership, it is certainly less than clear whether they would have been able to transform the basic nature of the union. Once in power, they would have had to negotiate periodic contracts with management and would then presumably have had to sell them to the membership, to learn to live with them themselves, and to enforce them among the rank and file.[33]

It is, of course, at least conceivable that once in power they might have provided a more militant form of leadership, less concerned with managing the contract than with promoting and relying on collective solidarity as a means of resolving problems and disputes. In terms of the character of unionism, this could have been a significant reemphasis. As it was, though, the militants failed in their bid to seize union power. Much of this, I think, can be attributed to their lack of sophistication. They had not anticipated that the union president would oppose them at the nomination stage and had not inquired about whether a worker could stand for union office while on lay-off. But what is more difficult to explain is the lack of any significant reaction by those attending the union meeting to the president's handling of nominations.

There is no doubt that workers were buoyed by the success of the January action—warmth in the break room was the tangible result of their militancy. Yet while the attempt to institutionalize this militancy through union elections was generally encouraged by the workers in the finishing department, it was not fought for or promoted vigorously by the workforce as a whole or by those attending the meeting.

One possibility is that the issue of Gage's politics made it more difficult for workers to defend him. Although there were only two open references equating his radicalism with communism in the finishing department (the foreman's query and the bulletin board posting), perhaps such rumors and suggestions were more widespread in other departments, where his militance might not have been defended as strongly. It may also have affected finishing department workers, who would not necessarily have raised questions and concerns about communist tendencies openly. Moreover, militancy might have been viewed as necessary in a crisis, but unappealing institutionally.

It is also possible, though, that Gage's politics were less important in the period before the union meeting than the message conveyed by his being laid off. Perhaps this served to remind workers of the fate that might befall others who transgressed in similar ways. Fear of the sack had been evident throughout each of the strikes, and outside of a collective action where workers are actively coaxing one another and openly displaying solidarity, the singling out of one activist might have served as a tangible threat.

Taylor workers may have rallied to the defense of a fired worker in October, but an unjust firing is not the same thing as a lay-off. There is no contract provision that stipulates the conditions allowing the company to lay off workers (as there is with discharge). A lay-off is considered a temporary status. The understanding is that workers laid off during a contraction in production will be reemployed when production picks up. Consequently, workers in American industry do not typically contest lay-offs, as they are not viewed as instances of managerial despotism (as the firing in October had been).

Anticommunism and the lay-off of a prominent activist may have been factors that contributed to the waning of militancy preceding the union meeting, but the closing of the plant itself turned out to be management's ultimate weapon in demobilizing worker militance. This effectively foreclosed any possibility of further growth of the culture of solidarity that had begun to take root. Neither bureaucratic social contract unionism nor more militant leadership could have prevented this, suggesting an intrinsic weakness of workers' power in one union local in the face of the power of capital.[34]

Taylor Casting Company announced that it was closing the New Jersey plant and shifting all production to its less labor-intensive, more profitable Southern plant because of economic factors. The Southern plant was non-union and located in a "right-to-work" state. Capital flight to the "sunbelt" has been one sure way in which corporations have been able to undercut unions.[35] The twenty-one "right-to-work" states essentially prohibit union security agreements, making union membership extremely difficult to maintain, and are another direct legacy of the Taft-Hartley Act, which explicitly permits states to impose more stringent regulations on union security than federal law allows. Because the South remains largely unorganized, this region of the country has served as a haven for companies like Taylor Casting seeking "union-free" status. Although it is impossible to know for sure, it is not unreasonable to suggest that the militancy of Taylor workers played a significant role in the company decision to shift operations when it did. Even the most conservative trade unions can be victimized by plant closings and runaway shops, and the specter of increased worker militancy is likely to influence corporate decision making in this regard.

The crucial point is that although a culture of solidarity significantly affected factory life at Taylor by promoting militant collective actions that could win (indeed won) concrete victories, there are powerful structural barriers to what can be achieved in any single workplace. As long as corporations have the ability to respond to unionism by extricating themselves from it, plant can be pitted against plant and region against region.

But "capital flight" is only one mechanism employed by corporations to undercut the prospects for labor solidarity. As noted earlier, managements have become increasingly aggressive in their attempts to prevent trade union organization itself, representing a critical shift in management approaches to labor. Not only do workers break the social contract by engaging in wildcat strikes, but in recent years employers have also found its maintenance less useful than its violation in achieving management goals.

In the study that follows, I trace the efforts at union organization by a group of hospital workers, mostly women, forced to contend with the sophisticated strategies of anti-union consultants. The solidarity that such an effort demands must extend through an entire workplace and be sustained for a protracted period (unlike a wildcat strike). Increasingly, managements are employing vigorous union-prevention tactics, not only to derail particularly militant expressions of solidarity, but also to contest the establishment of union organization itself. In this context, the "push-button" unionism of the postwar social contract is giving way to a unionism that must be aggressively defended—and perhaps to a more *defensible* unionism.

Chapter Four

Union Organizing and Collective Interaction: "Like a Thief in the Night"

As chapter 3 indicated, the legacy of the post–Taft-Hartley social contract weighs heavily on the structures and practices of contemporary trade unionism, which might serve as a pivotal basis for industrial action. But collective action is also often a crucial component of union formation, especially in the face of sharp employer resistance. This chapter examines the process of union organization by a group of women hospital workers. In this case, as in earlier periods of history, managerial counterstrategies combined paternalism and repression in an attempt to defeat the workers' efforts, highlighting the jaggedness of the terrain that is the field of collective action for American workers today.

Springfield, Vermont, rests on the New Hampshire border among the craggy foothills of the Green Mountains. The town, which has a population of about ten thousand, is divided by the Black River, a narrow band of water that rushes down a windy mountain corridor and along the main street. The mostly idle red brick mills that dot the river's edge serve as monuments to the steady decline of manufacturing industries throughout the region.

Springfield, once nicknamed the "Machine Tool Town" for the score or more machine shops that settled here during the "second wave" of America's industrial revolution, until recently employed most of the working men of Windsor County. The Jones and

Lamson factory, the area's largest employer, was transported to Springfield by ox cart in 1888, and later became one of the world's largest manufacturers of lathes, grinders, and optical machinery, supplying automobile, munitions, and aircraft factories through two world wars. Employment at the plant stood at a healthy twelve hundred workers until 1981, but by 1983 Jones and Lamson (now owned by the multinational Textron Corporation) had pared the workforce down to a skeletal two hundred and eighty workers, and in 1985 the plant was to close down altogether.[1] Thus, Local 218 of the United Electrical Workers (UE), whose contracts with the machine shops once provided a proud standard of living for many households in and about Springfield, was, at the time of this study, navigating its membership through the stormiest economic period in many decades.

Although the machine shops were the traditional source of employment for many of the region's working men, Springfield Hospital has been one of the few places where the women of Windsor County have found work. The eighty-one-bed hospital, which employs more than three hundred people, 90 percent of whom are women, is the primary health care facility for Springfield and the surrounding hill towns.

This chapter traces the development of a unionization campaign at the hospital that began in the spring of 1981 and culminated in a National Labor Relations Board (NLRB) election in February 1982. The campaign and its process of mobilization and countermobilization serve as the context for my analysis, but the main focus of inquiry is the culture of solidarity embodied in the organizing committee of women workers that represented the main vehicle of the union effort.

Rumblings of Dissent

At various points in the past, the employees of Springfield Hospital had voiced concern over workplace problems. For example, nine years before the union drive, thirty-five employees from the nursing staff wrote a letter to the editor of the local newspaper in response to a call to a local radio talk-show. The caller had spoken glowingly of his satisfaction with patient care at the hospital. But in their letter, the nurses replied in no uncertain terms that, although they were "dedicated to providing good nursing care," they were "totally frustrated, heartsick . . . our morale is nonexistent over the current situation." The "current situation" to which they referred in 1972 was characterized by dangerously low staffing, in which one registered nurse "must take charge, give medications for 40 patients and be a secretary-receptionist. . . . Nurses must take care of flowers, hand out fresh water, wash beds, admit and discharge patients, all in the course of trying to bathe, feed, and care for the acutely ill." "Is this satisfactory care?" they queried rhetorically. Their letter concluded with a plaintive cry for relief:

> Nurses have tried to go through the proper channels with these frustrations to try and correct a very bad situation. No one listens to us—we have no voice on the Board of Trustees to represent us. . . . The only chance for any changes to correct this intolerable situation is for you the public to apply the necessary pressure to accomplish this.[2]

The nurses' expression of powerlessness in 1972 was to give way to a decidedly more affirmative approach to their collective difficulties in the next decade. For many of the women who began mobilizing in 1981, conditions in the hospital had not appreciably improved since the letter of protest. Though a few had vague recollections of talking among themselves about the need for a union in those days, even fewer recalled that a nurses' association had actually been contacted to discuss the possibilities. Although nothing in the way of an actual union drive ever got under way in the early 1970s, the disaffection marked in that early statement reflected sentiments and concerns that remained for many a part of their work experience at the hospital.

For those nurses whose tenure had spanned the decade since the early outcry, the nature of the labor process had changed rather dramatically in the hospital, even though the problems of short staffing and heavy workload remained a constant source of strain. By the 1980s, the tide of specialization and mechanization, characteristic of developments in the health care industry nationally, had found its way to Springfield Hospital. As elsewhere, nurses were expected to develop highly specialized skills to meet technological changes. At the same time, the modernizing, cost-efficient management of Springfield Hospital, keenly attuned to industry trends, did what it could to trim the fiscal sails in terms of labor costs. The result was a heightened sense of professional responsibility on the part of the nursing staff, with a corresponding set of expectations about working conditions, and, concomitantly, the routinization or proletarianization of the actual labor process.[3] One RN who had worked at the hospital since 1970 noted with some pride the changing medical practices she had witnessed:

> Nursing is evolving into more and more trained things. We're getting more highly skilled surgeons here. When I first started we didn't do anything; we transferred any kind of chest surgery . . . very seldom did we do any major bowel surgery, which is the thing I kind of specialize in now as a sideline . . . we never did any large blood vessel repair work or anything like that. Now they're doing it. I had never heard of a respirator at that hospital; now we have three or four respirators at one time in there.

She went on to explain some of the attendant costs to both staff and patients:

> Years ago, you could handle six, eight patients without terribly big strain because all you did was custodial care for the most part. Now we get major gall bladder surgery, major bowel, chest surgery, critically ill patients. . . . It means we have the same amount of patients to take care of with a lot less time. Where you have a patient you should be spending two and three hours with per shift, you're spending maybe an hour if you're lucky, and this isn't fair or safe. You go home terribly frustrated, exhausted, and you know you haven't [given] the kind of care to a patient they should have had. It's not fair. It's not fair to the patients, it's not fair to us.

This seemingly contradictory set of tendencies toward the simultaneous professionalization *and* deskilling or proletarianization of the labor process took a toll on the employees of the hospital. For the RNs, a group that played a critical role in the nascent union campaign, it was perhaps the main underlying source of dissension.

For other employees who were drawn to the union drive, especially those less affected by technological change, complaints and problems centered around conditions that seem to echo more traditional industrial concerns. One forty-six-year-old "unit-aid" (nurse's aide), the wife of a disabled man, had tried in vain for a couple of years to move into a better paying, more interesting job as a ward clerk. Despite her dissatisfaction with her job, she was overlooked while ten new ward clerks were hired from outside the hospital in one six-month period. She and her daughter, who was also a worker in the hospital, were not unaffected by this treatment, and both became strong union supporters. An LPN (licensed practical nurse) with more than ten years' experience complained of similar problems: "I've seen people that worked with me, and myself included, get passed over for orientation to different units just because somebody else who happened to be a favorite of management wanted it."

Throughout the workforce, women are often located in positions of lowest status and pay. Although the desire to improve their economic situation is extremely important, it is often not the only factor of concern to women workers. Job upgrading and the possibilities of promotion can be among the most compelling issues motivating female workers to organize. After establishing themselves in the workforce, which in many cases is a new experience requiring a new sense of confidence, a concomitant desire for more responsibility and status may be created.

Among LPNs and dietary and housekeeping workers, pay levels were, however, clearly a critical issue. Many dietary and housekeeping employees had worked ten or fifteen years in the hospital, yet reportedly were on a pay scale that hovered just above the minimum wage. Groups of employees were sometimes pitted against each other for wage increases that were felt to be barely sufficient. One LPN noted that "some years we didn't get any raises at all," explaining sardonically that this was

> because the night shift needed it more than I did. Hey, the evening shift can't have any because "that poor night shift, they really need it," you know? I mean, "Sorry, Yvonne, you're a good nurse but you know there's no such thing as a raise this year." What really made us mad is when they would give us two- or three-cent raises. . . . I mean it was just really a slap in the face . . . and you didn't really argue about it because you knew everyone else got just as low.

One worker felt embittered by the treatment she had received from the hospital after she learned that she could have returned to her old job at her old wage when she came back to work after a pregnancy leave. Instead, the hospital had rehired her at minimum wage each time she had taken a leave. She was informed of her right to her original job only after her third pregnancy had forced her to quit her job as an LPN and return as a new employee being paid the base wage. Such treatment provided the low flame over which dissent simmered for many years among the workers at Springfield Hospital.

"Like a Thief in the Night"

Although a wide range of problems festered beneath the surface, the union campaign was precipitated, for at least one influential group of RNs, by the dissolution of a policy advisory committee by a new hospital administrator, Elliot Reich. Upon assuming his new post as executive vice president (the top administrative position in the hospital), Reich disbanded this joint administration/employee committee because of what his legal counsel determined was its increasing resemblance to a collective bargaining body. The committee had actually served as a liaison between the administration and the employees. Designed to facilitate administrative policy implementation, the committee was essentially a communicative device established to ease policy changes. Reportedly, the administration would explain new policies, while employee "representatives" could suggest modifications and offer opinions to be taken under advisement by the board of trustees. The committee had been established in the wake of the protest letter in the early 1970s, which was a period when fairly dramatic policy changes were introduced, along with the adoption of more advanced medical procedures.

According to the women who became active in the union campaign, the committee was ineffectual in bringing about any meaningful change in their working conditions, largely serving as a forum and a conduit for administration plans. So long as the committee existed, however, many felt a sense of hope that their long-simmering grievances might be aired and that conditions might eventually be improved. The dissolution of the committee was viewed more in symbolic than in real terms; although largely ineffective, it had provided a symbol of hope that change might occur, a sign that the administration harbored some concern for the feelings and needs of the workers.

For some workers the dissolution of the committee may have

been the last straw, but to others it seemed more important in retrospect than it did at the time. It clearly stirred some workers to act, however, and as such was an important factor. It served as further proof of the loss of control over their work lives, creating a conflict with their expanding self-image as workers needing and able to handle increasing autonomy and influence over their work—sensibilities not unlike those of traditional craft workers.[4]

The important point is that Reich's action may have played a significant role in engendering exactly what it was designed to prevent. One worker considered the consequences of Reich's decision in relation to the subsequent union drive:

> In the last ten years we've grown, a lot of things have happened. . . . They try to pull things over on you, see what they can get away with. And we had this committee which had some input to policies, and so people felt that maybe they had a little control over their working lives, you know? Then Mr. Reich came. . . . He did away with this policy committee, right? And one of the things that people were realizing on this policy committee *before* he came was that even though they were talking to people and getting ideas, that the hospital went ahead and put in these policies, whatever they wanted, regardless of what these people wanted. So we realized we didn't have any say. But then Reich comes along . . . and disbands this policy committee. That kind of set things off right there.

The policy committee may not have been a mechanism designed to represent the interests of the workers in any clear or direct way, but nevertheless the fears of the administration may have been well-founded, for it seems that the latent effect of the committee was to bring workers together in unintended ways. Left unchecked, it was on its way to creating the practical effect of unionism.

The latent unionism is apparent from the experience of an RN who, as a member of the committee and a representative of her co-workers, took her responsibility more seriously than the administration had intended. The committee had been set up with what seemed to her an arbitrary number of representatives for various employee groups within the hospital. As one of three representatives of a hundred nursing employees, she felt that to represent her constituency adequately she would "have to have meetings with them to know what they wanted." She called meetings of workers to which her supervisors were not invited, and together the nursing employees would read through the hospital policy manual, discussing changes they would like to have implemented. Through these meetings, the workers were taking the initiative in collectively formulating policy, rather than simply responding to administrative policy initiatives, as the committee had been expected to do. When a need was agreed on (such as vacation time, health insurance, and so forth), a proposal was drafted, signed by all, and submitted to the administration via the policy committee.

The dissolution of the committee was an attempt by management to end collective bargaining by petition. However, the worker who called these meetings had never thought that her actions would be viewed as seditious by the administration. When asked whether she had considered her activities an attempt to form a union, she replied: "No, no, no, I didn't. I thought of it as a good alternative, like an open door. . . . We weren't thinking it was a union at the time. We felt that at least something was being done, and we were talking amongst ourselves. . . . But I think it was just getting too serious for them."

Thus, "like a thief in the night," the practice of unionism tiptoed its way into the hospital. Just as many of the first industrial unions of the CIO in the 1930s were cultivated in the company unionism of the 1920s (see chapter 2), here a praxis of collective action was germinating within a similar managerial mechanism. Company unionism in the 1920s was largely based on an appearance of representation that depended on management's ability to maintain a separation between leaders and the rank and file. Workers were to be prevented at all costs from having a common forum to discuss mutual concerns. Here, too, the hospital management could not countenance a "representative" who organized and consulted her constituency. The process of organizing meetings and petitioning for change was apparently viewed as a threat to managerial prerogative.

The First Steps

Shortly after the policy committee was disbanded, two RNs contacted District 1199 of the National Union of Hospital and Health Care Employees. They had read about the union in a nursing magazine report on a nurses' strike in New Hampshire and wrote to an RN there about the union. Richard Sanders, an 1199 organizer, was sent to Vermont in May 1981 to meet with a small group of the workers. At this meeting, the seven workers attending asked Sanders a range of questions about the process of forming a union. He emphasized the difficulties and dangers involved—that the administration would most likely put up a formidable fight against such an effort by harassing union activists and spreading mistrust and fear among potential supporters. He warned that the management would spare no efforts in trying to turn workers against the union drive. He wanted the workers to consider whether or not they would be able to withstand such a vigorous countermobilization and whether the changes they sought would be worth such a trial. He clearly wanted to make sure that they were serious about what they were doing and realized what might lie ahead. He also sought to convey his vision of what a union ought to be, stressing that a union is not simply an election that establishes formal grievance machinery—a bureaucratic structure—but also a democratically organized configuration of workers that can effectively contest for power in the workplace. As many of the activists later recounted, Sanders inspired the group by offering a set of ideals and principles worth fighting for rather than by making promises of material improvement. At the next meeting a month later, between forty and fifty workers turned up, and the union drive was under way.

According to Sanders, the large turnout for the meeting was actually a mixed blessing. At such an early stage, a meeting this size cannot be kept confidential, and the management is thus likely to know about the union drive early on. Moreover, such a large meeting may accelerate the pace of the campaign prematurely by motivating large numbers of workers to act before they have carefully thought through all the issues and prepared themselves for the obstacles to organizing. It can also become difficult for the union organizer to coordinate action without a core of leaders who have been tested and who are certain of their own commitment. Sometimes the long, hard task of building a dedicated organizing committee may be deemphasized in favor of rapid movement toward an election as a concrete goal that can mobilize large numbers of supporters. This may not be to the best advantage for building a solid union that can sustain itself effectively in the workplace over time. While the union drive at Springfield Hospital did tend to emphasize an electoral strategy, the union organizer was aware of the dangers of an exclusive focus. And of course the size of an electoral majority *is* important because such a union campaign often continues beyond the day of the election, as employers (often with the help of their consultants) may try to reverse a successful union drive by endlessly delaying the bargaining process.[5]

A formal set of procedures exists for establishing a union. The National Labor Relations Board administers an election after at least 30 percent of the employees of an enterprise or within a "bargaining unit" (a group or groups of employees deemed to represent a "community of interest") indicate a desire to be represented by the collective bargaining agent, or trade union.[6] With this 30 percent "show of interest," the NLRB will make a decision on the appropriate bargaining units and schedule an election in which a majority of each unit must vote in favor of union representation before an employer is compelled to bargain.

From the perspective of the union, the bargaining unit(s) decided upon may or may not represent the most advantageous division of the employees in terms of garnering union support. Thus, while the union may feel that it can gain and maintain the support of more than 50 percent of the employees in a workplace, there may be more than one bargaining unit involved in the election, and all may not support the union to the same degree. The variability of support and potential support is an important issue during a contested union drive, and either management or the union can gain (or lose) from a particular decision about the proper bargaining units.[7]

Moreover, a 30 percent "show of interest" in petitioning for an election is not nearly enough to propel a union drive to a successful conclusion. If management engages in a concerted counterattack once a union drive is under way, it becomes extremely difficult for the union then to increase its strength above 50 percent. In fact, according to Sanders, there is an axiom among organizers that a union is strongest at the time of the petition for an election. From then on, the union is essentially trying to hold on to enough support in the face of the managerial countermobilization to win the election. A petition to the NLRB with only 30 percent of a bargaining unit "showing interest" is unlikely to later result in the 50 percent plus one vote that is necessary to win an election. Consequently, many union organizers want *at least* 50 percent of the workers to sign union cards as a show of interest *before* petitioning for an election, expecting that management actions leading up to the election will cause a decrease in support for the union. Although social scientists studying voting behavior and elections in the workplace and beyond may not always be sensitive to the shifting, dynamic quality of electoral social psychology, the successful union organizer must be.

In the case of the union drive at Springfield Hospital, it was felt that at least a 65 percent show of interest in each of the three bargaining units (RNs, technical staff, service and maintenance) would be needed to withstand a management countermobilization, given the fact that the hospital administration had retained a law firm known for combating unions and for working closely with anti-union consulting firms.[8] In a discussion of the strategy employed in this campaign, Sanders noted the critical nature of the percentage in gauging the collective strength of the workers:

> We had always made it very clear to the workers that unless we had at least 65 percent of each bargaining unit, we would not petition for that bargaining unit. You know, workers always think that their situation is different; "Well, we may only have 60 percent, but we know other people are with us, we know it, and this place is different, it's a smaller hospital . . . they'll never do to us what they've done at other places, they won't get away with it." They've got so many reasons to believe that this, their place, will be different, that 60 percent or 55 percent is enough, and we can win if we just push . . . but experience has taught us that you need at least 65 percent to have a chance in an election, especially with the consultants.

Although the goal of the union drive is to win a representation election so that workers may exercise the right of collective bargaining, to a large degree it is in the *process* of its formation that the character of the union is created. Generally, a successful union election represents the institutionalization of that which brought it about—namely, a praxis of worker solidarity, or, in the case of "business unionism," a more or less hierarchical union structure and a set of bureaucratic practices. District 1199, with its reputation for militancy and democratic, socially conscious unionism, would be expected to allow a good deal of rank-and-file initiative in the organization of a union and would be less likely to retard the development of worker solidarity than some other unions.[9] For 1199 as well as for many other unions, the vehicle that drives the process of union organization forward, that expresses in potential the solidarity to be realized in institutional form, is the rank-and-file organizing committee.

The Organizing Committee

An organizing committee generally consists of the most committed and most active supporters of the union drive, and in many respects it is the main actor in the process of unionization. The union organizer is essential in building the committee and giving it direction and guidance, and the workers as a whole must vote in the election and maintain the life of the union once it is established, but the union organizing committee plays the most critical role in the formation of the union and, from a sociological standpoint, provides an interesting model of emergent social organization. The organizing committee embodies the practice of unionism, exemplifying its values and sensibilities during a period when these are taking root and are subject to challenge, skepticism, and attack.

The members of the organizing committee carry out the daily tasks of union education, attempting to convince others in a systematic way of the power of collective interest and organization. This is a formidable task in most workplaces. Employers maintain considerable resource structures to control employees. Indeed, in a society in which individual initiative is held to be the only legitimate avenue of social mobility and improvement, collective action is a remarkable accomplishment. Organizing committee members not only must develop the fortitude to withstand the intense pressures brought to bear by the employer, but also must illustrate to others the possibilities and benefits of solidarity through their own activities and values. The committee must provide an area of social space within the employer-dominated workplace where an alternative definition of social relations and power can be provided and maintained.

Leadership ability is forged largely in the work of the committee, with the union drive becoming a critical training ground for activists. One key role of the union organizer is to identify potential members of the committee and to cultivate certain leadership qualities. At Springfield Hospital, Richard Sanders noted the elements he sought in forming the committee:

What we have to do is to identify the leaders, or the potential leaders, in every work area and on every shift. But it's not necessarily the person who promotes himself or herself as a leader, not somebody who stands up on a soapbox and engages in long speeches. They may turn out to be leaders, but there are other kinds of people who are leaders—the person who others clearly respect, who is paid attention to when they have something to say. That person is able to express and articulate feelings and sentiments that other people have but aren't able to [express]. The person who, in a very quiet way, has a dignity that not only the co-workers respect, but even the management does—those are the people you're looking for, who are the "natural" if unrecognized leaders.

The membership of the organizing committee at Springfield Hospital was somewhat fluid. At points in the campaign the membership swelled, and at others it shrank, but overall there remained a core of from twenty-five to thirty-five activists who were clearly identified by others as "the union." The makeup of the committee was never completely representative of the entire workforce. The nursing staff of RNs, LPNs, and nurse's aides made up the largest bloc of activists, with a few workers from the dietary and housekeeping departments. Committee members were concentrated on certain shifts. Certain departments (maintenance, switchboard operators, the central sterile department) were not represented, and this proved to be a critical factor in the development of the campaign.

Virtually none of the women on the organizing committee had ever had any direct experience with unions before and had not publicly or openly challenged authority in the ways they would be required to in this campaign. Many, however, were at least marginally familiar with unions from husbands, fathers, or other relatives who were union members. Although this certainly provided support for some, most found themselves on completely unfamiliar terrain.

New Forms of Activity

Most of the women of the organizing committee got involved in union activity with some trepidation, as it required public defiance of the hospital administration. One RN, a prominent activist on the committee, echoed the anxieties of others when she noted: "You're going against the system and you feel almost bad, like you're being bad and tricky." But initial anxieties were eventually faced, and union activities became a primary focus in the lives of these women for the better part of a year.

"House visits," calls on co-workers at their homes before or after working hours, were one of the first forms of activity. Some employees were approached at work or called on the phone and asked whether they would like to hear more about the union effort. Others were approached "cold"—paid a visit uninvited—which tended to be more difficult for committee people. This activity served different purposes for different people at different times in the campaign. Primarily, it expanded the union drive by recruiting activists to the committee and generally gaining sympathy for the cause. It allowed the committee members to discuss unionism openly, something that became impossible in the workplace with supervisors present.

The house visits also served as a method of self-education. For most committee members this was the first time that their ideas about solidarity and unionism had been tested publicly, and the first time that they had been expected to articulate an alternative set of principles, in addition to explaining the basic "nuts and bolts" of trade unions. Moreover, they were expected to persuade others of the righteousness of their approach, one that had not firmly come together in their own minds yet. A thirty-four-year-old LPN noted how gingerly she approached the issues during her first house visits. Her co-workers "felt a little shy . . . but we did too at that time; I mean this was all new to everybody, really." The early house visits provided the committee both with a means of testing their own ideas by articulating them to others and with an experience in mutual support that would be necessary in developing a collective self-confidence for the battles ahead.

For the most part, these experiences seem to have been very positive for the union activists. Most were treated politely, and though the visits did not always convince the listeners, additional activists were sometimes recruited in this fashion. As the union drive progressed, and the administration began its counteroffensive, the tenor and the function of house visits shifted somewhat. As tension in the hospital increased, house visits increasingly provided the space to counter management propaganda and to gauge its impact on the workers.

Elliot Reich, as chief administrator of the hospital, was well prepared for the union campaign and quickly took steps when it was learned that an organizing committee was forming. Not unexpectedly, the hospital hired Modern Management (MM), a consulting firm from Illinois with a national reputation among labor activists as the preeminent "union-busting" firm specializing in health care labor relations.[10] The hospital had already retained the services of a law firm with a similar sort of reputation throughout the New England area. The hiring of MM added a certain chemistry to the emerging conflict, as it represented an unequivocal warning that a formidable counterattack was to be launched against the union forces. Boasting a "success" rate in defeating unions of better than 90 percent, MM campaigns have a general formula, well known to union organizers such as Richard Sanders. MM consultants are never seen by the workers, but they work closely and regularly with supervisory staff. Supervisors essentially are formed into a cadre-like team to campaign vigorously against the union.[11] According to Sanders, the campaign run by MM at Springfield Hospital was "classic" in the methods it employed.

Collective Action and Interaction

Within days of the first mass union meeting in June 1981, the countermobilization began—predictably, according to Sanders— with a rather benign administration gesture. Two memos were sent to all employees. The first announced a list of health insurance "benefit enhancements" approved "at the Board's recent regular meeting."[12] The second, distributed three days later, announced an increase in the net assets of the pension plan. It began as follows: "As you may be aware, Springfield Hospital is trying, on a day to day basis, to enhance its communication with employees regarding their benefits and the many things that go along with being an employee of our fine facility."[13]

House visits by the members of the committee continued in the following weeks, and talk about the union was more and more open throughout the hospital. In spite of management's first efforts, activists were finding many receptive ears among the workers and were slowly overcoming their bashfulness and caution. Then, two weeks after the initial round of memos appeared, another was sent by

Reich, unequivocally setting out the administration's position on the question of unionism. Addressed to "Dear Fellow Employee," the letter explained: "My job is to explain why the Hospital is totally and completely against a Union. First and foremost, problems are not solved by bringing in an outside party; they are solved by people who know and care about this institution sitting down and working them out together." The letter went on to point out Reich's desire to work with the employees in solving problems, praising the employees for their "honesty," "integrity," and admirable attitudes. The second half of the letter reflected a somewhat different tone:

> But I must tell you, we cannot take this Union threat lightly. . . . The next few weeks will be critical to your future and that of Springfield Hospital. There will be more meetings, probably followed by false rumors, veiled threats, and pressure to sign a Union card. *Before signing a Union card, remember that it is a legally binding contract.*

The letter also encouraged employees to ask the union "about its record of strikes and potential violence [and] . . . payroll-deducted dues and how these will affect you personally." Noting that "the next few weeks will be emotional ones," it urged employees to "listen and respond as we feel as an individual, not as our friends demand."[14]

Although the workers had been prepared by their union organizer for such a letter, most were upset by its contents. The administration had set itself firmly against the union drive, portraying itself as the rational, reasonable figure in the dispute, whose concern and respect for the employees was paramount. The union was portrayed as an "outside party" that would threaten, pressure, and engage in violence to force workers to sign a "legally binding" union card. This set the tone and theme of a message that was to be repeated many times throughout the campaign, one designed to raise fears about the disruptive effects of unionism while reminding workers of the goodwill of the administration and its ability to provide (and withhold) employment.

Through the summer months, each side grew bolder in its attempt to spread its influence in the hospital. Besides the house visits, before and after working hours, the committee began to hand out leaflets in the employee parking lot during shift changes. The actions of the committee became more lively as the weeks progressed, with activists sporting bright blue union buttons in the hospital, a defiant gesture designed to demonstrate a certain fearlessness and resolve.

Buoyed by the enthusiasm of the committee, the union organizer encouraged more directly confrontational tactics in order to demonstrate the power of collective action to both the uncommitted and the administration. The union committee would have to establish itself as a militant presence in the hospital with regard to the issues that concerned the workers. The committee was encouraged to respond to instances of harassment by supervisors, and there seems to have been ample opportunity for such responses. For example, in early August, a group of women from the committee marched into the office of the supervisor of the housekeeping department, many with their children in tow. The group, made up of RNs, LPNs, nurse's aides, and housekeepers, was protesting what they described later as the "obvious harassment" of a union supporter. It is not clear whether this or any other of the mini-insurrections that took place had any immediate impact on the treatment of employees, but the actions *did* have an effect on the committee itself. The union supporters were "getting their feet wet" in confronting authority, which would appear to be no small accomplishment for workers with little history of collective struggle. Moreover, by addressing the administration collectively, in ways they probably would not have individually, they were learning lessons about solidarity, whittling away at the rigid occupational and status barriers that exist in a hospital setting.

These first collective actions were not undertaken easily by these women. After the first confrontation, they all met at a nearby McDonald's restaurant to "vent our feelings about it." By expressing their frustration, anxiety, and hope, bonds were being built, with emotions serving as a common denominator of experience. To a degree, these interactions began to level the status distinctions among RNs, LPNs, and housekeepers. As one RN pointed out, these informal sessions created a sense of common interest and a feeling of mutual aid:

> Once we started in on the union, we found out by talking to one
> another that we all shared common problems, like lack of staffing in
> all departments, things that were being done to people . . . and so
> we found that we were talking to other departments that were with
> us a lot more, watching out for them, because the administration
> would pick on people something terrible.

A union culture was forming, with opposition as its central, defining feature. Its strength, then, must be seen largely in relation to
the oppositional climate in which it was growing, for concurrently
the administration was developing its campaign against the union
by escalating its activity.

Supervisory personnel took on an active role in the anti-union
effort, coached by the management consulting firm. Some supervisors, many of whom were RNs and had worked "on the floors" at
Springfield Hospital, did not have any intrinsic antipathy to unions.
At the outset, some even supported the prospect of a union for the
staff and had been relatively candid about these positive feelings
until management escalated the campaign, placing heavy demands
on supervisors. Head nurses who had spoken favorably of the union
effort, and some who, as working nurses, had even been involved
in the discussions of unionism back in 1972, were rapidly transformed into anti-union activists. One nursing supervisor who was
drawn into the anti-union activities had played a central role in the
earlier discussions. Moreover, she was the daughter of a prominent
local labor leader from Local 218 of the Electrical Workers Union
(UE), a fact, many speculated, that was a source of great emotional
anguish for her. One union activist wondered "how she must feel
inside, when her father was so involved in 218, in building it, and
how she'd been so involved with trying to form a union eight years
ago. Now, all of a sudden everything looks so different, I just really
didn't think deep down inside that she could do some of the things
she'd be asked to do and that she could really feel this way." Another organizing committee member, explaining the impact of MM
on the hospital, underscored its impact on the supervisory staff:

> They had an effect on the supervisors. When we first started the
> union drive, we didn't know the head nurses could not belong to
> it. . . . We had a lot of head nurses who were pro-union until
> they found out through their meetings that they could not belong

to it. . . . I don't know what they said to them, but they filled them with a lot of knowledge of how bad and how devastating this could be.

The use of supervisory staff in this manner is not unusual. According to the Director of Organization of the AFL-CIO, anti-union consultants are being employed in most organizing drives, irrespective of the industry or the region of the country. In virtually all of these cases, the supervisor plays a crucial role:

> Supervisors are warned that the NLRB offers them no protection, then are indoctrinated in their role as the shock troops in management's campaign. Carefully coached on what they can say and how to get a message over just this side of the law, supervisors eventually spend much of their time pursuing the anti-union program, delivering management's message and closely monitoring employee sentiment. Defeating the organizing effort supersedes every other managerial objective. Employees sympathetic to management are mobilized and enlisted in the effort. Union activists are isolated from other workers and their every step is watched so that supervisors can start building a case for reprimand and/or discharge.[15]

Supervisors were trained as effective activists for the countermobilization in what were called "key management meetings." The meetings, which MM representatives reportedly led, took place during the supervisors' work hours. As the union drive intensified, these meetings became more frequent. The corresponding disruption of the work routine hardened the attitudes of the union activists and angered others who had maintained a degree of ambivalence toward the union drive. One RN specifically noted that the disruptions caused by these meetings angered her, but she did not direct this anger at the head nurses, whom she considered dedicated and hard-working. She felt that they had gotten "caught up in the system being imposed by the lawyers for the hospital," and that the nurses "were being taken from their duties in the hospital" to attend the meetings. She and others cited specific instances of patient safety being placed in jeopardy by the absence of a head nurse. Sometimes this provoked anger at the upper administration, rather than at the supervisors directly. In some cases, frustration over the situation was completely undirected, a potential advantage for management. If management can successfully avoid blame for a difficult work situation, it increases the likelihood that portrayals of the union as "disruptive" or even "violent" will be accepted by those who have experienced a generally troubled period at work over several months.

During the early stages of the countermobilization, supervisory staff were employed to execute what appears to have been a dual strategy. Union activists who had demonstrated a clear commitment to the union effort were now being monitored closely while in the hospital. *Potential* union supporters who had not registered their opinions openly, and who are crucial for both sides in such a dispute, were drawn into "one-on-one" conversations with Reich or department supervisors. These first "one-on-ones" seem to have been designed to assess union sentiments and convince those who might be persuaded to remain loyal to the administration. One worker whose sympathies lay with the union was called into Reich's office during the first months of the campaign in an effort to gauge her loyalties:

> He started by saying, "I want you to think of this hospital as your family" and things like that, and "If you have any problems I want you to always be able to come to me or Ruth," who was our director of nursing. He must have seen my attitude was very reluctant or whatever, or not very interested 'cause he said, "I have a feeling that you really would never trust me to come to me. Is that right?" and I said, "Yeah." That was my one and only "one-on-one."

Another worker, whose judgment on the union issue was unclear at the time, was engaged by her supervisor in a "one-on-one" and later recounted: "She just wanted to tell me about how she felt that a union would be a very poor idea because it sets up an adversary relationship between workers and management. She said that she felt that it would hamper the free and easy kind of community she said that we had." These sorts of encounters were really no different in form from the house visits by organizing committee activists, in that each side was attempting to persuade the uncommitted in a setting free from the influence of the other. But while similar in form, there were significant differences. For an employee to be confronted by an employer is intrinsically intimidating, because the employer controls the means of employment. However benign the employer may be, the inherent power relationship is unequal. In contrast, the union visits must be deliberately unintimidating because the union has no such power, and in such situations peer persuasion is completely ineffective if it is intimidating.

Those identified by the administration as solid union activists experienced quite a different sort of treatment from the supervisory staff during the first months of the campaign. There seems to have been a conscious strategy to monitor the most prominent activists and separate them from those who might be influenced by them. As one unionist explained:

> It got so frustrating because you were always being followed, so you felt like you always had someone looking over your shoulder or trying to jump in on the conversation, that you're never alone. You could be walking in the hallways and there would be people behind you, you know? And if you came to the hospital, people would know it immediately.

Although there might seem to be a dash of paranoia in this, the weight of evidence supporting such an assessment, particularly once the unionists filed their petition for an election, is considerable.

In October, the organizing committee and Richard Sanders, in consultation with the leadership of District 1199, decided to move ahead to petition the National Labor Relations Board for a union election. The committee had been soliciting signatures on union cards since August to petition for the election, and 65 percent of the workers in the service and maintenance unit and the technical unit had signed by that point. Only 55 percent of the RN unit had signed cards, however, and the union made a decision not to file for an RN election for several reasons. First, there was a possibility that the hospital (on the advice of its consultants) might petition the NLRB for an expanded "professional unit" (RNs plus other professionals defined by the board). This might well include doctors and others who, though staying well above the fray for the duration of the conflict, would, if brought into it, be likely to vote against a professional union at the hospital. If the union resisted expansion, the hospital could tie up the election in the courts for months. Second, even if the RN unit were uncontested, the union expected that the hospital would be able to overcome a 55 percent petition through additional hiring into the unit, natural attrition, and/or administration-induced attrition of the pro-union ranks. But the committee did feel that it had the support to win union representation among the two other units: the LPN/technical unit and the service and maintenance unit. It was felt that if the union could win one or both of these units, a union stronghold would be established in the hospital, and the RNs would be able to build on that later. Nevertheless, those RNs who had been active up to that point pledged their continued support and activism to try and win a union for the others.

On 13 October, about fifty hospital workers, many with their children and spouses in tow, marched through the front doors of the hospital to Reich's office. A local newspaper likened it to "a scene from a John Wayne western," as the organizing committee demanded recognition of their union by the administration (based on the support indicated in a packet of signed union cards).[16] An assistant administrator read a statement to the organizing committee and the press declaring: "At this time we're not in a position to recognize the cards of 1199 as a bargaining agent of this hospital. . . . We don't feel that a majority of employees want a union."[17] Their enthusiasm heightened by their show of strength, the workers left the offices to regroup for a brief rally in the parking lot. While praising the workers for how far they had come in their struggle in the previous six months, Sanders warned: "From now on it will get harder. It's been a long haul, but it's going to get worse," a point that was to become evident to these women soon after.[18]

Within days, the union filed a petition with the NLRB and simultaneously moved to tighten the activities of the organizing committee. Sanders knew that the march into the hospital and the petition would be viewed by the administration as having "thrown down the gauntlet," and he began to prepare the committee for an escalation of the struggle. The workers organized a "phone tree" to facilitate rapid responses to management provocations and tactics and to spread information quickly and efficiently. The need for such a system was becoming apparent. As one worker explained: "We were starting to get people pulled into the office either for menial things or to be reprimanded about things that had never seemed out of the ordinary before." The phone tree had hardly been established when it was called on to mobilize the ranks.

Confrontation and Emergent Culture

At the end of October, six union activists drove into Boston with Sanders for an NLRB hearing and stopped at the union office there to discuss the submission of the petition. Before committing the union and its resources to the battles that seemed to lie on the horizon, the union leadership asked the workers about their commitment at that stage. They all felt they wanted to move ahead, and though they did not feel they could speak for all the workers involved, they thought most would agree.

While at the meeting, an RN phoned home to check with her baby-sitter and was told about an urgent phone message from the director of nursing. Upon returning the call, she was instructed to report to the director's office that evening. She was not told the purpose of the meeting, and it seemed a curious order. The group was tired from a long day of meetings and apprehensive over what this summons was about. Before leaving for home, the committee decided to activate the phone tree. They wanted to be prepared for whatever management had in store for their fellow worker.

When they drove into the hospital parking lot, they were startled by the group gathered there. As one worker recounted:

> There's all these people there, and I'm so tired and I said to Jane, "My goodness, look at that group of trick or treaters," and she said, "Suzy you fool, that's people from the hospital!" I couldn't believe it; there must have been thirty people there.

Another noted: "They were all standing in a group and we were just so excited. This was the first time we'd used the call list and it worked this well." And another: "It was just such a good feeling, because it kind of pulled everything together, to know that you had all those people there supporting us."

They followed their co-worker who had been summoned to the office, filling it and the adjoining reception area, as the director of nursing and two other supervisors sat back in dismay. The director asked everyone but the summoned worker to leave the office, but the group refused, explaining that they had been asked to accompany her and would remain with her. One participant recalled the sense of collective power that she felt at that moment, a feeling she had never experienced before:

> [The director] wanted us all to go, and Karen said, "No." She wanted
> us to stay, so then right there I said, "Oh, this is really nice, power
> in numbers, you know." If there had been just one of us, I'm sure
> probably we might have left, been intimidated by her, but with that
> many of us there, not one of us was gonna leave.

With her hands reportedly trembling, the director began to
write down the names of all those present, in an effort to assert her
authority. But by holding their ground in the office in the face of
authority, many were gaining both an individual and a collective
self-confidence, as one worker emphasized:

> I think that was a real turning point, because it was very intimidat-
> ing for me to have my name written down. I mean, I figured, "Hey,
> we're all gonna be fired . . ." But I mean, if you stop and look back,
> I guess we were either dumb or pretty brave, I don't know which.
> But you had the support and you knew that they couldn't fire every-
> body, or they couldn't run the hospital. And they knew it.

Ostensibly, the worker had been called to the office for what
everyone felt was an unjust reason. A day or two earlier she had
agreed to work overtime to take the place of another nurse, who
did not feel she could manage working a certain shift because of
her pregnancy. But when the first worker reported to work to
replace the other nurse, she found her at her job, and so decided
to return home. Her supervisor told her to work in another unit of
the hospital, and when she balked (she apparently insisted that
she had agreed to work only for the pregnant nurse), her supervisor reportedly replied curtly, "Fine, if that's what you want to do,
then go on home." At the evening meeting, she was berated for
having "abandoned patients," and it was further announced that
from that night onward, employees would be fired for refusing to
go where they were ordered.

Many felt that the administration had actually planned to fire the
worker that night, that because she was a strong unionist, an example was to be made of her. Others felt that they had simply planned
to intimidate her, but it was viewed by all as part of the anti-union
strategy. And all felt that their collective response was a major step
in the campaign for the union.

The confrontation was clearly a boost to the committee. The
action demonstrated the power of solidarity in a practical way to all

who participated—a seemingly omnipotent authority could be overcome. As one LPN put it:

> Man, that felt good. It felt good because there was unity there.
> There were LPNs, RNs, maintenance people. It was everyone who
> went to pull for this girl. . . . We were all pulling together to help
> each other, and it was then, I guess, I knew that we had a good
> chance at this.

The clear demonstration of solidarity had lifted their spirits and
offered them a glimpse of what was possible. Most of the committee members viewed this experience as central in maintaining a
sense of collective strength through the campaign. When asked
about how the incident made them feel as a group, workers commented: "We felt like, if this is the beginning, we've got a fight
ahead," and "I guess it was a nice strong feeling of unity between us
all. That made us strong."

A layer of deference and fearfulness in challenging authority was
shed, or at least momentarily discarded, during the course of that
evening. This did not take place in any linear, gradual fashion, it
seems, but quite suddenly. For many, when the demon of their
fears was confronted directly by enough bodies and voices for them
to be assured of some success, timidity gave way to its opposite.
With the forces amassed in that office came the knowledge that a
weapon to confront authority now existed. This allowed them a
courageousness that would have been unthinkable in another context. For example, when asked whether she harbored any fears as
she contemplated the confrontation that was to take place, an LPN
noted emphatically that she had been scared to death. "Truthfully.
But we had been asked to come down there, so we came, and
literally we chased away a little bit of authority. . . . It was a good
experience because I think we showed a little force and a little
power. . . . I think we were all kind of shaking, you know? But we
had to show 'em too. . . . I think deep down, we felt that this was
our first 'flight,' it had to be good."

Another noted that she had "never done anything like that in my
life," and that she, too, had been "scared to death" upon entering
the office. "But," she stated triumphantly, "we all spoke up for our
rights." Although important lessons of collective action and solidarity were learned through that incident, it also marked a heightened

intensity of the conflict itself. As one of the participants observed: "They stepped up their stuff after that. . . . They really knew we meant business then. It was a turning point. . . . There was an increase in papers that came out, and an increase in the meetings."

Controlling the Atmosphere

Throughout the union drive, the business of healing the sick continued, though it was inevitably enveloped in the conflict. Each side maintained a view of proper health care that corresponded to its position on unionism. The organizing committee held that patient care would be one beneficiary of the changes union power would bring, that the optimum conditions for patient care would be achieved by a rectification of staffing problems, heavy workloads, low pay, and other union concerns. For management, however, the union was an illegitimate, "outside" body imposed on the hospital, which would bring disruption and even violence to the hospital and community, preventing the administration from delivering efficient, cost-effective health care. Each side thus tried to generalize its interests in order to establish the righteousness of its position against a competing morality.

By the first of the year, as the election neared, the conflict had become a struggle over social space within the hospital. Each side tried to control the "atmosphere" of the workplace and prevent the other from expanding its influence. A "turf" mentality had developed in which each side sought to impede the dissemination of propaganda by intruding on the "turf" of the other.

The supervisors frequently held meetings with small groups of employees to promote the administration's views on the campaign. At these meetings, according to committee members, there was a strong preoccupation with the issue of potential strikes and violence, with pictures of strike violence and news clippings of militant activity passed around. Numerous "one-on-ones" were held with individual employees who might still be convinced, as well as with union activists, in an effort to pressure and intimidate them. Organizing committee members began to intrude on these group meetings and attempt to break up the "one-on-ones." Apparently, things reached the point where not only would unionists "watch out for" one another, but when any worker was gone from her work area for what seemed to be an inordinate amount of time, a search was mounted in the offices and corridors. For example, one committee member noted:

> Anna was shipped out of the emergency room where she'd worked for years, fifteen years or more, and shipped up to the first floor to do meds. They were just picking on her 'cause she'd been very verbal, very open and everything. . . . I was out on the first floor to get something and the charts nurse on the first floor said to me, "The supervisor has Anna in the office and she's been in there an awfully long time." . . . So I thought, "Well, I'll just barge in there and see what's going on." . . . All of a sudden I noticed that Anna was in tears, and I asked her if she was all right, and she said yes, and then she asked the two supervisors if she could leave. . . . What they had been doing was attacking her. . . . They'd been picking her up on tiny insignificant little things . . . they would bring up things like "Your attitude is not right." . . . She'd been in there for about two hours!

Another activist spoke of constantly watching out for others and of patrolling the halls during off-duty hours to monitor one another (wandering the halls while on duty would have been cause for discipline or discharge):

> You kind of had to watch out for people. When people were missing more than ten minutes on the floor, even when you were doing patient care, it was on your mind: "Keep an eye on *that* one today, they're after *that* one." You could tell because there were little meetings outside in the hallways between the supervisor and the worker and all of a sudden they were gone. You just tried to find out where they were.

She had intruded upon a number of these "one-on-ones" and described one experience when she mobilized others:

> They took this girl off the floor. She was a ward secretary, and I knew what was going on. . . . There's a kitchenette right by the conference room and I peeked in and poor Lynne was stiff as a board. . . . I couldn't go in and they knew that, so when Lorraine and Joan walked by I just pointed, "Get in there," and they did. . . . They just sat down in there and listened. It lasted for over an hour and the girl came out and thanked us for coming in.

Another activist explained that such "patrols" were designed to "let the employees know that we were there if they had any questions to ask and to prevent any real hassles from occurring from the administration." An alternative source of authority was now operating in the hospital, an authority whose legitimacy was based on mutual solidarity but was not yet institutionalized. By "policing" the interactions between supervisors and workers, the women of the organizing committee were making forays into a sacred area of management prerogative.

The administration's countermobilization embodied a vigorous attempt to limit the social space and maneuverability of the union forces. Committee members recalled being followed and watched, and supervisors regularly attempted to eavesdrop on conversations. One likened the atmosphere to a "Nazi camp. . . . The surveillance was terrible, they were always on the floor keeping track of who was talking to who." Another worker, an RN who worked the night shift, spoke about her head nurse staying late at the hospital just to watch out for her union activities:

> My head nurse used to hang around for a few hours into my shift, and she intimidated me a little bit because I felt that she was just leaning over my shoulder and watching what I was doing. . . . Once she did finally leave to go home for dinner she would come back an hour or two later and stay for a few hours during the night. . . . Oh, I know she was there just to watch what I was doing and to see if I was holding any union meetings, who I was talking to, if I had any extra visitors, any extra phone calls, that kind of thing.

Supervisors began screening all incoming telephone calls for union supporters, something that reportedly had never been done previously. Callers now had to give their names and the reasons for the call before a worker was paged.

One primary locus of the contest over social space was the hospital cafeteria during lunch, dinner, and other break periods. Here the workers were relatively free to proselytize, as they were off duty in a setting with large numbers of co-workers. The organizing committee set up an information table with leaflets, where activists would sit to answer questions. Other activists deliberately placed themselves at tables where they could explain the union perspective during mealtime conversation. As the February election date neared, supervisors and top administrators began to place themselves near the activists to inhibit such discussions. Activists were verbally engaged by the administrators to prevent them from freely talking to workers. As an activist recounted: "When we did cafeteria visits, they tried to take up all of my time . . . all of a sudden I'd find myself sitting at a table with one or two administrators discussing the same things over and over again. After about the second time, I knew they were trying to keep me away from people."

This became a crucial area of struggle, because it was here that workers had the opportunity to ask questions of union supporters, and it was here that union supporters could counter management propaganda. Moreover, the cafeteria provided a visual illustration of the collective potential strength of the workforce as a whole. Feelings of isolation were more easily broken down in such a setting. The value of the physical setting for union propaganda was understood by the activists themselves. As one explained:

> We were downstairs in the cafeteria, and they would hear something on the floors from their supervisors, and they wouldn't go to another co-worker or another supervisor, they would come to us. . . . There'd be like maybe three tables with two or three of us at each one; there would be four maintentance workers and LPN/tech workers at the table with us, asking us to explain: "What does the latest paper mean?" or, "So and so told me that if I joined the union that I wouldn't be able to take my kid to the doctor's if they called and said he was sick at school. . . . that I wouldn't be able to do that on shop time," you know?

Winning control over the "atmosphere" of the workplace was thus an important part of the struggle, fought out in various areas of the hospital. But certain areas, certain social spaces, were "preserves" held by either union activists or management sympathizers and impenetrable to the other side.

The maintenance department was one prominent locus of anti-union sentiment among the workers. Except for the secretary, the seven workers in the department were all male, and most reportedly opposed the union drive from its outset. According to union supporters, the workers in the maintenance department had particularly close personal ties to their supervisor, cultivated over many years. These, combined with the character of the department as a "male preserve" within an overwhelmingly female workforce, would seem to have made for an unusual degree of insularity.[19]

Consequently, the organizing committee made little effort to persuade members of the maintenance department, essentially conceding it to management early in the campaign.[20]

Though small and tightly consolidated, this department seems to
have had considerable impact on those workers whose work stations
were nearby. The dietary department, part of the service and maintenance bargaining unit in the elections, was located near the maintenance department, and although a key potential source of union
support in the view of the activists, it was very difficult to penetrate.
Many of the activists felt that dietary workers were inhibited from
openly supporting the union because of strong pressure from the
maintenance workers, as well as the threat of management retaliation. In recounting the history of the campaign, the activists recalled
that many dietary workers had expressed strong pro-union sentiments in the first days of the campaign, but that this support rapidly
receded as the countermobilization was launched. For example,
Sam, a worker in the kitchen whose father had been a solid union
man for forty years, seemed to be strongly behind the union drive in
the hospital for the first months. According to Sanders, however, he
proved susceptible to pressure from the maintenance men, with
whom he had frequent contact, and his sympathies changed quite
dramatically over the months. He even reportedly began playing
racquetball with Elliot Reich after work. Although some male workers were active in the organizing drive, the emergent culture was
essentially viewed as a women's culture. This proved to be an important strength in the development of unionism, but it may also have
represented a liability in recruiting male workers. Only four of the
twenty-two dietary workers remained active on the union side
throughout the drive. At least twelve others eventually took positions against unionism, encouraged by the maintenance department. This area represented a formidable anti-union social space,
which the committee had great difficulty holding over the course of
the campaign.

Although spatial factors seem to have operated to prevent (or
dissuade) workers from actively supporting the union elsewhere in
the hospital as well, work-group interaction also created pro-union
"preserves."[21] Of the three work shifts, the evening shift (3–11
P.M.) was the most pro-union. Many of the first union organizers
worked this shift. In time, twenty-four of the forty-six employees

on this shift played an active role on the organizing committee, and nine others held consistently strong pro-union views. That this shift should have been so pro-union is not surprising: with fewer management personnel on duty during these hours, pro-union sentiments and activities could be openly nourished. Compared to the day shift at least, the evening shift was relatively free of management intimidation and coercion. On this shift, the culture of solidarity was firm among the RNs, LPNs, and nurse's aides who made up most of the organizing committee. Here, as elsewhere, a collective definition of the situation could be constructed among the activists, cultivating the values, ideas, and general ethos of solidarity to counteract both management propaganda and the traditional notions of professionalism among nurses, which would not seem to provide fertile ground for the cultivation of militant unionism.

At first glance, the strength of union solidarity among the nursing staff might seem surprising. It has generally been held that professional occupational groups (RNs included) have less of a propensity toward unionism than non-professional workers.[22] The ideology of professionalism, it is argued, maintains the status distinctions of professionals in relation to other groups of workers, while binding them to the sources of power that have conferred their status privileges.[23]

In fact, at Springfield Hospital generally, the strong current of "professionalism" among nurses seems to have prevented a good many from involving themselves in the organizing drive. Some felt that although unskilled workers might have a need for union protection, RNs should not resort to what was viewed by many as unprofessional conduct. Others felt that if a union were established, work rules might then conflict with the requirements of patient care, an argument promoted by management at every opportunity. One LPN, active in the union drive, expressed her frustration with those RNs whose notions of professionalism tended to blunt the union's appeal:

> The worst problem we had with some people, especially the professional RNs, was that there had never been a union in their lives, they had never come into contact with them, had no idea what the heck they were about. They just didn't understand, you know? "Why do we need a union, we can talk to these people." You know, bull! You can't talk to the administration. We kept trying to tell

them this but they always start: "It wouldn't be professional to have a union."

The professionalization of nursing has been under way for some time, and the expectations that derive from it can combine with proletarianization of the labor process to create a militant chemistry among nurses.[24] To a certain degree, this combination of factors seems to have operated at Springfield Hospital. Though a significant minority of RNs openly opposed the union drive on the grounds that it was not "professional activity," about half of the active organizing committee members were RNs, whose passion for unionism was fueled in part by "professional" concerns (staffing, quality of patient care, and so forth). These RNs viewed unionism as the only effective means of ensuring that their professional concerns would be enforced. For many, the union drive was seen as a mechanism that might gain them a degree of control over the work environment, thus improving the quality of patient care. The militance of one significant group of nurses, then, should be viewed partly as a reaction to the proletarianization and routinization of the hospital, as well as an affirmation of professional interests. Although it hindered the growth of union sentiments among some, professionalism ignited, or at least justified, such sentiments among others. The existence of a social space like the evening shift provided a forum where the union's definition of professional responsibility could be argued relatively freely, with a positive outcome for the union side.

The Election

The union election at Springfield Hospital had been set by the NLRB for 4 February. As the election neared, the hospital administration increasingly used official memoranda to promote its opposition to the union. Written communiqués to employees had been used successfully in earlier anti-union campaigns conducted by MM, and the form they took at Springfield Hospital seems characteristic. Written on official hospital stationery and signed by the chief administrator, such memoranda hold the legitimacy of an official communication from an employer, gaining wide circulation throughout the workplace. These memos were delivered personally by supervisors to the workers in their departments, and the organizing committee simply had no comparable means of communication with the workforce. Though only five memos relating to the campaign were distributed through the first five months of the organizing drive, thirty-eight memos were delivered in the last three months, with the rate increasing as the election approached. In November, seven letters were distributed; in December, ten; in January, fourteen; and in the three February days prior to the election, seven memos were handed out to virtually all employees. Basically, three separate, yet related, themes dominated these communications. The first conveyed the reasonableness and reliability of the administration. Memos emphasized the administration's desire to provide "facts." The union case, it was repeatedly asserted, was based on "empty promises" or lies. The following excerpts are illustrative:

> You can vote for the potentially empty promises of a union . . . or you can vote *NO* and give me the opportunity to continue to work with you, and for you, so that we may show continued progress together.

> Don't be misled by a salesman/organizer who will promise you anything to get your vote.

> Q. *The union says we will get "more" if they are elected.* Is this true? A. No. The union will tell you anything in order to receive your vote.

> Don't let the union deceive you into thinking there's something automatic about what they can do if they get in our hospital. The union desperately wants your vote and will tell you *anything* to get in. . . . Although the union organizers may tell you that you cannot lose anything if they are voted in, the *truth* is that *no one* can predict what would be in a contract. . . . The decision on the union issue is in your hands. Please take time to examine all the *facts* and make your decision based on *facts* not on promises that may not be delivered.

> This election will be the most important issue of your working career and we want you to know the facts regarding unions in hospitals. . . .

> Do I have to vote for the union if I signed an authorization or membership card?

ANSWER: No! The signing of an authorization or membership card does not bind you to vote for the union in the election. The election is by *secret ballot* so no one will ever know how you vote.

The second general theme raised questions about the interests of the union, the destination of future union dues, and the distant character of the union. Letters rhetorically asked (providing their own "answers") such things as: "Is the union interested in you or YOUR MONEY?"; "What control do you have over how the national union spends your money?"; "Have the organizers told you that *even* unemployed members must pay dues?"; "Do you really want to be bound by an Oath of Membership which restricts your individual rights and freedom?" Such questions might have been easily answered by union activists, but the purpose of these memos was to plant doubts in the minds of those not involved with the organizing committee on a regular basis. Not only did the committee not have a comparable system to communicate with uncommitted workers, but the *manner* in which management communicated its message also put them at a disadvantage. Frequently, while an employee read the memo supervisors would stand by to answer questions as the consultants directed, or to offer a similarly programmed speech if there were no questions. It was a distinct disadvantage that the committee could not talk about the union during working hours in work areas, whereas the supervisors could. Just as important was the effective way in which the administration exploited this advantage.

The third, and most potent, theme of management communiqués, emphasized by supervisors in group meetings and "one-on-ones," was the specter of strikes, violence, and disruption. Used frequently in the final weeks of the campaign, this issue was clearly raised to sow fears about unionism and to divide rank-and-file workers and potential union supporters from the members of the organizing committee. As in other memos, quotations from unnamed union supporters were offered as "evidence" of the administration's contentions. For example, the following was distributed to all employees two weeks before the election:

In their manipulating way to try and get your vote, union followers and their organizers have continually promised ". . . there will never be a strike at Springfield Hospital . . ." Others of you have been promised ". . . of course you are free to work during a strike . . ." We are not predicting a strike at Springfield Hospital, however. . . .

The letter goes on to point out the number of strikes in health care over a three-year period, and continues: "In many of these strikes, violence and injuries occurred and arrests were made; courts were forced to issue restraining orders to end the violent acts."

Other memos emphasized the issue of violence with reports of specific strikes, or included copies of NLRB complaints against unions for violence on picket lines. One seventy-page booklet, shown to workers in group meetings with supervisors, consisted of a series of photocopied news clippings about particularly violent past hospital strikes. Memos characterized the organizing drive as a "hate campaign" and extended sympathy to workers who

> . . . feel badly over the intimidation and harassment you are receiving by other employees who are soliciting for the union. I fully realize that many of you are fully disgusted with the continuing disturbances and demonstrations from the pro-union contingent. . . . If these activities continue to become more aggressive and violent the hospital will be empowered to take appropriate legal action.

Thus, through memos and letters distributed to employees on a steady basis, the administration sought to create fears about the consequences of a successful union drive, sow doubts about the integrity of the union and the character of the organizing committee, and generally offer a steady stream of anti-union sentiment in order to chip away at the support for the union that had been registered earlier in the petition for an election. While carefully cultivating an image of responsibility, fairness, and integrity, the administration's tactics were designed to disrupt the organizing activities of the committee. This was accomplished by separating the activists from other workers, shifting work assignments, closely monitoring the movements of activists in and around the hospital, and disseminating rumors about their violence-prone character.

The activists worked to counter this by trying to gain access to workers who either had not registered open support for the union or were viewed as particularly vulnerable to management propaganda. Generally, these workers were in departments and on shifts where committee members were less concentrated. In the dietary department, the housekeeping department, and on the 7–11 shift among the nursing staff, support for the union became more tenuous once the administration countermobilization began. One activist recalled having to reassure many workers who had registered support for the union at the outset. An alternative view had to constantly be offered to some groups to counter the hegemony of supervisors:

> Most of the energy went into talking to people in the service and maintenance unit . . . explaining to them what the union was and how it possibly could help . . . and we made a lot of house visits to these people, sometimes a couple times a week, and phone calls, continuing to reassure them. . . . That's why we went in several times to talk to the supervisor of housekeeping, to show the employees in that department that this guy isn't right, and what he's doing is wrong, and to prove to them that what we're saying is more true than what they're saying.

In the weeks prior to the union election, the organizing committee felt relatively hopeful, despite the flurry of administration memos. Though not well represented in all departments, support for the union seemed widespread throughout the hospital. In spite of the solid opposition of the maintenance department, the dietary workers and housekeepers who made up the balance of the service and maintenance bargaining unit still tended to give quiet support to the union during house visits and shift changes, though it was clear that the election might be very close here. Despite the strong pockets of anti-unionism among some groups of RNs, there would be no election for RNs in any case, and the LPNs and technical staff who would be voting seemed solidly pro-union.

On the weekend before the Thursday election, the administration took a fairly bold move. In an effort to ensure victory, they filled the hospital with administrators and supervisors, whether they were scheduled to work or not, in an attempt, as Sanders put it, "to put us out of the game." Their strategy was to provide one last push to prevent a pro-union vote by coming out in force to engage every worker they could throughout the weekend. But, according to Sanders:

> We anticipated their plans and sent the full group of committee people into the hospital in shifts. *We* followed *them* around and

clearly inhibited them in carrying out their plan. They were so confused and routed that they literally left the hospital en masse mid-afternoon on Saturday and didn't return at all on Sunday. For the rest of the weekend, at least, we controlled the hospital.

The committee felt elated at the end of the weekend. They felt that they had picked up support in the service and maintenance unit and now thought that they might be able to win that unit by a five- or six-vote margin. On Monday, however, the administration's response to events over the weekend came swiftly. In what was later described by Sanders as a "desperate, last-ditch attempt by MM" to derail the union effort, the administration orchestrated a confrontation designed to dramatically win over the undecided voters.

With three days left, a group of committee members spent the afternoon in the hospital during their off-duty hours, as they had been doing for months. They were talking with workers and simply making their presence felt in an effort to discourage "one-on-ones." As a small group stood in the hospital lobby talking with one another, two police cars pulled up to the hospital. A group of officers headed directly to the administration offices. Emerging shortly, they approached the workers in the lobby and warned them to cease their "picketing" and leave the hospital, to which one of the workers replied, "We are here to organize and talk to people on breaks, and we are in a legal area." An officer then returned to the administrative office, and the director of nursing entered the lobby to suggest to a group of visitors waiting there that they leave the hospital, as these workers were a "hostile group" and trouble might break out. Angered and confused by what they felt was an infringement of their rights and an insult to their character, but not wishing to be arrested, the workers dispersed. While they were in the discharge area of the hospital, the police officer approached them again and ordered them to leave the hospital. Because they were in an area they thought was acceptable, they declined, and the officer informed them that he would return at 4 P.M. to arrest them if they were still on hospital property.

The workers were angered by this threat. They felt that they were within their rights to be in the hospital and that they were doing nothing different from what they had done for the past nine months. They viewed these threats as another attempt to intimidate them, which hardened their resolve. They decided to call the union organizer to seek his advice, and Sanders called the state attorney in Montpelier to find out his position on all of this. The state attorney informed him that there would be no arrests if they did not disrupt patient care. They decided to stay in the hospital.

At 3:10 P.M., after a few of the activists had punched in to work, a small group gathered in the cafeteria to eat dinner and discuss the day's events. Suddenly a group of policemen appeared and arrested four nurses for unlawful trespass. Despite their acquiescence, they were led through the hospital in handcuffs to the waiting police cruisers, lights flashing, as other workers in the hospital stood by in the corridor watching in shock. The arrests were viewed by the organizing committee as an effort by the administration to confirm what had been a key element of its propaganda over the previous months—that the union would bring "violence and disruption." As evidence that the arrests were part of the MM strategy, committee members cited the fact that the following memo was produced just *prior* to the arrests:

> It is important for all of you to understand the reasons why a group of people who are involving themselves in disorderly conduct throughout the hospital were issued citations by the Springfield Police Department.
>
> These individuals who had congregated in patient care areas and various departments were asked to leave on numerous occasions by various administrative personnel. The request to disperse their group went unheeded. . . .
>
> It is our sincere desire to protect the rights of all employees from this type of behavior. This interruption very clearly disrupted the flow of hospital operations and ultimately, high quality patient care, a goal which most of us are here to uphold. We will continue to protect the rights of our employees and patients in the future.

Further evidence that the hospital had tried to provoke arrests as part of the anti-union campaign was offered months later during NLRB hearings on the union election. At the hearings, the chief of police testified that he was phoned by Reich on Sunday and told "to expect an arrest the next day," and was phoned again at 8 A.M. on Monday morning and told by Reich that he would "prefer an arrest."

Whether or not the arrests were part of a planned strategy, they clearly stunned members of the organizing committee. Most important, they caused a great deal of fear to spread through an already anxious workforce. This became immediately evident on the faces of those who watched the scenario unfold. As one of those arrested observed: "I can still see the expression on a couple of the dietary workers' faces when we were being led out of there . . . some of them are just kids, seventeen, eighteen years old . . . they got a job and you see these people that you kind of look up to and 'My God, they're being led out of there in handcuffs.' " As if to underscore the threat, police officers were deployed for the next three days, patrolling the halls of the hospital and standing guard outside as well.

On the day of the election, workers entering the hospital passed through a line of police cars parked in front. They were met at the door by officers inquiring whether they were entering the hospital to vote or whether they were scheduled to work. The activists viewed this strong presence as a symbol ensuring that workers voting would heed the warnings that associated violence and disruption with a vote for unionism, a symbolic gesture designed to confirm the management position on the effects of the union's presence. Responding to the explanation offered by the hospital that police protection was necessary, one activist queried rhetorically, "Protect whom? . . . Mind you, there'd been *no* tire slashings, no signs of violence any place . . . they were intimidating us."

Throughout the days preceding the election, the organizing committee had felt anxious about the outcome. Many workers whose sympathies had seemed to lie firmly with the union cause throughout the campaign would now hardly acknowledge the presence of union activists for fear of being identified as pro-union. The following statements by activists suggest the impact of the administration's tactics:

> That next day after the arrests when we went in that hospital, those people were scared. They would see one of us coming and they would all of a sudden be busy, take their tray and run. . . . People just couldn't look at the girls in the face . . . they were scared to death.

> Even a brother of Yvonne's [a stalwart committee member] who works in service and maintenance . . . was scared to talk to his sister afterwards, 'cause she had been arrested. He was afraid: he wouldn't look at me. . . . There were a lot of people that you couldn't even

talk to . . . when they were going in to vote in the election they wouldn't look at you.

Apparently, the image of these activists being led off in hand-cuffs remained a vivid one for some workers. One committee member explained: "After we were arrested, several people [said] (and they still say it to this day) that 'You must have done something wrong, you had to have. They wouldn't arrest you for no reason.' " By orchestrating these arrests just three days before the election, by immediately providing a clear, reasonable-sounding explanation of events, and, further, by maintaining a police presence up to and during the election, the administration, guided by MM, had essentially had the "last word" in the campaign. Unprepared for this tactic, the committee could not offer a persuasive alternative definition of the situation: it did not have the time to provide its own analysis of what had transpired. An effective alternative view would have had to convince the workers that the police were not a neutral force in the dispute. Such a perspective would have had to be cultivated over a good deal of time in various ways to be successful, and the time was simply unavailable at this point.

Even with the arrests and intimidation, the results of the election actually brought cheering news to the union activists. The bargaining unit composed of LPNs and technical workers voted in favor of union representation, though by a closer margin than anyone had anticipated (twenty-nine to twenty-six). The service and maintenance workers voted strongly against the union (sixty-two to thirty-eight). Though certainly not a smashing victory for the union-ists, the outcome did seem to establish a beachhead of unionism at the hospital, and was thus celebrated as a success against both the hospital administration and the consulting firm hired to derail the union drive. But whether or not this outcome can be considered a victory or a defeat for the union, the dynamic of solidarity among the workers in the context of this prolonged crisis is important as a sociological phenomenon in itself.

Sources of Support:
Beyond the Workplace

In attempting to understand the contours of the oppositional cul-ture that was being created, it is useful to look briefly at the outside elements that might have influenced the character of events within it. For the participants in the union drive were linked to families and a wider community that not only helped shape collective action, but also were, to one degree or another, shaped by it.

Though the union drive was certainly a new experience for these workers, most brought to it notions of unionism, however schematic and unconsolidated. It seems that many were predisposed toward unions, and a few against; some changed their views during the struggle, whereas others had their preconceptions confirmed by it. Family attitudes toward unionism seem to have been a key factor in shaping the views brought to the union drive. It was this sort of information gained through existing kinship networks in the community that the activists used in assessing the potential for activism among others. As one activist explained in discussing a group of teenagers who were hired to work in the dietary department during the campaign: "It really helped to have some background on their parents. . . . If their parents were union or pro-union in their ways of thinking, that helped a lot, because they supported those kids . . . they understood a little bit more what a union was about." In contrast, she noted, workers who had never "come into contact" with unions and "had no idea what they were about," especially RNs from middle-class backgrounds, tended to be the most difficult to organize. Negative attitudes on the part of influential family members could be decisive in dissuading someone from supporting the union cause.

For some of the organizing committee members, support for the union had its source in family histories and the value systems in which they had been reared. One forty-six-year-old housekeeping worker evaluated the administration's tales about union violence with reference to her father's experience as a union carpenter: "They were mentioning about tires being slashed and things like this when you're associated with 1199. . . . But that's what you hear about any union, and my father belonged to a union and they never slashed tires." She went on to describe the ideas that had been instilled in her by her father, who always "added an eleventh commandment: 'Thou shalt not scab.'" She explained that while she was growing up a neighbor had been a "professional scab," and "wherever there was a shop on strike, he would scab. We weren't allowed to say hi to the family or anything." She added that once, after the man's house had been burglarized, her father had said sarcastically: "It couldn't have happened to a better neighbor."

Such uncompromising socialization into the ethos of class loyalty was rare among these workers, but many did have relatives who worked in the unionized machine shops in the community. As one worker explained: "Either our fathers or aunts or our uncles, or our brothers, or our husbands work in these shops. I think everybody could sit down and write a long list of people we know that are working in these union shops." This meant that some workers knew what a union represented and were not as susceptible to management's anti-union propaganda. These workers had at least the rudiments of a perspective in which solidarity was viewed as a reasonable response to feelings of injustice. As one activist, whose father had been a union representative in the postal service, said: "My father was always trying to fight for someone's job . . . so I never had an idea in my head that unions were bad."

In some instances, family influences resulted in unexpected dynamics. A hospital supervisor whose father had been a prominent local union official played a major role in the anti-union effort. The fiancé of a key union supporter was the son of a member of the hospital's board of trustees (reportedly, his allegiances, torn for much of the conflict, were finally drawn to the union side because of his fiancée's influence and pressure). And two sisters who both worked at the hospital took opposite sides in the campaign.

The power of kinship seems most obvious within the nuclear families of the activists. Throughout the nine months of the union campaign, the women of the organizing committee essentially became full-time organizers. They planned and attended regular meetings (often at irregular hours) and spent a good deal of time outside of work mobilizing for the struggle. The tempo of activity intensified and slowed down at various points, but in general the time and energy devoted to the campaign were considerable for many of the activists, placing a heavy strain on their family lives. Household tasks now had to be negotiated with other family members and shared in new ways. In many instances, the responsibility for housekeeping had to be taken on by husbands and children. The negotiations over these changes merit some attention, as they represent one important factor in the ability of women to engage in sustained collective action and to transcend the limits imposed by the traditional public/private, work/home dichotomy.

In contrast to male participants in collective action, women often must gain the support of the men in their lives to ensure that the "private" sphere is maintained while they are engaged in the "public" one. Although men, too, must secure a modicum of support from women in such situations, it is largely emotional, and while such support is important, perhaps critical in some cases, to male participation, men's *ability* to be involved is not determined as directly. Men are usually expected to engage in the public sphere, whereas for women in traditional households, public activity is neither expected nor encouraged and is often resisted as a usurpation of the male role.

Consequently, when it was forthcoming, support by the husbands in the form of work in the home "allowed" the women the freedom to engage in union activity. For a few, such support was offered generously and continued beyond the immediate crisis. One activist emphasized: "If I hadn't had my husband's support, I don't think I would have been as active, but he was really understanding. . . . He helped an awful lot and he still helps me out." Another suggested that the reorganization of her family life had had a positive influence on her relationship with her husband. When asked how well he had adjusted to a regimen in which his role in the household was considerably greater than it had been before the union campaign, she replied:

> Very good. I think we strengthened our relationship because of it. We were both working then and we had a baby-sitter who was available up until 5:30. But we would meet at shift change and figure out what each other's plans were for the evening, and sometimes he'd go home and get supper for the kids, come back and get me, or meet me wherever. It really depended on what had to be done for the week. He was very supportive; much more so, in fact, than I ever expected.

Most of the husbands of activists took on greater responsibility for the home and children during the campaign, although many seem to have done so with a good deal of grumbling. Moreover, in some cases, the interpretation of how much support was actually provided differed depending on whether you talked with the man or the woman, as the following interchange suggests:

Husband: She was always on the go; I mean, she wasn't home at all. . . . I supported her; I didn't mind her doing it.

Wife: I don't feel you supported us completely. I remember saying that I had a meeting and you going, "Oh, again!" or some little remark.

Husband: Well, she wasn't around that much and it's harder for us in the sense that I'm self-employed and I do an awful lot of running around; I'm gone at least twelve hours a day on the average. So when she's not home it makes me have to get home earlier, 'cause the kids are coming home from school and everything, so that pressures me to get home.

Wife: I still did all the chores, though.

Husband: Well, most of 'em. There'd still be a lot of meals I'd have to cook, things like that.

Wife: But that was more during the NLRB hearings, though, really.

Husband: Oh yeah, we did a lot during the hearings.

The husband's apparent acquiescence to his wife's interpretation of his involvement suggests that his support for her activism may have been less than consistent, but it does seem significant that it was at least an issue in this and other seemingly traditional families. Though in some cases the workers had to continue to do the household tasks *in addition* to their union activity, they were not prevented from engaging in the union drive. (For this husband, responsibility for the children was, although probably not complete, the first time the issue had been negotiated at all.) These "negotiations" were not always simple or peacefully resolved; indeed, there was frequently a considerable amount of conflict. One woman, whose involvement was curtailed at points in the campaign, noted some of the dynamics of family life during the crisis in the hospital: .

I'd have to leave very, very early in the morning and then I'd come home at midnight a couple of times a week. . . . There were times when he's saying, "I don't want you to go and do this; I want you to spend more time with your daughter." He was doing a lot of baby-sitting . . . so he was feeling the frustration from that end of it, and the marriage was just definitely having a terrific strain.

After offering other specific examples of intransigence on the part of some of the husbands, another organizing committee activist (whose own involvement was not impeded by her husband) noted: "There were a lot of girls that weren't as active as we were because they didn't have the support at home, and basically either their husbands were just selfish or a lot of them weren't in unions and really didn't understand what we were fighting for."

In general, union husbands tended to play a more progressive role in relation to their wives' involvement than did those who were not in unions. The men who worked in the machine shops (members of Local 218) spent a good deal of time together during the campaign. While their wives were involved with the struggle at the hospital, these husbands had a forum where they could discuss, argue over, and generally develop a collective definition of the situation in which the wives' union activities could be sanctioned as legitimate and worthy of support. These associational bonds were largely unavailable to husbands who were not in unions and thus had no common forum. Non-union husbands had to contend with their wives' absence during the campaign with little or no peer support or encouragement, and this was doubtless one crucial reason why these husbands were more intransigent and less open to changing established patterns.

The women themselves tended to attribute the "enlightenment" of those husbands who supported their activity to the associational bonds among the men. As one activist noted of her husband: "He was really understanding, but of course he had the support of a lot of the husbands that were in 218, too. . . . Yvonne's house was a very common place to meet . . . the guys would stay there with the kids, and we'd take off and do whatever we were gonna do." Another activist, whose children were old enough to take care of themselves, recalled that she had taken her husband to meetings at the union hall and that this had eased the tensions caused by her frantic schedule during the campaign. When asked whether she had felt pressure from her husband, she replied: "Yeah, I felt it from him. A few nights he'd come home and say, 'Are you going off *again?*' But I made him participate a little, and that kind of helped because most of the meetings were at the UE, so he could talk to some of his buddies who were there."

It is conceivable that changes in gender relations in the context of crisis return to "normal" once that crisis has subsided. It is even possible that there may be an intensification of the traditional division of labor in the family.[25] Clearly, further research on the dynamics of family relations and the circumstances that disrupt them is necessary. But despite important questions of durability, significant changes clearly took place within many of the families of activists, loosening role definitions, or at least creating a context in which such negotiations seemed reasonable and change possible. In any case many of the women of Springfield Hospital felt that the experience of the union campaign changed them, if not the structures of their families. "Most of the girls have become much more independent, much more independent and free-thinking, using their own heads," one veteran worker observed.

Part of the difficulty in disengaging oneself from private life and becoming more engaged in the public realm lay in feelings of guilt that had to be overcome. Most of these women were also wives and mothers whose sense of value and duty was partly bound up with their family roles. Even the most staunch activists had to deal with the contradiction between their traditional private role and the liberating possibilities of a public one. As one key unionist noted pointedly: "I felt guilty about leaving the kids so much. . . . I was used to being here for all their little demands. . . . You feel guilty because you can't participate in a lot of the stuff they were doing in school. I had to give up the school science program and Girl Scouts."

To a considerable degree, these issues were addressed most directly through the associational bonds created among the activists themselves. Together they could discuss the feelings of guilt and inadequacy that often simmered beneath the surface in relation to their new-found identity as activists. Mutual support took a number of forms. Besides the emotional support and empathy they offered one another, they often assisted one another in managing child care and other tasks that, prior to the struggle, had largely been seen as private concerns. At points in the campaign, organizing tasks and responsibilities were reallocated to relieve the pressure felt by some activists. Such mutual aid not only facilitated the work of the organizing drive but also served to ease the problems and tensions generated by the campaign in the personal lives of activists.

Discussion

The campaign at Springfield Hospital was not part of a revolutionary upheaval. The workers there did not set out to overthrow a social order or transform "power relations at the point of production." They merely tried to gain union representation in order to bargain collectively with their employer, a status sought by thousands of American workers each year. But in the United States in the 1980s, the establishment of a trade union is no longer routine (if it ever was). More often than not, it is a fiercely contested conflict in which workers are forced to participate in a social drama for which they are ill-prepared. It is only when the struggle is under way that they begin to steel themselves for it organizationally, morally, and ideologically.

This is not to say that the process of unionization is free of the bureaucratic web woven over decades of labor legislation. Some have argued that the purpose of such regulation is to lubricate labor relations and minimize social conflict. Particularly in recent years, however, such legislation has been used increasingly to disrupt the mechanisms by which workers acquire and exercise their collective strength.

In 1937, a year when sit-down strikes swept the mass-production industries and forced employers to recognize unions, unions won 94 percent of representation elections in the United States. By 1966 this figure had slipped to 66 percent, and in 1979 (*before* President Reagan demonstrated his approach to labor by breaking the air traffic controllers union, PATCO), unions were winning only 45 percent of representation elections.[26] Although the lack of aggressiveness and creativity in post–Taft-Hartley unionism is responsible for part of this decline, more important in the current period is intensified employer resistance and employers' ability to use judicial structures effectively as weapons in their cause.

Management's increasing reliance on consultants such as MM is not only because of their expertise in exploiting the "worker's basic fears of isolation, powerlessness, and insecurity," though this is an important part of the formula.[27] Equally important in demobilizing union power is an ability to manipulate and use legal structures and procedures in the employer's interest. There are myriad ways in which this can be accomplished.

The delays allowed by the law in the process of obtaining union representation had the most impact on the workers at Springfield Hospital. As pointed out earlier, it has been shown that the delay between the filing of the election petition and the actual conducting of the election reduces the union success rate substantially.[28] What this meant at Springfield seems clear: 65 percent of the workers in general and 55 percent of the RNs expressed their desire for union representation after two months of organizing. In the seven-month interval preceding the election, the management and its consultants mobilized the entire supervisory staff to devote most of their time and energy to breaking down the union support that had been registered. Had an election been held promptly, one or two months after the petition, it is possible that management would not have been able to mount nearly as effective a countermobilization as it did.

Nevertheless, the workers at Springfield Hospital did manage to establish an initial union presence in their workplace through the victory of the LPN/technical unit workers. Or did they? Almost six years have elapsed since the union election, and it now seems that the first union contract with management will not be negotiated. The union has never been recognized by management. It took the Reagan-appointed NLRB more than four years to issue a bargaining order to Springfield Hospital. This state of affairs is not uncommon in the recent climate of labor relations, where appeals to the NLRB by management attorneys can delay union recognition for as long as five years.[29]

The women of the organizing committee at Springfield continued to meet for several years, though less frequently than before. But they were severely—and it seems perhaps fatally—weakened as a group by the long delay. Their contact with the union waned considerably after the organizing drive, and this angered many of them.[30] With the shutdown of the Jones and Lamson factory in town, some of the women moved away with their husbands to seek work elsewhere. Among those who stayed, some have seen their standard of living decline precipitously, with a union wage from the factory now replaced by unemployment benefits. They speak of FOR SALE signs sprouting in front yards like weeds as the town's industrial base has deflated.

Conditions within the hospital have perhaps had the most impact on the culture of solidarity. Working conditions deteriorated, accelerating the normal rate of job attrition, so that at the time of the bargaining order, only a small handful of activists remained. Although they had been bitter about management's ability to tie up their legal status as a union for so long, some members of the original organizing committee had actually maintained the group in relatively strong condition for three years after the election. The bonds established through the organizing drive endured throughout that period, and the workers continued to share information and provide mutual support. They realized that they would have to organize their co-workers anew when a bargaining order was eventually issued, but they also recognized that they had successfully fought a sustained battle and thought they could do so again if necessary. As one committee member explained in early 1985: "There was such a lull after the election, but we kind of needed that, I think. There had been so much pressure on everyone that we needed a rest. But we didn't need *this* long a rest! . . . We haven't given up at all." But by 1987, they *had* essentially given up. With their ranks largely depleted, no union representative on the scene, and a constantly changing workforce to be organized, they evidently could not summon the resources a new battle would have required.

Whether or not these workers would be able to withstand a renewed management mobilization in such a weakened state is clearly open to question. But at no time has their union activity and mobilization been simply a result of their own initiative alone. Contrary both to romanticized perceptions of workers storming barricades in pursuit of class interests and to the more prevalent view of American workers as collectively quiescent while individually pursuing status rewards at work and consumer goods at home, it is in fact the character of workers' interaction with employers and their expectations based on previous interactions that shape their ability and inclination to act collectively. No matter how hard some try to persuade us otherwise, labor-management relations in American industry occur in an acutely oppositional context.[31]

But, it might be asked, why do workers engage in such battles if the odds against a clear victory are so heavily stacked against them? This is a question that can be asked of all subordinate groups. The powerless are subordinate precisely because the potential power they embody cannot be realized in the normal institutional functioning of the organization within which they find themselves. Workers are subordinate to management because management has the institutional power to realize its interests, whereas workers lack the institutionalized power to exercise theirs to the full. As Michael Schwartz notes: "Its [the subordinate group's] power becomes real only when it can form and maintain an organization independent of the original structure," because the original structure is "based on the exercise of routinized power by the dominant group."[32]

At Springfield Hospital, workers knew that they would have to create an organizational form independent of the hospital administration if they were to realize their potential power. Some might once have thought that the "management advisory committee" would be capable of addressing their concerns, but they soon learned that it would not be allowed to do so. Indeed, as soon as a worker "representative" on the committee met with her co-workers to articulate demands and petition the administration independently, the committee was disbanded on the advice of the administration's lawyers. Thus, when they decided to build a union, the workers understood why an organizing committee, independent of managerial influence and drawn from the ranks of workers throughout the workplace, would be the proper organizational vehicle for it.

But having an independent organizational form was not in itself enough to mobilize them for such rough passages as they were to endure throughout the conflict. What maintained their morale was the recognition that their organization might establish their collective power institutionally. What workers here (or anywhere) will fight for is largely a function of what they can reasonably expect to win. In the case of workers who have little or no experience with unionism, what they think can be won must be demonstrated and reinforced over and over in the course of the process itself. For any subordinate group to maintain the discipline and coordination of its members, as well as attract new members, it must demonstrate its ability to exercise power. As Schwartz has shown, every such organization is faced with "two related but distinct problems:"

> On the one hand, it looks out to a possible membership which must be convinced of the efficacy of the organization in winning the changes they wish. . . . On the other hand, those already inside the

organization must be constantly reinforced in their belief that the organization is succeeding."[33]

It was precisely these two problems that were addressed in the confrontations with supervisors during the union drive. The large confrontation in the supervisor's office in late October was an important assertion by workers of their own collective power. The lesson learned by the organizing committee was summed up in one worker's recognition that "we were all pulling together to help each other, and it was then, I guess, that I knew that we had a good chance at this." Similarly, the march into the hospital to present the signed union cards to management and the numerous smaller confrontations to break up "one-on-ones" or confront supervisors harassing union supporters had the effect of reinforcing the resolve of the organizing committee members, while demonstrating to others the efficacy of a collective response to grievances. In fact, many of these confrontations were actually extra-institutional attempts at grievance resolution, inasmuch as the committee addressed the sorts of problems (harassment, firings, job transfers) a recognized trade union would confront.

What we seen, then, is an independent grouping of workers in the process of becoming established as a permanent organization, with regular skirmishing between workers and formal authority defining and maintaining the internal coherence of the group, as well as demonstrating the potential practical value of an alternative source of authority. A union was being formed in the vehicle that was advancing it.

A question often asked of protest groups and social movements revolves around the issue of rationality. Do the participants in such actions or movements proceed in a rational way, assessing the costs and benefits of their own participation? In the case above, were the "demonstrations" of the organizing committee "data" from which participants took an "accounting" in order to assess the value of their personal participation as well as the efficacy of the union drive itself?

Many of the activities of the organizing committee had the effect of demonstrating collective power to members as well as to potential members. Clearly, this was a conscious aim in the program introduced by the union organizer. However, as I have tried to stress, the union drive was not simply a matter of a conscious strategy being set out and followed point by point on a clear field. At Springfield Hospital the field was littered with many obstacles, and even had a mine or two strategically planted. With the union drive taking place in a highly conflictual context, one important factor was the ability of the combatants to obscure each other's field of vision, as well as the vision of potential recruits. In such cases, rational calculation is thus not based on a simple "inventory" of available resources, but on socially constructed appearances as well.

For example, the union confrontation with supervisors created an *appearance* of collective strength and clearly maintained the morale of the committee. However, relative to the power of the administration, they were still unequal opponents. If the union committee had actually been as strong as it tried to demonstrate in confrontation, it would have been able to demand union recognition at any point and received it. It was not, but it acted in a way that in largely symbolic fashion demonstrated the potential collective strength it strove to achieve. Small, but very real, victories were won. The worker who was called to the head nurse's office in October might very well have been fired had thirty co-workers not accompanied her. The administration could conceivably have responded by calling in the state police or the National Guard to have the whole group forcibly removed, but such measures might have been disastrous for its anti-union campaign, and so they were not taken then. As it was, though, the worker was most likely called to the office not simply in order to fire or intimidate a union supporter (although that was doubtless one purpose), but to give a *symbolic* example to others of what the consequences of union support could be.

Indeed, one of the reasons for the high success rate of anti-union consultants like MM is their ability to construct a scenario that obscures the aims and character of an organizing campaign. "One-on-ones" and memoranda that warned of the likelihood of strikes, violence, and intimidation were thus, in the end, buttressed by symbolic depiction of what a union victory would allegedly bring to an otherwise peaceful workplace. Three days before the election, arrests were orchestrated that sought to *demonstrate* a reality the administration had been trying to assert all along. The police presence in and around the hospital in those last days before the election must also be seen in this light. Unjustified from any reasonable security standpoint, the police presence was designed to heighten the atmosphere of fear that MM had been cultivating and associating with the union forces. This tactic assured that undecided workers would not be voting based on a rational calculation of interests alone, but in the midst of a distorted social-psychological climate.

Socially constructed realities, drawing on symbolic representations as well as on tangible expressions of institutional and extra-institutional power, should be taken into account in discussions of rationality and irrationality in collective action and social movements. The classical debate has one side emphasizing resource mobilization and rational, cost-benefit calculation, while the other relies on social-psychological explanation. Recently, Lewis Killian has eschewed traditional social-psychological characterizations of collective action as somehow pathological, but has concluded that "while organization and rational planning are key variables, social movement theory must take into account spontaneity and emergence and the forces which generate them. It must treat as important, not as irrational, the feeling states and the cognitions which sometimes cause individuals to throw caution to the winds and act in the face of great or unknown odds."[34]

In the struggle at Springfield Hospital, management attempted to manipulate "feeling states" and "cognitions" as part of its rational, programmatic effort to defeat the union drive. Similarly, heightened feelings of solidarity allowed workers to confront authority in spite of rational fears of discharge, isolation, and arrest. Thus, a socially constructed social-psychological climate played a significant role in the calculation of resources and the process of mobilization on both sides in the collective action.

Moving from the opposite camp in this debate, but arriving at a destination not far from Killian, Bert Klandermans has attempted to use social psychology in an effort to expand the resource mobilization approach "by revealing processes of social-movement participation on the individual level." By interviewing workers repeatedly over several months during the course of a mobilization campaign conducted by their union leaders, he was able to document the changes in commitment over time in response to "maneuvers by their opponents," as well as other "external events." Among other things, his findings refute the claim of Mancur Olson that people are not motivated to engage in collective action because of the "collective good," but only by virtue of "selective incentives," and they support the view that group solidarity is an important determinant of participation.[35]

Although Klandermans' analysis is a significant contribution, data from the Springfield Hospital case would seem to suggest the need for a modification. At Springfield it was an emergent culture of solidarity, a collective association of workers, that negotiated and collectively defined reality and that navigated a course through "maneuvers by opponents" and "external events." Workers did not simply respond individually to initiatives, but to a large degree did so as a group in mutual support, with (and sometimes without) the backing of family and friends. Klandermans' reliance on the individual as the key unit of analysis may be necessitated by his use of survey methodology, but the actual process of mobilization is rarely the result of a multitude of individual responses and is shaped considerably by the collective chemistry of intragroup relations. As Kistler stresses in discussing union organizing drives elsewhere: "The individual's decision whether or not to support unionization is not made in isolation. It is influenced by the experience of collective action during the organizing campaign itself and the subsequent contract negotiation process."[36]

Not only are decisions made in collective action but also, I would argue, something new is created in the context of conflict. An emergent culture is created in which new values are incubated, new forms of activity generated, and an associational bond of a new type formed. The organizing committee in the union drive at Springfield Hospital served as a structure for solidarity. Not only was the commitment of each activist sustained in it, but a collective identity was formed as well. By the end of their campaign, activists thought of themselves as a collective entity that embodied a certain vision distinguishing them from others and representing a new approach to authority, hierarchy, and relations to one another.

This emergent culture may have been an episodic phenomenon, ultimately dissipated by subsequent events (it certainly was tempered as the crisis waned), but it did serve as a vehicle that sustained the workers and changed them during a significant period in their lives. Through it, in the heat of conflict, they shed some old ideas about hierarchy in the workplace as well as in the family. The moments of confrontation allowed them to see that authority could be challenged, and the culture in which they were enveloped gave that challenge direction, continuity, and support in the face of a formidable countermobilization.

That most of the activists were women clearly shaped the character of the oppositional culture. To some degree it may have inhibited recruitment. For example, the male maintenance workers who opposed or kept their distance from the union drive partly sought to preserve the occupational status accorded their skilled work. Their occupational status as skilled manual workers, as well as their maleness, set them apart from much of the organizing committee, and though there were other factors involved in their reluctance to join (their relationship to their supervisor, their resentment of members of Local 218, and so forth), we cannot discount gender as a factor.

The organizing committee was always in danger of violating the standards of behavior for women in the hospital and in the surrounding community. The administration often pointed to violence and aggressiveness as characteristic of the union drive. Although the uncommitted knew that there had been no incidents of violent behavior, the "aggressiveness" of the organizing committee may have been viewed with suspicion by those not accustomed to a group of women acting in such a forceful, assertive manner. Recent analyses of the militancy of women workers show that traditional notions of their acquiescence have been misinformed,[37] but for some workers at Springfield Hospital, female militancy was most likely not accepted easily or simply.

The overwhelmingly female character of the organizing committee also meant that ability to participate was linked to the successful modification of traditional roles in the home. Without some modification, responsibilities for maintenance of the private sphere would have made the demands of involvement in the public one largely impossible for activists with families. As Kate Purcell has shown, family life can be a significant obstacle for women shop stewards in established unions, even when their families are supportive of their union activity. In interviews with married women shop stewards, Purcell found them generally unable to attend union meetings or weekend conferences, "not because they were uninterested or were less interested in the union than in their families, but because they were prevented from doing so *because of* their family commitments, often mentioning that their husbands discouraged or forbade such activities."[38] Purcell found that women's acceptance of the domestic role was more pragmatic than ideological, and the same seems to have been true for the workers at Springfield Hospital. For women to participate fully in the union drive, family members had to take more responsibility for child care, housework, and other domestic tasks. The union campaign created a set of conditions in the lives of participants that required a degree of reorganization or loosening of traditional roles. The process essentially embodied a practical critique of privatized social relations.

Changes in the home were not simple, direct, or even. Union husbands tended to be more responsive than non-union ones, but they, too, often resisted. With reference to the men of Local 218, one worker noted that views were changed gradually through the course of the campaign: "They saw it as 'these little women, we'll have to go up and protect these little women' . . . then, as things progressed, their attitudes changed, they began to understand more." She explained that it was a struggle for the women to retain their own leadership and autonomy in the face of the paternalistic attitudes of the men:

> It was like, "We're going to stand on our own two feet and you're not going to tell us what to do. You can help us, but you're not going to tell us." We needed the emotional support but we didn't need leaders. We could handle it on our own.

The culture of solidarity they formed in the workplace, and that reverberated through their families, also touched the wider community. Political configurations were now understood with reference to their own experience, and for some this raised significant questions about politics and the wider society. After pointing out that the union drive had been "an education in the way management worked," one LPN explained the links between "the personal" and "the political" growth of the women of the organizing committee:

> It was an education in knowing ourselves, too. I think a lot of us grew a lot through it. We did things that we never thought we were capable of before. We went and talked to management, made our

ideas clear, made our thoughts clear, our wants clear, our needs
clear, which I (ten years ago) probably would have sat back and said,
"I can't do that, I'm just a lowly LPN." But it really strengthened us.
It broadened our ideas as far as general politics in the town, and
state politics [are concerned]. During this [time] we got very active
in Peter Welch's campaign for state senator. He had helped us an
awful lot during the campaign, and we had gotten aware of how you
put the politicians in and they can work for you or against you. We
were more aware of it than ever before. I think we all had kind of
been nonchalantly taking it for granted that the only ones who could
change things around us were people with money or people with
power, and in this town they're usually one and the same.

She went on to describe how many of the activists had been involved in the formation of a town labor coalition "to help all different unions . . . to give advice and moral support during contracts
or if there was to be a strike."

During the union drive at the hospital, Local 218 organized an
"Unemployed Council" in Springfield. Prompted by the struggle at
the hospital, as well as the increasing lay-offs in the machine shops,
the council established a food bank to distribute food to laid-off
workers, raised funds to maintain their health insurance, and mobilized a series of marches and community forums to build community solidarity. In many ways, the union drive had galvanized the
men of Local 218 to organize their own membership as well as the
wider community on behalf of a larger community of labor.

Although the political perspective of the workers in the hospital
may not have been a global one, it did represent a new way of
considering one's interests. Political interests were no longer simply conceived of in individual terms or in terms of the general
"attractiveness" of a candidate, or even in terms of traditional political allegiances, but roughly in class terms. Activity in the state
senate campaign was viewed in terms of the interests of "labor,"
with the policies of politicians evaluated on the basis of their potential impact on unions. One couple—the wife an organizing committee member, the husband a member of Local 218—spoke enthusiastically at the end of the union drive about the prospects of the town
labor coalition serving as the seed of a possible statewide labor
party that would ensure that labor's interests would be represented
in a wider political arena. They viewed this as a necessary check on

the mobilization of the business community, who, represented on Springfield Hospital's board of trustees, was seen as the impetus behind the hospital's anti-union efforts. Although this rudimentary class analysis of politics was not shared by all the participants in the campaign, it was a view of politics that in the context of this conflict was considered eminently reasonable by many.

But does talk of a labor party and the class character of politics signify that these workers had arrived at political class consciousness, that long-awaited station that figures so prominently in Marxist social theory? Or were their experience and the political articulation of it simply momentary echoes from the past, unconnected to the enduring sense of class versus class implied in common notions of class consciousness? To venture answers based on this case will of necessity seem inadequate, for such questions are based on a conception of class "writ large" as a national phenomenon in which a priori notions of class consciousness require a global awareness. The scope of this case study, as well as of the previous one, has been not only more modest but also of a different order. I have sought to examine class conflict as it is expressed on the local level, as it is lived. In the course of these collective actions, the workers at Springfield Hospital and Taylor Casting Company did develop a heightened sense of mutual solidarity and did organize themselves to pursue their interests against their employers. In neither case did workers clamor to join a revolutionary political party or demand control of the means of production in the society (though political conceptions of authority in the workplace were certainly issues in these conflicts). As I will argue more fully later on, the fact that the empirical fabric of this sort of conflict does not seem to fit the classical design of class consciousness does not mean that there is no connection to larger class forces at the national level or a generalized sense of class versus class.

It was the Taft-Hartley Act (which itself was meant to resolve previous conflicts with labor for American industrialists) that established the current terrain of conflict by limiting the means by which workers can fight collectively (in the local workplace and community). The fact that wildcat strikes are one of the few openings for workers to engage in self-organized activity independent of the overall structure of labor-management relations is a direct result of a national phenomenon. Similarly, the effects of the Taft-Hartley legacy are revealed in the subversion of the industrial relations system by management in its drive to prevent unionism in places like Springfield Hospital. That is, in many ways the expressions of conflict at the local level (such as in our case studies) have been shaped by national historical forces.

But are cultures of solidarity of the kind that have been documented movements that exist at the level of the work-group and the workplace alone, or do they ever expand outward (toward the "national level")? In the study that follows, we will move beyond the processes of interaction at the micro-level of the work-group (as in chapter 3) and in workplace mobilization (chapter 4) to examine broader social interaction at the community level. Labor-management conflict can spread beyond the factory gates to encompass a surrounding community, and the study of this development will add to our ability to assess the limits and possibilities of such cultures of solidarity.

Chapter Five

The Strike as Emergent Culture: Community and Collective Action

It has been argued in different forums and in different ways that contemporary American society is immune to the open class warfare that once punctuated its history and that conflict, if it is expressed, remains contained within the workplace. This is certainly the case for the most part and reflects an important reality, as the previous accounts demonstrate. But as the third study in this book will indicate, the tenor of recent conflict sometimes recalls the battles of an earlier era in many important respects, though there are crucial differences.

As pointed out previously, strikebreaking has a rich history in American industrial life and is again being freely resorted to by employers in the current period. However, the field upon which this is now occurring was shaped in significant ways by the Taft-Hartley Act and the postwar social contract. The Taft-Hartley Act is largely responsible for a bureaucratic grievance system, prohibition of wildcat strikes, injunctions against mass picketing, and the possibility of strikebreakers voting in government-sanctioned elections to decertify established trade unions, as well as for the existence of "right-to-work" states, which weaken union security. All of these are ingredients of the following conflict, and, together, they make contemporary strikebreaking an essentially new phenomenon.

Clinton, Iowa, is a city of 35,000 people that stretches for more than six miles along the banks of the Mississippi River. It is located in the eastern part of the state in fairly close proximity to the riverfront cities of Davenport to the south and Moline and Rock Island, Illinois, on the eastern bank.

From the middle to the end of the nineteenth century, Clinton was an important center of lumber industry activity, as the river fed the town's sawmills with a constant diet of logs from the north. Settled by a population that was mostly German and English, Clinton was a town largely inhabited by the sawmill workers, shopkeepers, and riverboat workers who made their living from lumber. Nineteenth-century Clinton was also the home of lumber barons such as Chancy Lamb, of whom it is said that he "came to the Midwest with 25 cents in his pocket in 1832 and stayed to turn lumber into gold."[1] By 1900 most of the steamboats that had guided the logs downriver had disappeared, and the sawmills had given way to millwork and furniture manufacturing.

In 1980 Clinton's riverfront was lined by the smokestacks of factories stretching the length of the city. The soot from the factories coated everything along the riverfront, and the small residential enclaves interspersed among the plants, the taverns, and the fast-food restaurants spotting the river's edge seemed hopelessly tainted by the dirt and the dust.

Just behind the riverfront was a commercial district of shops, small shopping centers, and low-rise office and government buildings. Beyond that were tree-lined residential communities of small, boxlike dwellings, parks, and schools. On a hill overlooking the city sat a number of large, stately homes, owned formerly by the lumber barons and more recently by local corporate management and wealthy professionals.

Throughout the postwar era the "Quad Cities" region of the Midwest has been a highly concentrated manufacturing area, with major farm-implement and machinery plants, metal works, and food-processing plants employing about 80 percent of its manufacturing workforce.[2] In Clinton itself, food processing, chemicals, and plastics have been the predominant manufacturing industries, although a large Chicago-Northwestern railroad yard and other smaller factories have also employed large numbers of workers.

The two largest employers were the DuPont Corporation and the Clinton Corn Processing Company, each one employing about

1,300 workers. The DuPont plant was built at the time of America's entry into World War II and was reportedly the world's largest cellophane wrapping factory. Clinton Corn Processing Company was built at the turn of the century as the city's lumber industry was declining.[3] In 1956 "Clinton Corn" was acquired as a fully owned subsidiary by Standard Brands Incorporated, a major multinational manufacturer, processor, and distributor of food and related products, and in 1977 it was merged with the parent firm. In 1980 it formed the Clinton Corn Division of Standard Brands.[4] The Clinton operation was the third largest corn refinery in the United States, with a production capacity four times larger than the company's next largest corn processing operation.[5] It processed corn into syrup, starches, feeds, and alcohol for the production of gin and bourbon.

Corn processing is a highly mechanized operation. Machines clean the raw material, move it through various mill processes (grinding, sifting, cooking, drying), and package the finished products. High rates of capital expenditure and a high ratio of capital per worker have yielded productivity gains in the grain mill industry in general, and in corn processing in particular, well above the average productivity gains in American manufacturing.[6]

Clinton Corn's production workforce of 750 was more than twice the size of the average processing workforce at other plants in the United States.[7] It was made up of relatively skilled machine tenders and operators at each stage of production (converting starch into glucose or corn syrup, blending and drying, degerminating and grinding, filtering, cooling, evaporating) and packers (who tend packing machines and weigh products). A large skilled maintenance department of about 200 electricians, general mechanics, millwrights, oilers, sheet metal workers, and other construction tradesmen was kept busy, in addition to an "unskilled" workforce of laborers, forklift drivers, warehousemen, and janitors.

The workforce at Clinton Corn (and throughout the city) was overwhelmingly white, with many workers of German, English, and Polish heritage. At the time of this study, only a tiny fraction of the workforce was female.

As is true of virtually all corn mill workers in the United States, the Clinton Corn production workers were unionized.[8] The major union representing such workers has been the American Federation of Grain Millers, which is based in Minneapolis and represents 38,000 workers nationwide. At Clinton Corn, workers were members of Local 6 of the AFGM, which had represented workers at the plant since 1937.

The American Federation of Grain Millers was small in relation to most national unions, but politically and organizationally it seemed a fairly typical American trade union. The national union supported key AFL-CIO legislative objectives and sponsored resolutions on a range of pro-union issues.[9] Though occasionally endorsing contract strikes among the 203 local unions under its jurisdiction, the AFGM has not been particularly militant. In recent years it has been one of many unions that have recommended that striking locals return to work before winning all their objectives, and it has signed contracts providing concessions to management.[10] In short, the AFGM is not atypical of postwar American trade unionism and generally falls within the mainstream of that movement.

Local 6 had been organized in 1937, and in 1980 still retained among its membership a few who had been present in those formative years. For example, the father of Pete Hardy, a fifty-five-year-old active trade unionist, had been one of the original union organizers and the first president of Local 6. The younger Hardy told of licking envelopes when he was thirteen as part of the organizing drive, and his knowledge of the union's history made him (and a few others) unofficial historians of the local. Joe Petovich, a thirty-eight-year-old electrician, was the business agent of the union. He served as chief liaison between the local leadership and the leadership of the national union and was the main negotiator for the local in its dealings with the Clinton Corn management. Most of the day-to-day affairs of the local were handled by the president, Ted Bridges, a twenty-four-year-old worker. Together, he and Petovich represented the apex of the local union power structure, although they were part of an elected executive board of fourteen members, which voted on many of the key decisions for the union.

Dissolving the Social Contract

Clinton Corn had been the scene of occasional labor disputes that flared into strikes between 1937 and 1980, but in the mid 1970s the management began to adopt an extremely aggressive bargaining

posture, which created a particularly bitter labor relations atmosphere at the plant for an extended period. An incident that signaled the deterioration of labor relations took place in February
1975 when a worker found taking two night-light bulbs from the
plant in his lunch bucket was summarily fired. Under the terms of
the union contract, the company had a right to suspend the man
until he was found guilty, but only then could he be fired. Reportedly the worker had not been particularly well liked by his co-
workers (he had evidently failed to support union action in defense
of others in the past), but the workers nevertheless rallied to his
defense and began a wildcat strike that lasted for seven shifts over a
fifty-six-hour period. In general, the workers did not doubt the
company charges against the man. Although technically he was
guilty of theft, the use of company materials for personal needs was
a common practice among Clinton Corn workers—a practice with
long historical precedent at this plant and among workers generally.[11] Reportedly, it was not very unusual for Clinton Corn workers to use company tools and wood found in and around the factory
complex to build small boats for duck hunting and furniture for
their homes; thus the discharge of a worker for taking two light
bulbs was seen as an unusually harsh punishment.

A week after the wildcat strike, the company retort was swift and
furious. Forty-five workers were discharged, and a hundred and
fifty others had their seniority eliminated as punishment for participating in the wildcat strike. Union members were stunned and
embittered by this action because they had understood that in
exchange for ending the strike no reprisals would be taken against
the participants. But instead of risking another escalation by further industrial action, the union decided to settle the issue using
legal channels. Numerous meetings were held between company
and union officials to discuss the issue, but after two years of arbitration hearings, legal suits, and an unfair labor practice charge by the
union, the situation remained unresolved.[12]

The severity of the discipline had placed the union in a very
difficult position. In addition to having forty-five of its members
discharged, the assault on the seniority process represented a
direct blow to what is probably the most basic of all union protec-
tions. The establishment of a seniority system ensures that hiring,
job bidding, and lay-offs will take place in an ordered, specified

manner, largely beyond management control and discretion. It prevents the company from easily pitting worker against worker by favoring those whose sentiments and actions are pro-company and anti-union. The seniority system lies at the heart of unionism, and undercutting it represented a clear challenge to the existence of Local 6.

The wildcat strike and its aftermath typified the deterioration of the collective bargaining relationship at Clinton Corn, but there were other, less dramatic indications of a management offensive as well. Although it was not apparent until 1979, the whole grievance system had deteriorated during the period from 1975 through 1979. As noted earlier, the grievance system in American industry established a mechanism for the resolution of problems between labor and capital and, strengthened by an elaborate government bureaucracy, has often been used as a weapon in the struggle between workers and employers. At Clinton Corn, the grievance system entailed a four-step process designed to deal with disputes over the contract through a progression of meetings between workers (or union officials) and company officials until the problem was resolved to the satisfaction of both parties. If problems could not be solved within the plant at one of these levels, the last resort was to bring in an outside arbitrator at the cost of approximately $1,500 per party (company and union) per arbitration. In many ways, the grievance system can serve as a barometer of labor-management relations: a large number of arbitration hearings suggests that union and management are not able or willing to resolve contract problems promptly on the shop floor.

At Clinton Corn, data on the grievance process indicate a fairly dramatic increase in the number of arbitration cases after 1975. From 1937 (when the union was first organized) until 1975, only fifteen grievances had to be taken to the fourth step of arbitration, whereas from 1975 until August 1979, the union was forced to pursue twenty-two grievances through to this step (virtually all formal grievances are worker grievances against the company rather than the opposite).[13] The union at Clinton Corn won eighteen of these.

This fairly dramatic increase in the number of arbitrations suggests that management was less than enthusiastic about making the collective bargaining process work on a day-to-day basis. The arbitration decisions make it fairly clear that the company rather than the union was "misinterpreting" the contract. Although the union could (retrospectively) claim management intransigence during this period and take some satisfaction in the fact that it was abiding by the contract, this could not make up for the enormous amounts of time, energy, and financial resources that were necessary simply to *maintain* the contract (without improving it in any way). The deterioration of the grievance system was the backdrop to a concerted offensive against Local 6, which included the company response to the 1975 wildcat strike, a brief lockout of all union workers in 1976, a company refusal to continue having union dues automatically deducted from payroll checks (making it more difficult to maintain paid membership and to keep union funds in order), and the rehiring of a tough "employee relations" manager known for his anti-union posture.

Retrospectively, it seems clear that Clinton Corn was engaged in a sustained offensive against Local 6, although very few union activists ever considered that the company was actually preparing to break the union altogether. Because the union had been in the plant for more than forty years and because many union members had twenty-four, or even thirty-five, years of seniority, the notion that the company might attempt to break the union was not widely entertained. Although this may seem naive, it is really not very surprising, given the experience of most American unions in the postwar period. From the late 1940s, when the Taft-Hartley Act was introduced, through the 1950s and 1960s, when the expanding economy buttressed a relatively stable collective bargaining climate for unionized workers, few American unions faced such a severe corporate assault. The labor relations experience of most union members and activists in the 1970s had been drawn from the period when the social contract seemed solid, and any suggestion that it could or would be broken would most likely have been given little consideration.

However, the company's continuing intransigence and unreasonableness had made workers at Clinton Corn more restive than usual as the expiration of their contract approached in the summer of 1979. More than anything else, the issue that fueled discontent was the unwillingness of the company to compromise on the discipline meted out to those who had lost their seniority, yet who were still working—a daily reminder to all of the injustice of the company. As one worker recounted: "By taking their seniority, it was like they were being punished every day they came to work." Throughout the stormy negotiation period, this problem hung over the union side, while management refused to treat it as a negotiable issue. Had the traditional social contract remained intact, it would have been reasonable to expect bargaining on this point. But the union, though slow to accept or understand what was taking place, was soon to have incontrovertible evidence that the old relationship with management was over.

In order to press the seniority issue, the union submitted a written petition from the members. This was not accepted by the company, and Petovich, the union business agent, decided to make it a public issue by telling newspaper reporters: "We submitted this to the company and they told us to go to hell!"[14]

While it recognized that rulings by the National Labor Relations Board and an arbitration panel had validated the company's right to take the disciplinary action, the union also felt that if the company were interested in maintaining a healthy labor relations climate, it would be more flexible and compromising on this all-important issue. To the union, negotiation of the 1979 collective bargaining agreement seemed a logical place to accomplish this.

In order to offer a clear public statement on the issues involved and allow the membership to vent their long-simmering frustrations, the union leadership recommended that the membership reject Standard Brands' final contract offer on 28 July 1979 and called for a short "protest strike." The workers voted for a limited strike of twelve days in an effort to appeal to Clinton Corn management. In such a strike, management would lose some production but would not be crippled by it. The union had decided that if management still would not bargain over the seniority issue during the strike, workers would return to work after twelve days under the terms of the previous contract and continue to press for resolution of this question.

As planned by the union leadership, the protest strike was to be a completely controlled affair. By declaring the limits of the strike beforehand, management was made aware that it was not being challenged in a "fight to the finish." Most likely, the strike was planned more as a gesture to the union membership than as a message to the management. With worker frustration running fairly high, and with the credibility of the union leadership in jeopardy, the union executive board needed to show the membership that they were taking some initiative. Even a limited strike might allow workers to regain some of the dignity eroded through company actions over the previous few years and might restore a sense of justice to labor-management relations at Clinton Corn.

But as the protest strike got under way, the company response seemed to pour salt into the wound. The company immediately placed quarter-page ads in the local newspaper announcing job openings for "permanent replacement workers." The union was shocked and infuriated by what it viewed as a clear provocation. The anger spread rapidly through the ranks of the membership, and within days workers came together at a meeting to vote 559 to 57 to continue striking indefinitely. It was later learned that the company had retained the services of a Milwaukee-based law firm well known among midwestern trade unionists as a "union-buster."[15] There was suddenly little doubt among the ranks that the company was unequivocally moving to break the union completely.

The strike at Clinton Corn, which began in August 1979 and lasted for eleven months, was reminiscent of industrial conflicts of the 1930s in its intensity and duration. In recent years, such strikes have become increasingly common again as corporations seek to break unions with which they have had long-standing relations. Conflicts such as the Browne and Sharpe strike in Rhode Island, the Phelps-Dodge strike in Arizona, and the Iowa Beef and Hormel strikes in the Midwest are illustrative of an emerging pattern of corporate anti-union policy in which the Clinton strike figured.[16]

In examining this strike, my concern will not be to detail a day-to-day account of events, but rather to outline the key components of the strike community. Because the Taft-Hartley Act has limited the ways in which solidarity can be expressed in American industry, unions have generally had no fully prepared repertoire of responses when the social contract is broken at the local level, and consequently militancy, social structural supports, and ability to sustain collective solidarity over time are untested elements. The focus here will be on the ways in which a response to union-busting was actively mounted by strikers and their supporters and on the dynamics of crisis that enveloped the community as a whole.

Strike Activity

Most strikes are rather extraordinary phenomena, for when workers decide to collectively withhold their labor from their employer, their daily life changes quite dramatically, as do many of the references that guide it. As T. Lane and K. Roberts observe in their study of an earlier strike in England, "To go on strike is to deny the existing distribution of power and authority. The striker ceases to respond to managerial command; he refuses to do his 'work.'"[17] When workers are hired to replace those on strike, it represents a direct challenge to future employment and immediately raises the stakes in the dispute. With the union suddenly engaged in a battle in which compromise by either side seemed unlikely while *permanent* replacements maintained production, the picket line at Clinton Corn became a center of conflict rather than the symbolic formation it might have been in a strike where management allowed production to cease. Throughout the day and night, and especially at shift changes, a strong picket line became necessary at all plant entrances to attempt to prevent the strikebreakers from entering and goods from leaving.

The psychological climate of a strike "under siege" by strikebreakers and a management determined to break it is perhaps as different from a routine strike as a routine strike is from a nonstrike workday. Although the withholding of labor represents a denial of authority, life on the picket line in a typical strike can quickly become as tedious as the drudgery and boredom of routinized work itself (and without a paycheck to help sustain it). In a union-busting strike, however, the psychological climate is heightened considerably by the assault on the picket line, with those who defend it anticipating daily conflict with those violating it and each side constantly monitoring the actions of the other.[18] Not only was the survival of the union at stake under these conditions, but also the employment of a new workforce held the threat of redundancy. The strikers knew that the only way to limit their "substitutability" was to show those contemplating strikebreaking that the price would be high.

The intensity of the atmosphere on the picket line extended through all aspects of the strike as it developed. Daily tasks were coordinated and organized for hundreds of strikers, who each took one shift daily on the picket line in addition to any employment they could muster in the community. Local 6 had no regular strike fund with which to pay even a token amount for picket duty (as many unions do), and many workers scrambled to obtain at least part-time employment to help sustain them through what was apparently going to be a long strike. Thus many strikers (employed or not) suddenly had a daily schedule that was a good deal more irregular than when they were in the plant, making flexible picket duty fairly simple to coordinate, but also breaking many of the everyday patterns of life that develop after years on the job.

The families of those on strike were inevitably affected by the disruption of normal patterns. Within many families, the wives of strikers (in the mostly male Clinton Corn workforce) had to either take jobs for the first time or take on second jobs to try to keep the family finances together. With a husband and wife working a combination of two or three part-time jobs, or a wife working two jobs and the husband none, patterns of family life inevitably shifted. A twenty-seven-year-old worker noted about his wife: "Right now, she's working third shift, so she gets a rest—I'm there—I'm a mother—right now I'm a mother and she's the father." Such changes, as in the Springfield Hospital case discussed earlier, were not made easily or consistently. The wife of this striker had taken two jobs during the strike, and she clearly appreciated his willingness to take over the household chores—at least during the first months: "In the beginning he could clean and I'd wash. He'd get the clothes and fold them and hang them. [He did the] cooking: I'd come home between jobs, eat, wash my face, and go off to another job. Everything that had to be done—he was there." By the end of the strike, though, this husband summarized the extent of his responsibility differently: "I supervise the kids—and make the kids do the housekeeping."

But whether or not family roles changed completely during the strike, many wives did become the sole or major breadwinners for the first time, and many of the male strikers were forced to take more responsibility for children and household tasks. As at Springfield Hospital, crisis required many of these traditional families to consider other ways of organizing their lives. With the men on strike and many women at work for the first time, it was reasonable to expect men to collect children from school, prepare meals, and so forth. This became a fairly normal procedure for many strike families. Although the loosening of gender roles was largely a pragmatic adjustment to accommodate problems caused by the strike, it does further suggest that such roles may not be so rigid that they cannot be challenged.

The changes in daily tasks and schedules wrought by the crisis were not unusual in a prolonged strike situation, which, almost by definition, must be disruptive. The strike at Clinton Corn, however, quickly became defined by the strikers as a battle against union-busting—a crusade in which militant action was justified. During the course of the strike, mass marches and demonstrations were organized in order to gain public support for the cause by highlighting the injustice of the company, to raise money for striking families, and to demonstrate to the strikers that other workers were in solidarity with them. In the first few months of the strike, statements of solidarity from other unions were read aloud at marches and rallies, providing the strikers with evidence that they were not isolated in their battle. At one rally about two months into the strike, a United Auto Workers official from Des Moines told the assembled Clinton workers, their families, and supporters: "Iowa will not allow this company to break the union." And a member of another union from Dubuque said: "We'll support these people to the bitter end . . . we're just supporting ourselves." Such simple statements of support went a long way in maintaining morale. When the president of the International Association of Machinists from Washington appeared at a rally in the first months of the strike, his statement to the workers articulated the connection between the local struggle and a larger world-historical conflict, a link that was to provide ideological sustenance throughout the course of the strike. He noted in part:

> This assault is no different than Nazi Germany's attack on trade unions, no different than every tin horn military dictator that rules in the third world where Standard Brands operates. . . . We must deliver two messages to corporate America: We won't tolerate dictatorial rule within the borders of Clinton, within the state of Iowa, or within this country. This is America, and free trade unions are here to stay. Fight on![19]

What is important for our purposes, though, is not simply that unionists from elsewhere came to Clinton to show their solidarity, but that members of Local 6 organized and conducted the events.

Workers who had never attended a political demonstration of any kind suddenly had to learn how to organize a demonstration. They leafleted plant gates throughout the area, spoke at meetings of other unions to discuss their plight and to build up their strike fund, and otherwise made contact with trade unionists outside their immediate union local. To do this effectively, strikers had to reach active unionists at International Harvester, McLaughlin Steel, Wesco, and other nearby plants. Regional contacts between different unions and among workers in different industries had to be made for the first time in many cases. Such ties, which would seem to be basic links in union solidarity, have generally not been firmly maintained in the post–Taft-Hartley period.

Essentially, the necessity of expanding contacts to gain support demanded that workers develop a "class analysis" of the area. By going to another group's union meeting and speaking about the situation at Clinton Corn, the strikers learned a great deal about the conditions of other workers. A typical view was expressed by one middle-aged striker when he exclaimed:

> This is not just happening in Clinton, you know. Those guys at Harvester are facing the same kind of stuff; the Delevan workers got busted, just like they're trying to do to us. . . . It's happening all over the country but everybody thinks it's just them—when you get out to talk with these other guys you see how bad it is all over.

The strike also provided the rank and file of Local 6 with opportunities to get to know one another in new ways. Word of strike developments and other news was generated by, and passed along at, the Clinton Labor Temple, where the Local 6 union hall and offices were located. The Labor Temple became a central meeting place for strikers, where workers came for information, had problems solved, kept abreast of strike news, or simply congregated when they were not on picket duty. From twenty to forty workers were almost constantly gathered at the hall, smoking and drinking coffee, laughing, talking, and generally spending a good deal of time together. Some fortunate enough to have found temporary jobs often stopped at the Labor Temple after work for an hour or two; those without work sometimes stopped by two or three times during the day. The Labor Temple was the "command center" of the strike, and the long hours spent there enabled relationships between workers to be cultivated in new ways. Here workers discussed strategy, assessed strike developments, and kept up one another's spirits in difficult times. Inside the plant, breaks had often been the only occasions when workers could talk together without a foreman present to inhibit conversation, and even then it had been difficult to get to know workers outside of one's immediate work area. At the union hall, there were no such limitations.

The Labor Temple also became a center of social activity for families and supporters of the strike. Dances and catfish fries were regularly held at the union hall throughout the strike, bringing the families of strikers together. At these affairs there was a picniclike atmosphere. Music was played, union songs were sung, and people talked, laughed, and shared meals while their children played throughout the large hall.

These events served a number of purposes. They constituted social activities for a strike community whose members could not afford to maintain an active social life with their finances in deep crisis. They also provided a context in which those in hardship could socialize with others confronting similar circumstances, preventing a sense of isolation and despondency from setting in too deeply. By bringing families together, the pressures on family life caused by the long strike were eased and the sense of community was made tangible.

An important dimension of developing strike support from outside, as well as of activities designed to maintain and develop the strike community itself, was that these were *collective* activities that created a sense of mutuality and sociability. These workers and their families had been loosely associated for many years, but had not previously shared the intense sense of community nourished by the strike. The strike added a whole new set of activities that were other-directed (toward co-workers, their kin, and between families).

Counterinstitutions of the Strike Community

Organizational forms had to be created to mobilize and sustain the struggle against Standard Brands. As the institutions of the local community registered their support of the employer, the strikers largely filled the vacuum with institutional forms of their own making.

The scale and developing intensity of the strike made it virtually impossible for members of the Clinton community and its institutions to remain outside the conflict for long. A strike at one of the largest employers in an industrial town the size of Clinton, especially an employer with such a long history in the community, would be an important event no matter how peaceful and ordered it was. The importing of replacement workers across the picket line, and the consequent angry (and sometimes violent) reaction of the strikers, thrust the conflict onto the front page of the *Clinton Herald,* the town's only newspaper, where it was to remain for much of the duration of the eleven-month strike.

But the strike's prominence in the life of the town was also the result of personal ties linking many residents to people on both sides of the picket line. More than seven hundred strikers, half as many replacement workers, and their families, friends, and neighbors were all directly touched by the conflict, as were the police who worked picket duty, the shopkeepers whose business shrank, and the churches and civic institutions whose allegiance was sought by both sides in the dispute.

One of the most contentious elements of the strike for many was the role of the police. The Clinton Police Department was immediately thrust into the conflict by its legal responsibility to provide safe passage into the plant for replacement workers crossing the picket line. This meant that large groups of strikers and police faced each other daily in the first weeks of the strike. Typically, the picket line would swell as the cars of replacement workers lined up behind police ranks before a shift change. Picketers hurled a steady stream of verbal abuse at strikebreakers while the police readied themselves. Once a signal was given, a phalanx of police moved on the picket line, forcing an opening for the cars, while the strikers attempted to hold their ground. This daily pushing and shoving on the picket line steadily increased tensions until, about one month into the strike, a particularly violent confrontation took place at the plant gates that seemed to harden attitudes and firmly set a tone of animosity that lasted for the duration of the strike.

The violence erupted at the end of a large Labor Day rally and march through the town by 2,500 strikers and supporters. Seventeen people were injured, ten were arrested, and scores of car windshields were smashed when several hundred of the crowd marched to the plant gates at the conclusion of the rally to meet the afternoon shift of replacement workers.[20] The interpretation of events surrounding the confrontation highlights the hostility of the strikers toward the police.

According to the accounts offered by strikers, the demonstration was peaceful until a car driven by a strikebreaker lurched forward into the crowd of picketers, flinging a striker into the air and injuring him. But the immediate shock quickly turned to fury when the police seemed more concerned with getting the car safely inside the plant gates than with the condition of the injured man. To those on the picket line, it appeared that the police had helped the strikebreaker from his car as he entered the plant grounds and let him walk freely into the plant. A striker recalled, "That scab almost killed someone, and those bastards just let him in to work—then all hell broke loose."

At that point, company security guards emerged from behind buildings inside the plant gates, armed with high-velocity waterhoses, which were turned on the demonstrators. Whether they were provoked by missiles thrown by picketers or whether their action was planned to provoke conflict (as strikers insisted) is not altogether clear, but the "Labor Day Riot," as it was called by the local media, set the tone for relations between police and the union for the rest of the strike. Strikers battled the police, who moved forcefully to clear the area, and, as one unionist who found himself in the midst of the struggle later put it, "It was like a war—no, it *was* a war."

After this incident tensions were exacerbated both on and off the picket line. The police became a frequent target of strikers' verbal abuse, as it had become clear that their role was to protect the property of the company and to escort strikebreakers across picket lines. As the strike wore on, the actions of the police became more menacing to strikers. Many of the most prominent union activists and their families recounted numerous incidents of police harassment. The president of Local 6 reported that his wife was followed by police on her way from work many times, and the business agent claimed that police cars drove slowly past his house continuously throughout the day and night during the strike. He told of being pulled over in his car and being handed speeding tickets and of being verbally abused by police officers; he was particularly incensed by one incident in which two police officers confronted him with their hands on their guns, despite the presence of his young daughter, for what he considered no apparent reason.[21] Others told of being tailgated by police cars as they drove through town, being repeatedly stopped for "routine checks," or being stopped on the street and asked for identification. In filing harassment charges against the Clinton Police Department, the attorney for the union asserted that the police department "has been engaged in fishing expeditions. There is a thread in common among those being stopped—people in support of the union and the strike."[22]

The strikers described a pattern of violence against union families by strikebreakers or "persons unknown" that the police did little to stop or even investigate. One widely discussed example was recounted by the wife of a union activist who was on the picket line when gunshots were fired from inside the company grounds:

> After the shots were fired, we called the police, but they didn't even show up to investigate until the next day.
>
> Back at the union hall, some of the guys were listening to the police band radio when the police called the company security office. The guard told the police that everything was OK, that they had it "under control." The security guards are the only ones who had guns and the police just took their word for it that everything's "under control." Is that justice or what?

In response to this and other cases of what was felt to be police bias, the union created its own informal "police department." The union hall served as the strikers' police station and was staffed on a twenty-four-hour basis by volunteers, who sat at a police band radio and telephone. Union activists and supporters who feared that the police would respond late (or not at all) to emergencies used the twenty-four-hour union telephone to summon help. As one of the three strikers on duty by the phone one night noted: "If you got a problem, call the union—they're quicker than the Clinton Gestapo. When people hear a noise at night outside their house, they call the union hall, not the police."

In explaining the need for such protection, workers reported a brick being thrown from a car at the child of a striker. Another told of an arrow being shot at his window a few months earlier and of numerous break-ins at the homes of strikers (which they were convinced were strike-related). It was common knowledge that strikers had broken the windows of strikebreakers' cars and homes, had slashed their tires, and had painted *scab* on selected garage doors throughout the town (an interview with a crime prevention officer revealed that three hundred cases of vandalism had been reported during the strike). Because the strikers felt that the "real" crime was strikebreaking and union-busting, almost anything that attempted to combat it was justified, while acts of violence and vandalism against the strikers simply heaped injustice upon injustice. Most felt that the police protected the company and the strikebreakers while leaving the union completely vulnerable to criminal acts by strikebreakers.

The strikers spoke with pride of how their policing had successfully tracked down the person who had fired three or four shots into the windows of their business agent's home and car. Though the police took responsibility for the arrest, a union supporter had overheard a drunk in a tavern bragging about having "taken care of Petovich." Strikers investigated and reportedly turned the culprit (a strikebreaker) over to the police.[23]

The members of Local 6 had always viewed themselves as law-abiding citizens. They had implicitly respected the police department of Clinton before the strike, yet they developed a deep mistrust of the police during it. When police officers entered restaurants and other public places where strikers congregated, they were met with what one officer described as an "uncomfortable silence." The bitterness engendered by the strike forced at least one police officer, with twelve years on the force, to find a job elsewhere. With one sister who was an avid union supporter and a brother who was part of Clinton Corn's middle management, the man was probably under a good deal of family pressure. In tendering his resignation, he explained:

It's been a very stressful year. . . . It made me definitely sure I wanted to get out of law enforcement. I had enough of the stigma. . . . It's not over even after the strike is "officially" settled because it's not going to end the hatred. . . . A lot of good men on all sides of this dispute will leave town before it's over with. It leaves a bad aftertaste in your mouth.[24]

Although many individual police officers probably felt similarly torn in a town where many had friends, relatives, and neighbors on both sides of the conflict, the community of strikers considered the actions of the police a betrayal of their role as public servants.

Other strike developments reinforced the strikers' widely held view that they had been betrayed by once-respected institutions. When the courts granted the company an injunction against mass picketing at the plant within hours of the first outbreak of violence, the neutrality of the legal system was called into question. Such injunctions, a direct legacy of the Taft-Hartley Act, substantially shape the character of strikes by limiting the scope of collective action and making union-busting a much simpler affair than it would otherwise be. With picket lines limited to six picketers per entrance, the movement of strikebreakers into a struck plant is relatively unimpeded, and fines and jail sentences threaten workers who violate the injunction. This probably heightened the violence in the Clinton community, inasmuch as the strikers could not legally mass at the plant to dissuade replacement workers, and without the ability to dissuade the strikebreakers in some way, the union lost much of its leverage to win the strike.

This legal protection of strikebreakers enraged members of Local 6, who had little prior knowledge of the mechanisms corporations can employ to break strikes. In their view, the "theft" of their jobs by strikebreakers was the cause of hostilities at the picket line, and the fact that the judicial system would not acknowledge this seemed a grave injustice. They spoke with incredulity at the apparent disparities in the sentencing of strikers and strikebreakers. One unionist remarked on how "the guys who shot at Joe's [Petovich's] house ended up doing forty-five days in jail, when our guys arrested on the picket line were doing ninety days." When the judge who had presided over many of the court cases justified his stiff sentencing of strikers by asserting that they had "totally abandoned every principle of good law and order and became a wild and ranting mob," the emerging characterization of the legal system as "company-owned" was given credence.[25]

The cynicism of the strikers was reinforced when it was learned that the public safety committee of the Clinton City Council (the body responsible for overseeing the police department) embodied what many believed to be a clear conflict of interest. One of the three members of this committee owned a job placement service that had provided jobs for strikebreakers in the plant and jobs for strikers elsewhere, and some questioned whether he might have benefited from the prolongation of the conflict. The daughter-in-law of another member of the public safety committee reportedly was the secretary of the plant manager who had managed Clinton Corn's labor relations policy. This, combined with the fact that the chief of police had been appointed by the previous mayor (who served during the strike as the head of security for the company), convinced the strikers and their supporters that the city government was firmly on the side of the company. City council rulings that seemed to go against the interests of the union were interpreted as a reflection of the class allegiances of local government.[26]

The strikers countered this sense of betrayal by creating their own institutional structures and arrangements. For example, the *Clinton Herald* was widely viewed as anti-union. It was seen as a newspaper that editorialized against disruption by strikers on the picket line while virtually ignoring the violence of the scabs and the police. Many felt that it reported incidents out of the context of the overall situation, which isolated strikers from potential support. Not only did strikers boycott the *Herald* by driving across the river to Fulton, Illinois, to buy their papers, but they also began publishing their own newspaper, the *Voice of Labor*.

In the first edition of the *Voice of Labor*, which was published every few weeks throughout the strike by "Concerned Citizens of Clinton," a group formed to mobilize activity in support of Local 6, it was made clear that the paper would "report the facts about the *workers'* plight truthfully and without prejudice."[27] The *Voice of Labor* was read by virtually all the strikers and their families and was handed out at factory gates and in certain taverns throughout the city.[28] Its publication was just one of many projects undertaken by Concerned Citizens in support of the strike.

Concerned Citizens was a loosely knit group that numbered from fifty to a hundred people at different points during the strike. It was organized, led, and coordinated by an executive board made up of five women—all wives of strikers. The core of its membership consisted mainly of wives, children, and trade unionists from other plants in town, but strikers often attended Concerned Citizens' meetings and participated in the group's activities, though they played only a minor role in its coordination and perpetuation.

Strikers considered the work of Concerned Citizens a crucial part of the mobilization effort. In addition to publishing the *Voice of Labor,* the group collected food and raised money for the strike fund, conducted regular Sunday vigils and marches to the jailhouse to lift the spirits of jailed strikers, and organized contingents of strike supporters to attend city council meetings (as one executive board member put it) "so that they can't get away with anything without us having something to say about it." She noted that they often brought their children to the picket line to provide them with "a real education about this country." To educate themselves, they organized a weekly labor history study group, which was attended by more than fifty people during the last four months of the strike, providing an opportunity for them to consider their struggle in a wider historical context.

None of the organizers or members of Concerned Citizens had ever been involved in this sort of activity before. Some spoke of their experience during the early days of the strike and their initial shyness and embarrassment at the shouting and chanting on the picket line. But eventually they overcame their reticence and became an important component of the overall strike. Although the involvement of the women reportedly led to strains and tensions in some of their marriages, just as it did among some of the hospital workers discussed earlier, here, too, it generated a loosening of the traditional division of labor among activists. Participants in the group became highly respected for their enthusiasm and ability to organize, respected by men raised with traditional notions of gender roles. In many discussions of the strike and people's experience of it, the work of Concerned Citizens was highly praised. During one conversation among a group of strikers, a young worker made a lighthearted remark about the organization, and a seventy-eight-year-old retired Clinton Corn worker lectured sternly, "Don't you go makin' fun of the Concerned Citizens. You ought to know those women are the *backbone* of this strike." He went on to recount his experiences during World War II in a local tractor plant where the women workers seemed "more militant than the men would ever be."

Concerned Citizens helped maintain the spirit of solidarity so necessary in the face of tremendous hardship. It allowed whole families to involve themselves in a struggle whose resolution would ultimately affect not only the strikers but their kin as well. Had families not been involved, the strike might have been broken much earlier, as the strikers' sense of isolation would have been heightened. In effect, Concerned Citizens, and other elements of the general mobilization (social activities, mass demonstrations, strikers' police department, strikers' taverns, the *Voice of Labor*) created the rudiments of a "community of solidarity" in opposition to the company and those considered company "agents" (strike-breakers, police department, courts, city council, *Clinton Herald*). But the institution that played perhaps the most powerful role in this emergent culture was St. Mark's United Methodist Church.

St. Mark's United Methodist Church

St. Mark's is located in the village of Comanche, Iowa, about five miles from Clinton. Its pastor, the Reverend Gilbert Dawes, was a slim man then in his mid forties, whose almost boyish face and frequent smile made him appear much younger. He had been pastor at St. Mark's for about eight years before the strike, and before that had served as a missionary in Latin America, where he had learned the perspective of "liberation theology." Although his small-town congregation of largely working-class people (as well as a few professionals, managers, and farmers) was perhaps not the most sought-after position in the Methodist Church, for Dawes, a native Iowan, it embodied the sorts of characteristics compatible with the project he hoped to develop. In writing of his experiences later, he noted that "for my part, the pastorate in Comanche was an experiment to see if Christians in a typical small town setting in the United States would respond to the gospel message from a liberation theology perspective. My feeling was that 'if it played in Comanche,' it would play almost anywhere."[29]

Over the years, Reverend Dawes and members of the congregation had voiced opposition to the war in Vietnam, had raised funds for the Patriotic Front in Zimbabwe, had picketed in support of American Indians at Wounded Knee, and had otherwise distinguished themselves politically from standard religious perspectives in the midwestern Bible Belt. Since 1972 Dawes had served as chaplain to the Clinton County Labor Congress, familiarizing him with the overall labor situation in Clinton and introducing him to the leadership of Local 6, an affiliate of the Labor Congress. When the 1975 wildcat strike took place at Clinton Corn, Dawes sent a letter to the company protesting the harsh treatment of the wildcatters. At that time, he spoke to a meeting of the Local 6 membership in the wake of the firings and explained the relevance of the Bible to their situation: "'Being your brother's keeper' and 'loving your neighbor as yourself' means standing in solidarity with him when he is out of work or his job is in jeopardy."[30]

Although the preaching of the social gospel has historical roots in Methodism in some regions of the country,[31] in the Bible Belt in the late 1970s it represented the outer reaches of a leftward pole. Dawes's ideology and practice found a receptive constituency among the men and women of the Clinton Corn strike, however, who gravitated toward the pole that offered their struggle both material and spiritual sustenance. Dawes held weekly prayer vigils at the plant gates at Clinton Corn, visited strikers in the hospital and in jail, and otherwise became an integral part of the strike movement. He enjoyed a great deal of respect from the membership of Local 6 and other unionists in Clinton throughout the conflict, and his beating and arrest by Clinton police as he left the scene of a plant-gate demonstration in April generated an outpouring of esteem for a man who, as one striker put it, "stood with us, and even spilled his blood with us."

St. Mark's United Methodist Church is a simple white steepled structure, with a brick addition containing the church offices and meeting rooms. The church had an official membership of about 150, with attendance ranging from 75 to 135 on any given Sunday. Its congregation was made up largely of working-class families, but its political orientation was more important than its composition.

The class composition of churches has been a subject for sociological investigation at least since Liston Pope's classic *Millhands and Preachers* was published in 1942. St. Mark's Church was not merely a "class church" in composition. It became, in many respects, a "class-conscious" church for the duration of the conflict and a center of strike support activity where the word of God was interpreted to instill a strong sense of class pride.

On a typical Sunday morning during the strike, the church parking lot would begin to fill at 8:30 A.M.[32] Families entered a church whose interior was simply furnished. A painting of Jesus hung above the pulpit in front, and aside from a few lighted candles along the walls and a red cloth with a yellow cross on the pulpit, there were very few adornments. On the wall behind the pulpit there was a large cloth banner that read: "Faith Without Action is Dead."

Sermons were designed to appeal to the class consciousness of the congregation. For example, on one Sunday during the last part of the strike, the pastor entered and requested two young boys from the congregation to join him on the pulpit to read a description of the conditions of child mill workers in Clinton County in the early twentieth century. The pastor then began to describe the struggle against child labor. During this portion of the sermon, he rhetorically asked God to "be with the strikers of Local 6 who sit in jail at this moment; and be with all those imprisoned around the world, and those unemployed, and those struggling against dictatorships in El Salvador, South Korea, and Zimbabwe."

Addressing God as "the creator, sustainer, liberator," he continued with the day's sermon, a lesson about Saint Paul, who "lists children and women among the slaves." Emphasizing that "workers are also slaves," he castigated Paul for having accommodated the exploitation of workers, women, and children, and he criticized fundamentalists and liberal theologians alike:

> Christians have found ways to justify imperialism, exploitation of workers, child labor, the exploitation of women—and they felt secure with the writings of Paul. . . .
> Paul was wrong—when he justifies and accommodates exploitation, he is wrong. . . . Just as Paul was blinded by the slave-based economy of this time—we can accommodate exploitation, blinded by our capitalist system and its powerful media blitz. . . . We cannot idolize the status quo while it is unjust.[33]

As he spoke, the congregation sat quietly nodding in agreement. At the end of the sermon, the pastor engaged in a twenty-minute question-and-answer session with members of the congregation. Those who commented agreed in one way or another with the content of the sermon, with constant analogies made to the strike from the pulpit and by the congregation. Afterwards, a collection was taken up for the Local 6 strike fund—a weekly ritual. At the close of the Sunday worship, the pastor concluded: "Love God and serve the people." The congregation responded in unison: "Serve the people and love God." As the churchgoers filed out, the pastor stood on the steps greeting people and exchanging pleasantries and spoke briefly about the strike to individuals, inquiring about their welfare, their children, and so on.

St. Mark's provided a powerful moral and spiritual legitimacy to the strikers' cause. Though castigated in the press and opposed by most of the local institutions of power, Reverend Dawes and the church continually reminded strikers of the justness, righteousness, and "godliness" of their struggle. Moreover, the church represented another setting where strikers could associate with one another and with others who supported them. One twenty-nine-year-old Du-Pont worker became involved in support for the strike through the church. He had been married at St. Mark's, and his son had been baptized there. At the time of the strike, he was one of the lay leaders of the church. He spoke of how his future security and the destinies of other Clinton workers were tied directly to the Clinton Corn struggle: "If they break Local 6, it'll set us all back fifty years. . . . At DuPont, we have a company union; but DuPont sets its wages according to the wages in the community and Clinton Corn has always set the wage standard here. If they break these guys, every worker in town will get hurt."

But not all church members had always agreed with the politics of Reverend Dawes. When the strike began, Dawes estimated that approximately a third of the membership opposed many of his political and religious teachings; another third tended to be fairly neutral (or only agreed with some of his interpretations); the remainder were solid supporters of the direction the church had taken since he had become pastor. The division in the church was not fully reflected in Sunday attendance, however, as the composition had changed during the course of the strike. According to church records, when the strike got under way (and as church activities and sentiments in direct support of Local 6 became more pronounced), there seems to have been a shift in the class character of church membership.[34] Of the eleven church families with at least one family member in a management position (at Clinton Corn or elsewhere), seven left the church completely during the period of the strike, ending their official membership. During the same period, ten families of striking Clinton Corn workers officially joined the church, and fifteen to twenty other strikers' families began attending regularly or periodically (without becoming official members). It is important to note that many of those joining were not Methodists; many were Catholics, some were Baptist. The criteria for church membership and attendance during the strike ceased to be based primarily on theological principles and interpretation of the Scriptures, but rather came to be based on the strike sentiments and class stand of the pastor and the congregation. At the same time, the other Methodist church in Clinton, First Methodist, which took a more "neutral" stand on the strike (deploring violence on all sides, praying for a peaceful resolution, or not mentioning the strike at all), acquired some of the "management families" that had left St. Mark's[35] and became the object of severe criticism for not offering direct and explicit support to the strikers.

In general, as the neutrality of civic, media, legal, and religious institutions was called into question by the strikers, the vacuum of institutionalized support was filled by institutions of their own making (the *Voice of Labor*, strikers' security force, Concerned Citizens) or by an intensification of the partisanship of already existing institutions (other unions, St. Mark's Church, and taverns that catered to strikers and extended credit during the strike). These institutions were part of the general mobilization for the strike, nourishing working-class sympathies, traditions, and a sense of mutuality among workers. Strong attachment to them was fueled by the sense of betrayal that was felt when workers saw previously respected institutions of government and community supporting the company.

For most in the strike community, trust in the larger society was shaken considerably during the strike. The notion that state institutions were somehow neutral was viewed as folly. Indeed, the concept of the "state" as a class antagonist emerged for the first time as a reality. The institutions and agencies of government were viewed as a coherent body, unified through a pattern of actions in opposition to the cause of the strike—a cause that was passionately felt to be just and morally righteous. The realization that the corporation could mobilize the resources of the police, the courts, the city council, and the NLRB on its behalf was a sobering one for many in this community.

As the power of the corporation was revealed in its ability to maintain production while limiting the actions of strikers, commonly held notions of "freedom" and "democracy" were raised frequently and subjected to new scrutiny. In David Halle's recent study of American working men, he found that in contrast to common claims of a strong working-class attachment to the political status quo, "most of these workers believe that the American political system in theory confers both democracy and freedom but in practice delivers only freedom."[36] In the context of the Clinton Corn strike, however, one widespread view denied even this. One striker who had worked in the plant for thirty-four years asserted, "We ain't got no freedom in Clinton—we got Standard Brands." Another worker noted, "It's a free country if you have power—and you have to have money to have power." Yet another explained pointedly: "We have a dictatorship right here in Clinton. It's a dictatorship by the rich—Clinton Corn, DuPonts, the city fathers control all of Clinton." In general, when community institutions were discussed, reference was often made to their control by "the rich." Although American workers often gravitate between the twin poles of nationalism and populism, as Halle has shown, in the context of a crisis such as this strike the latter can easily become the dominant ideological position.

For many in Clinton, the task of reconciling deeply held beliefs about the freedom of American society with the strike situation was a painful process. For example, one striker, an immigrant from Eastern Europe, sat beneath pictures of John F. Kennedy and the pope in his living room, explaining the disappointment he felt about the lessons he had been taught by the strike. "People in this country are free, but in theory, not in practice," he concluded.

The Moral Economy of the Strike

In general, the crisis of the strike caused a community to engage in activities and create organizational forms to defend itself against the real threat of job loss. Many had devoted the greater part of their working lives to the Clinton Corn Processing Company as members of the union, and the ferocity of the company assault was forcing them out of their everyday routine and forging a new sense of community. The strike created a context in which values and moral sensibilities were reframed to buttress the definition of the new situation. Although sometimes muddled in expression or inconsistent in application, there were clear patterns in the interpretations that emerged from the strike community.

Strikebreakers (those hired from "outside" to replace the striking union members) and "scabs" (union members who crossed the picket line during the strike) were, not unexpectedly, widely viewed with contempt by strikers and their supporters. They were frequently characterized in terms of the parasitical nature of their behavior, with words such as "leech," "bloodsucker," and "vulture" expressing resentment at those who would take the jobs of striking union members. Greed and selfishness were the motivations attributed to non-strikers. As one striker noted: "A lot of 'em got more money than Carter's got liver pills. . . . I know one guy who's a realtor, he sells houses. . . . I know another guy who inherited money and he was doin' OK." Another striker commented: "There are people down there who don't normally work steady jobs all the time—a lot of these people are just trying to make a fast buck and get the hell out right away."

Some, however, felt more disappointment than anger that their fellow workers would betray the cause for monetary reasons. The daughter of one worker (who was nearing retirement age) tried to explain her father's feelings:

> Dad couldn't understand why workers would go back who didn't have to. He understood and held no animosity for those who he knew had no money and went back because they couldn't hold out anymore—but those who went back who he knew had the money hurt him. He couldn't understand how they could do that to him.

In discussing their own reasons for remaining on strike for eleven months, in spite of the financial hardship, the strikers upheld their cause as a noble and morally righteous one. They spoke of the strike as a struggle to maintain dignity in the face of degradation. As one worker put it: "The common laborers are not tools— they are human beings. They do the dirty, stinking jobs, but they are human beings—and they want respect." When asked how she would feel if her husband were to cross the picket line, the wife of one striker insisted, "I would never let him go back—I wouldn't want him to be a super scab down there."

It may be simplistic to attribute strong altruistic principles to strikers and selfishness to scabs and strikebreakers, but the circumstances of the strike meant that strong feelings of mutual solidarity were generated in the strike community, whereas financial difficulty (or the prospect of financial gain) was the most compelling reason to subject oneself to threats and intimidation in crossing the picket line. As a thirty-five-year-old woman who was hired during the strike explained: "I took the job for the money; we were building a house but on his [her husband's] salary I couldn't even see a way to buy a curtain rod, and there were things I needed and things I wanted."

When asked if she would continue working after the strike, she replied: "No, I got my curtain rod and my washer—the children are at an age where they need me. I've accomplished what I set out to accomplish and now I'll find another goal."

In order for strikers to collectively sustain their community for eleven months, families and individuals had to "look out for one another," a phrase heard repeatedly, though this was not an expression of pure altruism: Solidarity was a relationship entered into with expectations of reciprocity, as a mutual affair. For example, when asked what solidarity had come to mean for her, the wife of one striker emphasized, "You always gotta help somebody else, because there's gonna be a day when you need some help."

In order to "look out for one another," rigid conceptions of private property gave way to a more collective sense. The difficulties of survival with little or no direct income for eleven months could be devastating, and workers told of their savings being depleted, their credit terminated, the threat and reality of houses and cars being repossessed during the strike. Survival demanded sacrifice and necessitated a good deal of sharing among families. Reportedly, as the strike wore on, many families were forced to share bank account reserves, and one striker gave the last of his savings to a family in dire need. Another, who took a job as a painter, helped find jobs for other strikers, and many strikers who found full-time jobs during the conflict donated one dollar per hour of their pay to the strike fund. One worker, a staunch unionist with two children, spoke of the tremendous strain the strike had placed on his nine-year marriage. Distraught because he feared his marriage would break up, working only part-time, and on the verge of losing his home, he contemplated crossing the line. When the strike fund eased the burden by helping him meet his mortgage payments, he "realized what this whole thing was for—solidarity." For many, private property had given way to what approached a sense of community property. "We all take care of each other and share what we've got with each other" is how one unionist described this sentiment. He wondered why a worker who had crossed the picket line for fear of losing his home had not realized this: "Why didn't he come to us? Somehow we would have found the money to make his bank payment."

Alternative conceptions of property were evident when workers referred to the company. The typical notion that a company owns and provides jobs for "employees" was shelved. Strikers asserted an alternative sense of ownership: "We built this company," and "those are our jobs." They generally viewed the scabs as taking "their" jobs and working "their" machines, reflecting a view of property at odds with traditional notions. Such a lack of respect for basic property rights might not have surfaced outside the context of such a struggle, but neither would the issue of communism, which was forced to the surface by a mixture of design and caprice.

Communists and the Strike

With the possible exception of freedom and democracy, there is probably no political impulse in American society as emotionally powerful or as pervasive as anticommunism. Yet, during the Clinton Corn strike, this ideological bedrock was shaken considerably by a combination of events and personalities that converged in the midst of the struggle.

About seven months into the strike, it was revealed that Tom Jagger, a Clinton-based legal aid attorney, was a member of the Communist Party. Throughout the strike, Jagger had been an active member of Concerned Citizens and was known and liked by most in the union as the man who sometimes played organ at the church on Sundays and who entertained with labor songs on his accordion at many union functions. Angela Davis, who was campaigning for the vice presidency on the Communist Party ticket, was in Iowa on a campaign swing. The time for the Iowa caucuses was approaching, and other presidential and vice presidential candidates had also traveled through Clinton County, but though many were asked by the union to speak on its behalf, all declined to get directly involved in the strike. When Jagger consulted with members of the Local 6 executive board about inviting Davis to address the strikers, they viewed it as a way of drawing attention to the conflict. Jagger, with the consent of the local union leaders, invited Davis to speak to strikers at the Clinton Labor Temple on a Saturday morning in early March.[37]

When this was announced, a storm of controversy erupted. Immediately, the president of the national union sent a telegram to the *Clinton Herald* stating that the American Federation of Grain Millers was "100 percent American" and that the union did "not accept or want [Communist] support."[38] The telegram went on to denounce "unauthorized and unofficial activities of Angela Davis, the Communist Party and any Communist ad-hoc committee wishing to support our local union in Clinton, Iowa, or anywhere else." Rumors of a threatened imposition of a "trusteeship" over Local 6 circulated. A trusteeship would have taken all power out of the hands of the local leadership, placing it in Minneapolis with the national union.

A struggle ensued during two days of meetings of the executive board of Local 6. Some reportedly felt that if Davis spoke, it would jeopardize the union's public relations, while others defended her right to speak on their behalf. After a series of heated meetings, arrangements were made for Davis to speak at St. Mark's Church instead of the Labor Temple. But what emerged from these meetings was a growing anger toward the leadership of the national union for the public telegram, the threat of trusteeship, and what appeared to be a lack of guidance and support for the local. The local's business agent offered a statement to the press that revealed the growing frustration with the national union: "I don't support or endorse the Communist Party and it's a shame that they're the only ones who speak out in support of us. Then when they do, the [union] hierarchy denounces them."[39] A few weeks later, at a union meeting attended by the membership and the national president of the AFGM, who had traveled from Minneapolis to attempt to quell the frustration, the local's business agent used the "Angela Davis affair" to further criticize the role of the national union for a lack of leadership: "I supported the freedom of speech. I didn't endorse Angela Davis, I didn't endorse her party, but I endorsed the fact that she's got a right to say any goddamn thing she wants to."[40] And amid sustained applause from the membership, he continued: "Everybody's got that freedom, because I believe in the Bill of Rights—the same goddamn right that lets the *Herald* print the garbage they print—that's why I'm a union man."

By attacking Local 6 for inviting Davis, the national union president had crystalized frustration and feelings against what many viewed as a general lack of support and clear leadership from the national union. After clarifying his position on Davis, the business agent elaborated on his criticisms, to sustained interruptions of applause from the ranks. According to Petovich, the national union had been "telling us everything that went wrong—everything we shouldn't have done, and never has a goddamn answer for what we should do now. . . . What I want to hear and what everybody wants to hear is what we can do today, tomorrow, and the next day to end this strike."

Davis's visit to Clinton and the prompt attention it received from Minneapolis served to underline feelings about the lack of support the local was receiving from its own union. Many felt that radicals such as Jagger, Dawes, and now Angela Davis had stood with them while the union leadership had offered little in the way of support. It highlighted for the strikers the lack of forceful, militant leadership at the national level. After months of picketing, marching, organizing, and building their strike community, the workers had begun to realize that the national union leadership had no strategy to defeat union-busting on this scale, no tactical experience with such a strike.

Even though the local leadership, under pressure from the national, rescinded the invitation for Davis to speak at the Labor Temple, the fact that her invitation was debated for two days seems revealing. It suggests that, to a significant degree, traditional alignments, prejudices, and beliefs had been opened up to scrutiny and even modification.

Before her speech at St. Mark's, two carloads of strikers met Davis at the airport and escorted her to a meeting room at the church. There, before her scheduled speech, she held a meeting with about twenty-five strikers, including about half of the executive board of the union. She discussed the strike and how it was connected to other struggles nationally and around the world, things those who had attended sermons at St. Mark's Church had heard before. One executive board member said later: "Getting to talk with Angela Davis was the high point of the strike for me. She was great. She showed me that we're fighting for a lot more than just this strike, and I really believe that."

Approximately seventy-five people heard Davis speak in the church, and about fifty others waved American flags in protest outside the church, including a contingent of management employees from Clinton Corn.[41] Considering that the *Clinton Herald* had written an extremely anticommunist editorial, uncharacteristically bordered in red ink, that the company had held a press conference in an attempt to emphasize the communist links to the strike, and that the Minneapolis-based union leadership had denounced the visit, many felt that the turnout was quite substantial.

Discussions of the Angela Davis affair with strikers showed a range of responses, but little support for the red-baiting campaign. Many expressed regret at having felt too intimidated to hear Davis at the church. When asked, others simply had difficulty reconciling the communism associated with dictatorship and totalitarianism with their positive feelings about Jagger, Dawes, and Davis. Many now agreed with a good deal of what they had to say about the nature of, and conditions in, the United States and could disassociate these ideas from competing notions about communism. For example, while discussing how he felt about the activity of communists in the strike, one striker, a long-time union member, expressed what seem to have been contradictory views. When asked about his feelings about the role of radicals in the strike, he quickly became defensive:

> Nobody can tell me who we can and can't talk to! Tom Jagger may be a communist or he may not, but he's been one hell of a supporter for this union. . . . If I lived next door to a black man no one is gonna tell me that I can't associate with him, and no one is gonna tell me that I can't associate with a communist—so long as he's for our union.

During the same discussion, he also complained about "those damn Commie Cubans" who had just emigrated to the United States and were being held in a federal facility in Iowa. The point is that he, like other strikers, was forced to deal with and "negotiate" the involvement of communists in some way. Although anticommunism seems firmly embedded in the fabric of American culture, in the midst of this struggle it was something that had to be dealt with in a new way. Red-baiting, something that might have seemed perfectly reasonable in another context, suddenly became highly problematic in the midst of the strike.

But while the circumstances of the strike may have made many of the strikers, their families, and supporters a good deal more "soft on communists" than they would otherwise have been, it most likely also made it more difficult for the national union to support the strike itself. The swiftness with which the national union leadership responded to the news that Angela Davis would openly support the strike suggests that it was viewed as a grave matter. Moreover, the harsh reception received by the president of the national union when he arrived to address the membership would probably not have prompted him to mobilize union resources enthusiastically on behalf of the strike thereafter.

In a sense, the strike threatened the national union with two separate, but related, dangers. On the one hand, although it was certainly clear in 1980 that corporations were becoming a good deal more aggressive toward unions on a national scale, with a Democratic administration in the White House and a Democratic majority in Congress the leadership of a national union would not necessarily have seen it as a period in which union survival was at stake.[42] As such, the militance of Local 6 (a large local within the national), while justifiable by the union in terms of management intransigence, would not have been seen (particularly after the union meeting in Clinton) as something that was easily manageable or controllable from Minneapolis. Without such control, the stability of the national union was threatened both by the potentially unbounded militancy of the Local 6 strikers and by the strike leadership, who in the advent of victory might have been well placed in the union in terms of experience and notoriety to challenge the national leadership electorally.

On the other hand, by raising the "specter of communism," the Clinton strike appears to have become much more of a political liability to the national leadership than it would have been otherwise. With anticommunism the mandatory ideological pass-key to trade union political discourse, the prominence of radicals in the strike and their enthusiastic reception by many of the participants no doubt made it exceedingly difficult in a political sense for the national trade union leaders.[43] Although it is not clear whether or not national support by trade unions who generally regard such militancy as anathema would have been effective in any case, it *is* likely that the failure of the proposed boycott of Standard Brands' products to materialize was a result of the political threat posed by Local 6.[44]

The Decertification of Local 6

The Clinton Corn strike was defeated after an eleven-month battle. Although the ambivalence of the national union toward the strike probably played some role in this outcome, broader, more compelling factors underlie it—not the least of which is simply the raw advantage that corporations enjoy in their dealings with unions in the 1980s. It seems that many (if not most) companies with reasonably sound legal guidance, a strong stomach for a period of severe social conflict, and financial backing can "legally" break unions with little difficulty. A fundamental legal mechanism for demobilizing unions has been the process of decertification, which, as I have noted previously, is an important element of the Taft-Hartley legacy.

At Clinton Corn, the Standard Brands management, guided by a legal team with previous experience in defeating unions, maintained production during the struggle with a large force of strikebreakers as well as 150 union members from the 750-member Local 6 who eventually crossed the picket line to work during the course of the strike. Though the plant's production undoubtedly fell considerably with a largely inexperienced workforce, a decision had evidently been made to sacrifice short-term profits in favor of the prospect of long-term operation of the plant with a non-union workforce. Presumably, with no union contract to bother with, management would gain virtually untrammeled control over work rules, safety standards, job design, wages, benefits, and even the average age of the workforce, and thus would quickly more than recoup profits lost during the strike.

Of course, such intentions were never stated publicly. Throughout the eleven-month strike, management kept a low public profile, periodically providing brief, concise statements to the press of its views on the lack of progress in "negotiating"; its revulsion at the militancy and violence of strikers; and its hopes that with a reasonable settlement of the dispute, the plant would remain operating in Clinton (a thinly veiled threat that was not taken lightly by many in the community). However, as strikebreakers had been hired as "permanent replacement workers," the community of strikers and their supporters knew that an attempt to destroy the union altogether was likely. About nine months into the strike a petition signed by the replacements was submitted to the NLRB for a decertification election.

The election was held on 13 June 1980, under the supervision of the NLRB. It was to be conducted at two separate locations. Replacement workers were polled in the plant throughout the day, while a polling place for strikers (forbidden to vote in the plant) had been set up in a firehouse away from the center of the town, to be open for two designated three-hour voting periods. This electoral arrangement favored the company in several ways. By holding the election on a Clinton Corn payday, it ensured that a large percentage of the active workforce would be present. Because their voting place was open throughout the entire day, various departments in the plant could take turns voting so as not to create long lines or crowds. At the firehouse, however, company observers challenged each one of the strikers' votes, slowing the process considerably. The strikers had limited voting periods, and some had other jobs to attend to, and the process thus seemed designed to discourage voting by strikers.

Although the election procedures had been the result of an agreement between the company and the union, circumstances virtually forced the union to agree to company terms for the election. As a right-to-work state, Iowa denies strikers the right to vote in a decertification election if that election is held after the one-year mark of a strike. Because the company knew that those working in the plant outnumbered the strikers, and because it was confident that with no union representatives present it could ensure a pro-company vote, it agreed to an election in which strikers could vote in exchange for the favorable polling arrangements. This allowed the company to enhance its already favorable electoral circumstances, while placing a "democratic" stamp on the destruction of the union. The union was decertified by a margin of fifty votes in June 1980.

Discussion

After one year on strike, a union local of 750 members was decertified by a determined employer relying on a legal weapon that has been in place for four decades, but has only recently been utilized on a regular basis. After the defeat, ex-union members were placed on a "preferential hiring list" as the law requires, and over the course of the following year several hundred were gradually hired by the company on a non-union basis. Those rehired tended to be production workers. Most of the skilled maintenance workers, many of whom had played a particularly militant and active role in the strike, were generally not rehired. Because they seemed to have such a difficult time finding work elsewhere in the state (in spite of a continual shortage of skilled electricians and other maintenance workers), there were strong suspicions that a blacklist had been circulated among employers, and many left the state in search of work elsewhere.

Concerned Citizens, which played such a prominent role in building and maintaining support during the strike, continued to meet and publish the *Voice of Labor* for several months after the decertification. But the defeat of the union, the rehiring of strikers, and the migration of some of the most active strike families made it more and more difficult to carry on as before. Although the organization gradually dissipated, for many the activism that had been sparked by the strike continued through St. Mark's Church, which consolidated the militance of a strike community that had lost its strike.

Opposition from within and from without to the political directions of the church and its pastor had reflected the strike conflict occupying Clinton for eleven months. Opposition from those in the congregation who had management sympathies and associations, as well as opposition from the church hierarchy, had reportedly served to sharpen ideological lessons being learned by strike supporters. As the pastor noted: "The significance of describing the kind of opposition we faced is to point out that its result among us was to clarify our minds and strengthen our solidarity. It made clear to all that a class struggle was taking place in the church as well as in the community, and this in turn made such struggle around the world much more understandable."[45]

For three years after the strike, many continued to meet as a political and religious body, though their organizational form was modified significantly after the departure of the pastor. After remaining in Clinton for two years "to help people put the pieces of their lives together after the strike and decertification of the union," Dawes requested a transfer to another church. The bishop replaced him with a pastor instructed to "bring back and 'reconcile' those who had left St. Mark's with those who had remained and gone through the struggle." Instead of submitting to what were viewed as counterinsurgency measures, seventy to eighty activists formed themselves into a branch of the "Methodist Federation for Social Action," meeting independently each week for a Wednesday night study group and a Sunday morning sermon, with pastoral duties performed on a rotating basis. As Dawes observed, "They have clearly learned that 'the church' is not to be equated with the pastor, a building, or a denomination, and in so doing they are stronger than ever before."[46]

An organization of seventy to eighty radical Methodists and social activists would seem to represent a potentially major political presence in a city of this size, but the defeat of the strike created a situation very different from the charged atmosphere when the energies of hundreds of people were devoted to organizing material and spiritual support for the cause. Through their activities, values, and organizational forms, the strike community created an alternative cultural formation in many respects distinct from, and in opposition to, the dominant society. In the course of the conflict, the hegemonic fabric of their world—its practices, expectations, and perceptions, the "lived system of meanings and values . . . which as they are experienced as practices appear as reciprocally confirming"[47]— was ruptured for a year of their lives. Such a break was necessitated by the character of the conflict and the demands it raised. By its extreme intransigence before the strike and the use of replacement workers in response to it, the company had broken the unstated "social contract" that had governed labor relations in Clinton and elsewhere for much of the postwar period. Largely unprepared for such an assault, and perhaps slow to recognize it as that, the union was forced to mobilize previously untapped resources to address this new relationship. Similarly, as the intensity of the strike and the prominence of the company in the life of the community drew the police, the courts, the city council, the local newspaper, the chamber of commerce, and other bodies into the conflict, it became necessary for the strike community to make sense of these developments and to respond. To a significant degree, the collective definition that emerged characterized community institutions as agents of the corporation, and the strike community created organizational forms of its own to fill this vacuum in institutional support. The strike, then, served as a catalyst in challenging existing relations of domination and subordination, not only in the workplace but in the surrounding community as well.

It should be noted that for both Katznelson and Halle, in two recent (and important) analyses of American workers mentioned previously, the contrast between the consciousness of workers in the workplace and in their communities has been seen as crucial.[48] For Katznelson, working-class political culture has been essentially "schizophrenic," with workers maintaining a fairly clear language of class division at work, while community politics is expressed through a language of ethnicity and territory. Similarly, in Halle's account, "America's working man" maintains a blue-collar identity in the factory, while images of the class structure appear more fluid outside it.

In the Clinton strike, however, a more unified definition of reality emerged, in which imagery of class conflict predominated in the wider community. The crisis of the strike caused a temporary breakdown in the work/community dichotomy. A rough, but consistent, language of class division and a class identity characterized most aspects of the strikers' political culture. Similarly, the crisis of unemployment and industrial decline in many industrial cities often precipitates political and conceptual links between power relations in the workplace and outside it, as labor, religious, and community organizations join forces to prevent plant closures by corporations. In recent years, such coalitions have often acted to break down this work/community divide (successfully at times).[49] Although American working-class life is indeed fractured in the ways Katznelson and Halle have shown, industrial crisis can force people to consider relations at work and in the community in new ways.[50]

But there is nothing inevitable or automatic about this conceptual breakdown of the work/community dichotomy. Although many of the activists involved in the union drive at Springfield Hospital made a link between power relations at the hospital and the surrounding community (prompting a degree of local political activism), this link was not as central to the rhetoric of the conflict there as it was among the Clinton strikers. With Clinton Corn workers "on the street," forced to rely on community resources to maintain their strike, the ability of the corporation to divert and direct those resources in its favor raised unavoidable questions about the allegiance of many institutions in the community. Among the wildcat strikers at Taylor Casting Company, in contrast, class relations in the wider society only received fleeting attention when radicals made an occasional reference to them in their rhetoric and never became a serious issue during a conflict that was kept contained within the plant gates. But in Clinton, where a scab workforce was escorted across the picket line daily by a tax-supported police department and sanctioned by a legal system with links to the company, as well as supported by a city council and other elements of the community such as the daily newspaper, churches, and the chamber of commerce, broader class allegiances became an issue throughout, as they doubtless do in other industrial conflicts that have an important bearing on the future of a community.[51]

Though the strike occupied the lives of a large segment of the community for almost a year, clearly not everyone played an active role. Among the 750 workers who made up the union local, 57 voted against the strike at the outset, in the face of what seemed to most an obvious company provocation. Picket lines were honored by all during the first few days, but about 150 union workers had broken ranks and crossed the picket line to work by the end of the strike.

Moreover, approximately 450 non-union replacement workers were hired over the course of the year to take the jobs of strikers. So while 600 union members remained on strike for the duration, 150 others crossed the picket line, and while active strike supporters numbered close to 1,000 (including active family members and unionists from other plants), 450 workers were recruited as strike-breakers to continue production during the strike. This is a considerable number given the verbal (and sometimes physical) harassment one could expect when crossing the picket line, as well as the threat of violence occurring elsewhere. But there is some evidence that only a relatively small number of Clinton residents took jobs as replacements. Many of the strikers insisted that except for their fellow union members and a handful of community residents whom they could identify, most "scabs" were from the "outside."[52] Although the identification of scabs as "outsiders" would seem to represent one means of bolstering a sense of community, more than 50 percent of the cars lined up to enter the plant during the strike did not have Iowa license plates, suggesting that there may have been some truth to the strikers' assertions. Moreover, one replacement worker, who emigrated from as far away as Louisiana, reported that he knew of others who had also traveled from out of state to take jobs at Clinton Corn.[53]

There were different levels of participation among all groups involved in strike activity. Among strikers perhaps no more than 50 came forward as secondary leaders who directly organized activities, from coordinating picket duty, working with support groups, collecting funds, and setting up meetings, to writing and distributing leaflets. Another 150 to 200 were active strikers who could be depended on to participate in most strike activity, and 200 to 300 others participated at various points (attending rallies, demonstrations, and walking the picket line). Similarly, among strike supporters involved in Concerned Citizens, and the members of St. Mark's Church, there were "concentric circles of participation," as the church's pastor put it,[54] with some more involved in strike support than others.

However uneven the participation, the strike served as a significant vehicle for the political participation of women in the community. The strikers themselves were overwhelmingly male, but the importance attached to the work of the largely female Concerned Citizens gave the strike community as a whole a cross-gender composition. Led by a committee made up of wives (and an ex-wife) of striking workers, Concerned Citizens was not simply a "women's auxiliary" subservient to the demands of a male union local. To a significant degree, it maintained an autonomy that allowed the members to act on their own initiative and by their own organizational efforts. The "male" strike was certainly what brought them together and shaped the direction of their efforts, but the issues they raised broadened its political character in an important way.

One critical set of issues raised by the women of the strike revolved around education in the community. Angered by the extent of institutional mobilization against the strike, Concerned Citizens organized "field trips" to the picket line for strikers' children so that they might "learn things they'd never learn in school," as one mother put it. (Although bringing children to the picket line might be construed as an attempt to gain sympathy for the strikers' cause, it frequently occurred at times when publicity was neither available nor sought.) Similarly, the labor history study group Concerned Citizens organized represented an attempt to rectify educational deficiencies of the adult members of the community.

Concern for the educational welfare of children can be seen as part of the traditional role of mothers, and the women of Concerned Citizens would thus appear simply to have been acting out that role. I would suggest that although the nature of some of their concerns, such as education, did reflect traditional roles, the relative autonomy of their organizational vehicle began to undermine the basis of the role dichotomy itself. That is, by forming an organization like Concerned Citizens in support of the "male strike," women created a mechanism and a forum in a traditional community to speak and act *as women*. Concerned Citizens regularly organized mass attendance at city council meetings to pressure the local government to support the strike in various ways. Moreover, with this organizational base of support, the women of Concerned Citizens could become involved in political issues beyond the strike as well.[55]

In both Clinton and Springfield, collective action served to bring many of the women participants across the private/public divide for the first time. In both cases, though, the crossing had to be negotiated with men to some degree. As we saw in the case of Springfield, male union members with their own associational network offered less resistance than men with no such forum, but it was not a simple process, and in many cases led to substantial discord within families. In Clinton, some women took jobs to lend financial support, and some engaged in strike support activity. Although their involvement was provided with a strong stamp of legitimacy from the union hall by strike leaders and from the pulpit by the pastor of St. Mark's, they, too, faced opposition by men unable or unwilling to adjust to new patterns.[56] Other studies support the view that autonomous organization is a precondition if women's support activity in strikes is to serve as a bridge from domestic concerns to public activity.[57]

But to what extent do these organizational forms sustain themselves after the precipitating collective actions have subsided? This is a crucial question, to which there is no simple answer. In Springfield, the organizing committee stayed together for several years after the union election. The women continued their associational ties, but the intensity that bound them strongly during the union drive eased considerably when it was over and eventually dissipated. It is possible that although they were organizationally prepared to mount further challenges during those years, gains made *as women* in the community and in the home have not been sustained.

In Clinton, it is even more likely that the changes made have been reversed by the outcome. The destruction of the union seems to have gone a long way toward dissipating the oppositional community that emerged around it. The majority of women active in the strike either left Clinton with husbands blacklisted from employment in the region or stayed on when their husbands returned to work at the plant. In a few cases, activism may have led to divorce and separation. Nowhere is there any evidence of whether the changes wrought during the strike have endured. It is likely that without a firm organizational base for themselves, most women would not easily have been able to reverse a slide back into traditional pre-strike roles.

The issue of organizational autonomy as a key factor in the ability of subordinate groups (women, workers, and others) to mobilize themselves in opposition figures prominently in the earlier case studies too. In the Taylor Casting case, workers mobilized themselves outside the union structure in order to enforce a definition and a practice of unionism restricted by the bureaucratic channels. The organizing committee of women hospital workers, independent of the hospital administration by definition in many respects, served as a women's organization as well. Both groups of workers demonstrated their potential ability to exercise power in collective actions independent of the dominant structures.

In the Clinton strike, the relationship between independent initiative and bureaucratic structure was more complex and somewhat contradictory. As noted earlier, the actions of the Clinton Corn management that led to the strike represented a gradual movement, beginning in 1975, away from the implicit social contract that for decades had governed relations between the union and the company. But in subverting the social contract, the Clinton management did not have to act independently of the "original structure," as subordinate groups are often forced to do in trying to achieve *their* ends. The company could use elements of the bureaucratic structure precisely because it was "based on the exercise of routinized power by the dominant group."[58] The Taylor Casting workers, in contrast, had to circumvent bureaucratic processes (which represented the routinized expression of their subordination) to enforce their interests promptly and effectively. In pursuing a counterinstitutional method of grievance resolution (wildcat strikes), the Taylor workers were implicitly (albeit briefly) breaking the social contract by circumventing the bureaucratic structure. The Clinton Corn management did not have to circumvent bureaucratic procedures in order to break the social contract; its power (as a dominant group) could be expressed and enforced through those procedures.

On the union side, once it was clear that management was severing the traditional relationship, a response appropriate to the revised circumstances had to be mobilized. But most unions have generally operated in an atmosphere of more or less peaceful coexistence with management, and they have no well-prepared response to meet an assault that threatens their existence. For the members of Local 6, ties of solidarity with other unions in the area, the mobilization of mass marches and demonstrations, the construction of an alternative welfare system and support network, as well as the militant tactics employed against scabs on the picket line and off, represented a repertoire of responses that had to be created anew.

With the proverbial "gun at its head," the leadership of the local had to scramble to address this crisis. In a way, no amount of militancy was too dramatic to consider, nor was any analysis of the

situation that could make sense of the new circumstances and provide a language to articulate it too radical to adopt. Consequently,
over the course of the conflict, the socialist ideology of Reverend
Dawes gained a great deal of currency, and the presence of communists as open strike supporters was considered reasonable by many
and extremely positive by a few.

Meanwhile, the heads of the national union were at a loss to
provide militant leadership or direction and remained at arm's
length throughout. With their approach to the struggle essentially
phrased in the language of the social contract (publicly calling for
the company to resume negotiation and filing unfair labor practice
charges against the company, while distancing the national union
from the militancy and radicalism expressed in Clinton), they provided little new that the local could use to meet the challenge.
But had the national union played a more forceful role in running
the Clinton strike, it is possible that the culture of solidarity that
was generated would never have been mobilized to the same extent. Recent accounts of strikes similar to the one in Clinton suggest that when national unions (even unions with a particularly
militant history) intervene on the local level, they bring an un-
imaginative, hierarchical, and bureaucratic approach that can sti-
fle the creativity, spontaneity, and militance necessary to respond
to union-busting.[59]

Thus, though militant leaders of the local severely criticized the
national president for not providing proper guidance and for publicly "red-baiting" a communist strike supporter, in my view it is
likely that more "guidance" (of a bureaucratic nature) would simply
have squelched a good deal of the initiative unleashed in the struggle. In other words, even though the odds are stacked against
union victories in such strikes, the "independence" that was forced
on the local and that allowed it to consider a fairly wide range of
resources in its mobilization might have been a better "guide" to
responding to union-busting than the bureaucratic approach the
national union might have taken.

With the language of the social contract increasingly discredited
within the strike community as the strike wore on, the language of
class struggle that emanated from St. Mark's Church tended to gain
wider currency. Reverend Dawes and the church had promoted a
radical perspective for a number of years, but it was in the context

of the strike that people began to gravitate toward this political pole in relatively large numbers. A militantly class-conscious political perspective became an acceptable part of political discourse in the strike community.

Perhaps ironically, for many within the strike community only radicalism and militant action seemed capable of defending traditional arrangements. With the social contract shattered, Clinton workers could not easily sustain its language. With the reality of a "class struggle" facing them, radical definitions of the situation and mass actions that seemed able to respond effectively were embraced by a large segment of the community—definitions and actions that bureaucratic social contract unionism could not easily provide. In a provocative analysis of collective action, Craig Calhoun argues that the crucial source of radical mobilization among people lies in their defense of traditional community; that "revolutionary and other radical mobilizations take place when people who have something to defend, and do have some social strength, confront social transformations which *threaten* to take all that from them and thus leave them nothing to lose."[60]

It thus seems that in Clinton the corporate threat to traditional arrangements *was* a crucial impetus for mobilizing a culture of solidarity. Now, as in the 1930s, the very existence of unions is at stake in many local conflicts, and it is in this oppositional habitat that the sensibilities and the practices of solidarity are forged—sometimes throughout a workplace, and sometimes across a whole community.

Aren't such cultures of solidarity doomed to failure, however, as in the Clinton strike? Moreover, are their small and partial "victories" capable of creating a wider political culture of labor, or are they simply overturned later? The following chapter discusses the significant limitations of localized cultures of solidarity and the difficulty of rooting a more enduring cultural formation in American society. But it also addresses the possibilities that lie in such local collective action, which may not be as inconsiderable as sociology's lack of attention to them would suggest.

Chapter Six

The Limits and Possibilities
of Trade Union Action

On 13 December 1981 a tiny (one square inch) news item appeared in the *New York Times*. Datelined Brindisi, Italy, the item read in full:

> Workers protesting the layoff of 25,000 employees by Italy's ailing chemical giant, Montedison, briefly closed down this southern industrial city today. The police said that the workers occupied the airport, sealed the main railroad station, blocked major highways and took over the Montedison plant. They left peacefully in the afternoon.

That was all. Apparently no *Times* reporter was on the scene (the story was taken from the AP wire), and there were no follow-up stories to my knowledge (I scanned the paper carefully during the following days). The *Times* may perhaps have overspent its quota of labor news on the PATCO strike and the Polish Solidarity movement that year, but I rather doubt that that was the reason for such limited coverage. More likely, it was because labor militancy is just so commonplace in Italy that a one-day factory occupation or general strike hardly merits much attention as "news."

But what if this same event were to take place in, say, Schenectady, New York? What if General Electric workers occupied their plant to protest lay-offs, occupied a local airport and a railroad station, blocked the New York State Thruway, and were home in time for supper and to watch themselves on the six o'clock news? In an American context, this would be a truly extraordinary event, which would probably be front-page, lead-story news for days on end.

First of all, a strike to protest lay-offs would be surprising in itself. A factory occupation would doubtless be viewed as a mortal sin against private property, and the state police would be called in to forcibly evict the occupants. Any attempt to seal the city of Schenectady off from the outside world would likely be considered an act of revolution calling for the activation of the National Guard. The Schenectady insurrectionists would no doubt be roundly condemned by politicians from both parties, nightly newscasters, and hordes of "responsible" labor statesmen, who, though perhaps empathizing with their goals, would certainly "utterly abhor" their tactics.

Yet in Italy and elsewhere, such events are hardly newsworthy, underscoring the relative nature of the repertoires of collective action and the consciousness of workers in various settings, as well as suggesting the variability in the obstacles to solidarity and militant action that workers must negotiate in different industrial societies.

But it is not simply that American workers do not have the "will" to strike over the laying off of co-workers or that they do not have the "courage" to occupy their workplaces in protest, for that is precisely what Americans once did fairly frequently. But as I have argued earlier, the degree to which American workers can express their solidarity against the actions of their employers has been severely circumscribed by law, by the structures of industrial relations, and by their unions, which have accepted these limitations. As I have shown in the case studies of collective action presented above, workers sometimes step beyond those limits and sometimes are forced outside them. The important point here is that attention should be paid to the terrain that must be traversed in collective action, and not simply to the will, the ideas, and the attitudes of participants in the abstract.

In the discussion that follows, I will draw out some of what I consider to be the most important and most interesting patterns that are revealed in these case studies, as well as discussing the key implications raised by them in general. The studies cannot be properly reviewed in a strict comparative fashion because in each of the cases there were differences in levels of analysis, the substantive events, and the characteristics of the participants. Nevertheless, though each must stand on its own as a somewhat distinct example of collective action, their common institutional context and the similarities in their interactive dynamics call for some measure of comparative attention. I will provide this as judiciously as possible, while also taking the opportunity to range beyond the case material to discuss the American labor movement more generally.

In each of these studies, more or less bounded communities of workers were formed in and by industrial conflicts, representing emergent oppositions to the individualism of American culture and the atomization and acquiescence often held to be characteristic of the common, everyday existence of American workers. As noted earlier, standard social stratification approaches often reify this seriality, and analyses of overarching cultural hegemony often ignore emergent oppositional cultural practices.

I have not wanted to suggest that day-to-day working-class experience in the United States is dominated or defined solely by the cultures of solidarity that coagulate periodically—that the marginal represents the central. Rather, my aim has been to suggest that the collective initiatives that impinge on industrial practices and structures deserve attention precisely because they depart from the routine, and thus may illuminate its complexities, contradictions, tensions, and limits. This focus would seem particularly salient in the study of American workers. What little attention there has been has almost invariably emphasized the American workers' "exceptional" lack of class consciousness relative to workers elsewhere, while ignoring their collective actions and the resources utilized by employers to prevent them.

As I have stressed, a level of everyday, serial existence is sustained by the ossified structures of labor relations through the rigidly routinized practices of the collective bargaining system—a system that has hinged on the postwar social contract. But as I have also shown, this is only one part of the reality, and there are significant countercurrents to this overall regime. Though opposition can form only in the fissures of this system, the fact that the system engenders opposition at all is too rarely recognized.

But recognition is not enough, and thus my emphasis in the case studies was not simply on the existence of oppositional cultures of solidarity, but on the *processes* of their development. Although survey methods focus on the existence of class consciousness within a sample population, my concern was not to treat class consciousness as a fact to be uncovered, but to understand cultures of solidarity as active processes best understood in their oppositional context and their motion, with attention to the dynamics of group fusion and the institutional forms that generate and shape them.

In these studies, the relationships between bureaucracy and conflict, routinized procedure and direct action, institution and counterinstitution were not simple and linear, but complex and often paradoxical. The workers at Taylor Casting Company appealed to the letter of the grievance system in order to transgress it in defense of a fired worker. Their wildcat strikes represented a direct challenge to the routinized collective bargaining system, while at the same time they enforced and defended a trade unionism that served as party to it.

At Springfield Hospital and Clinton Corn, it was the employers who largely undermined the incorporative institutional social contract by intensifying conflict and forcing workers to confront the limits of their collective strength within established constraints. The women at Springfield Hospital found themselves treated as subversives for relying on the formal NLRB mechanisms of union representation. Their activities in response were not the "push-button" unionism of a routinized social contract, but were framed by the necessities of a conflict that demanded militance and solidarity in the face of a managerial countermobilization. The employer used the long-standing grievance system to undermine the union in Clinton before provoking a strike and using an NLRB-supervised decertification election to destroy the union altogether. The union was forced from the mold of routinized, incorporating practices that characterizes labor relations in the United States, mobilizing a heightened solidarity across the community to confront this challenge.

In each case where workers mobilized their solidarity in conflict, a degree of independence from bureaucratic constraints was required. As long as workers kept within the bounds of the routinized industrial relations system—a system designed to prevent rank-and-file workers from drawing on mutual solidarity as the basis of their power—they were necessarily shackled in their battle against the employer.

The organization of wildcat strikes to defend a co-worker or improve conditions in the factory, collective confrontations with supervisors in the halls of Springfield Hospital, and the creation of counterinstitutions to sustain a strike community represent initiatives relatively independent of the dominant, routinized collective bargaining practices imposed to ensure labor peace in the postwar period. I say "relatively" independent, because while militancy and rank-and-file solidarity can be achieved only with some measure of independence from the structures designed to prevent them, the character of militancy and solidarity is also spawned and shaped by those very structures. That is, repertoires of collective action are not chosen or determined by abstract ideological criteria in order to achieve a certain score on the scales of worker militancy, but are shaped in the context of institutional practices that constrain workers from achieving realizable goals (the rehiring of a fired worker, the establishment or preservation of collective bargaining rights, and so on).

For example, the tactic of "working to rule," whereby workers protest by conforming strictly to the letter of their job description and procedure, only makes sense as a tactic where there are clearly specified "rules" to begin with. Similarly, the wildcat strike as a form of protest exists because the strike has been routinized or "defanged" in various ways, limiting its usefulness for winning concessions on the shop floor. Workers become militant and draw on previously untapped reserves of solidarity in organizing unions or defending existing ones because there is little in the codified industrial relations system to protect them from employers who are not bound to the social contract on which it is based.

In each of the conflicts examined, workers sought a measure of independence from the traditional, routinized practices of collective bargaining in order to mobilize effectively, even as their demands, expectations, and scope of their actions were drawn from and shaped by those practices. Distinctions between "offensive" and "defensive" action are rendered almost meaningless as a duality where both elements are embodied in the same collective actions. For example, a wildcat strike essentially represents a form of grievance resolution independent of routinized grievance practices that are viewed as ineffectual, and thus it has an "offensive" character, at the same time as it implicitly reaffirms and defends established rights of grievance resolution. In the confrontations with their supervisors, Springfield Hospital workers had a collective sense that they had a right to bargain collectively, and they enforced, demonstrated, and defended that right. Similarly, the strike community in Clinton created new forms of organization to defend traditional union bargaining rights and the jobs through which those rights could be exercised.

Craig Calhoun has found militancy and radicalism among early nineteenth-century English artisans to have been based not on yearnings for a proletarian revolution, as many have supposed, but on attachment to "traditional communities." He argues that these artisans were actually "reactionary radicals" defending established premises of thought and action and traditional ways of life against fundamental attacks.[1] There is much that is worthy of attention in this analysis, especially Calhoun's contention that in contrast to earlier "reactionary radicals," who paradoxically had little alternative but rebellion to preserve traditional ways of life, workers in advanced capitalist societies have reformist alternatives to social revolution. However, I think that one can easily overstate the contrast between the experience of nineteenth-century workers confronted by great social transformations and that of modern workers who at times also face acute industrial dislocation. The fiercely militant strike by British miners of 1984–85 was fought, after all, in defense of traditional mining communities threatened by pit closures, and, as I pointed out earlier, unlikely coalitions of religious, labor, and community groups have sometimes coalesced in the United States in recent years to fight to preserve jobs and defend communities in the face of plant closings threatening those jobs and communities.

Moreover, I would argue that "defense" in such cases is not simply a matter of holding traditional ground. In the process of defending rights and ways of life, new associations, institutions, and valuations may be required, representing a significant social *creation*. In defending traditional communities, the women of the British mining villages formed powerful organizations that served as new vehicles for political participation and linked them to feminist, labor, and community groups throughout the nation. These groups continue to raise fundamental questions of gender in their communities, on picket lines, and in the miners' union itself.[2]

Historically, while strike activity served to defend American miners against coal operators' attempts to increase control, it also created and extended long-term institutions of self-defense. As Jon Amsden and Stephen Brier have shown: "The necessity of constant conflict with the employers . . . resulted in the creation of a trade union organization which did not rest exclusively on the narrow base of craft skill. This organizational form represented an advance in working class consciousness and is reflected in changes in the form and content of miners' strikes."[3]

There is a danger in drawing the implication that workers defending traditional rights are simply expressing a conservative reaction to change. Though Taylor Casting Company workers "merely" defended or enforced the notion of a "right to grieve," they did so in a way that challenged existing authority relations, created an emergent grouping of activists, and reproduced this activity in a second wildcat strike. The hospital workers in Springfield were forced to defend their right to union representation, and in the process organized militant action, broke down barriers among themselves, and, as women, challenged male authority and played a significant role in "public" life for the first time. In Clinton a year-long strike was fought in defense of jobs and collective bargaining rights, and an oppositional community with solidarity as its defining feature was created anew in the process.

I would suggest, then, that the forms of collective action by workers were to a significant degree shaped and influenced by the structures and practices of institutional life that dominate labor relations in American society. The issues over which workers sometimes risked their livelihood were not drawn from an abstract ideological agenda but were things they felt they could reasonably achieve, based on rights that were codified in, or closely related to, those bureaucratic structures and practices. In a sense, workers defended these rights, but because institutional practices also limit their ability to pursue collective interests effectively, they had to pursue a measure of independence from those routinized practices. In the process, workers then engaged in new forms of activity (militant, direct action), created new associational bonds in practical forms (essentially emergent social movements), and developed new-found values of mutual solidarity (a new sense of "us," a new sense of "them," and emergent moral sensibilities about the values associated with each).

It is not a simple matter of workers *preferring* solidarity over individual responses. What the case studies have shown is that whereas corporate praxis and the system of labor relations create formidable obstacles to solidarity, cultures of solidarity are formed out of friction and opposition itself. That is, solidarity is to a considerable degree formed and intensified in *interaction* with the opposition. This was seen fairly clearly at Taylor Casting Company, where, for example, the spatial positioning of strikers was influenced by interaction with the foreman to create an initial appearance of solidarity, which quickly became a reality in the early stages of the first wildcat strike. The intensity of the first wildcat strike was in part dictated by the threat of management retaliation; the mobilization of solidarity in the second one was narrower and less dramatic partly owing to the more cautious response of a management that feared a wider conflict.

In the union drive at Springfield Hospital, the solidarity of the organizing committee was clearly heightened by the intensity of the countermobilization by management and its consultants. Had the management not contested the campaign, and had it recognized the union in the first stages, militant action might not have taken place, and there would have been no immediate, apparent need for strong bonds of solidarity among the activists. Similarly, though the face-to-face interactional detail cannot easily be traced in the data from Clinton, the employer's hiring of strikebreakers created circumstances that demanded a level of solidarity and militance that would generally be unnecessary in a routine strike that all parties expect will lead to a reasonably prompt compromise. Moreover, the counterinstitutions created by the strike community to nourish and sustain its solidarity were premised by the "support" that other institutions of the community seemed to provide for the employer. The point is that in each of these collective actions, the militancy of employers was not just a barrier to be surmounted in forming cultures of solidarity, but to a considerable degree served as the *source* of solidarity—as a fire that tempered the steel of solidarity.

Two interpretations emerge from a focus on the interactive quality of collective action: reliance either on social-psychological determinants or on the resource mobilization perspective. Synthesis of the two approaches is useful in understanding the dynamics of these conflicts. In none of the case studies did workers act "irrationally" in the sense that their collective actions somehow embodied unconscious individual or collective motivations; nor did they act according to a strict utilitarian model of individuals rationally calculating costs and benefits.[4] In seeking to discard such rigid models, I have found it useful to consider spontaneity and planning, relatively unstructured and relatively organized action, and social-psychological and structural determinants in light of the interaction between workers and employers.

As already explained, the forms such actions take, and the issues over which they are contested, cannot be separated from dominant institutions and preexisting practices, but they are not identical to them either, for conflict necessitates degrees of independence and the creation of structures of an emergent extra-institutional nature.

In analyzing the dynamics of these collective interactions (of opposing forces), I have had to consider the relationships of spontaneity to planning and social-psychological manipulation to rational resource mobilization, rather than posing one against the other. The wildcat strikes at Taylor Casting Company suggest that spontaneous action takes place and is important but that spontaneity is itself structured and can give rise to organized forms that can then lead, plan, or harness spontaneity in a more systematic way.[5] The first wildcat strike was largely a spontaneous reaction by workers to the sacking of a co-worker. But the first stages of the action revealed an organization of solidarity by workers in collectively negotiating a common stance toward the foreman in order to prevent being isolated and punished. These workers created an appearance of solidarity that demonstrated the potential power of collective strength to those uncommitted and persuaded the foreman that attempts to divide the workers were futile. The demonstration of solidarity and the active struggle to create its appearance in the work-group were important elements. Although quickly harnessed and organized, such spontaneous action cannot easily be understood without reference to the social-psychological dynamics that go into it. Moreover, had the first wildcat strike not "spontaneously" erupted, the second one three months later would most likely not have been planned, let alone executed.

In the Springfield Hospital organizing drive, collective actions were similarly "structured" in relation to the actions of the employer and the need to consolidate internal solidarity and mobilize new adherents to the cause. The march into the hospital to present union cards to management, the mass action in the offices of the supervisors, the numerous confrontations to break up "one-on-one" meetings or to confront supervisors for harassing co-workers—these actions, though sometimes spontaneous in the sense that they were not always pre-planned, were structured by the need to reinforce the resolve of the organizing committee members and to demonstrate to others the power of a collective response to grievances.

In both of these case studies, where the micro-processes of interaction are most apparent, socially constructed appearances and symbolic measures were employed in the mobilization of collective actions. At times, action was provoked, demanding a "spontaneous" response. Collective action was not a simple matter, then, of social psychology, spontaneity, emergence, and unstructured action *versus* organization, pre-planning, and the mobilization of resources. Rather, it was a complex set of interactions in which structured activity (whether rationally planned or spontaneously provoked) drew on available social-psychological weaponry as well as on more obvious resources (pre-existing networks, work-group culture, familial support) in developing nascent organizational forms. Clearly, the social-psychological climate of Springfield Hospital was an important factor in the union drive. Although the ability to manipulate it is partially traceable to access to other resources, it remains an important mobilizing resource on its own and should not be abandoned by social analysts understandably critical of traditional social-psychological approaches to collective behavior.

In contrast to the Taylor and Springfield Hospital actions, where the workers could continue to collect their paychecks and where mobilization took place within the workplace, the Clinton strikers were out of work for a year, with production continuing in the plant. In some ways, a more standard resource mobilization approach is better able to inform the dynamics of strike development in this case. Attempts to activate a wider labor community and to create and maintain institutions of support figured strongly in the strike culture, and the power of the corporation and its ability to mobilize strikebreakers, the police, the courts, the city council, and so forth ultimately proved decisive in the defeat of the union. Powerful, if less tangible, "spiritual" elements nonetheless sustained the strike community for a full year against "objective" odds that, "rationally considered" by the participants, might have spelled an earlier end to the strike.[6]

The strikers were sustained by their moral outrage and their sense of the righteousness and justness of their cause, in addition to the more concrete resources they could muster. While the mobilization of "objective" resources for strike support was critical, the spirit of solidarity that was promoted from the pulpit of St. Mark's Church and demonstrated in strike activities was a powerful social-psychological resource as well.

To what extent do such collective actions indicate a working-class consciousness? At the outset of this book I criticized previous sociological studies for relying on survey techniques that have limited the field of investigation to static, individual responses to attitudinal or ideational questions, often posed with a priori expectations and drawn from a rather narrow theoretical conceptualization. Echoing the concerns of others, I argued that ideas should be considered in the context of class behavior and that more attention should be paid to the chemistry of collective action—the praxis of class conflict.

Contrary to the belief of many academics and radical activists that it is necessary for people to have an intellectual grasp or "correct line" on society before they can change it, this book argues throughout that in the process of change and crisis, ideas are rendered a good deal more fluid than they are at other times. Militant action creates a context in which ideas may emerge, change, and be subjected to scrutiny and renegotiation.

Meanings and interpretations are not revised by individuals alone, but in a social context, intersubjectively. In intense industrial conflict this often means that consciousness is expressed and reevaluated in terms of associational bonds. Because the power of workers is largely based on the ability to combine when it counts, in a crisis the character of combination is subject to renegotiation.

Whether considering narrowly defined class consciousness or

wider cultures of solidarity, the political implications are, however, as important as the metabolic processes that bring them about. Lenin's classical view of the political implications was, of course, to emphasize the limitations of the "spontaneous working-class movement," which, on its own, could not develop more than a trade union consciousness, or "the conviction that it is necessary to combine in unions, fight the employers, and strive to compel the government to pass necessary labor legislation."[7] Lenin argued that "the 'spontaneous element' represents nothing more nor less than consciousness in an embryonic form" and that a revolutionary consciousness would have to be brought to the workers from without for them to overcome their ideological enslavement by the bourgeoisie.[8]

The categorization of consciousness forces one to deal in ideal types and to compartmentalize social reality, and for this reason I find the Leninist conception somewhat problematic. Rather, I would agree with Gordon Marshall, who argues that "to study class consciousness as if it were a simple continuum from Right to Left, or from Trade-Union to Political-Revolutionary awareness, is to exclude an enormous variety of other dimensions of class consciousness."[9] At the same time, if one were required to categorize the types of consciousness evident in the three cultures of solidarity I have documented, one would certainly have to place them a good deal closer to the trade union variety than to the revolutionary one.[10]

These cultures of solidarity do not reveal workers who are capable of, or interested in, making a revolution. They must be seen to have produced merely a trade union consciousness in Leninist terms. One could argue, however, that trade unionism is not a simple, narrow, or "mere" anything, that when trade union action remains closer to its basic values than it usually does in its American context, it can represent something quite radical. As V. L. Allen has argued, "Solidarity, equality and democracy express the antithesis of capitalist values and are the essence of collective action . . . individualism, the core of capitalist activity, is confronted by collectivism."[11]

Capitalist values and goals have hardly been challenged by the postwar social contract unionism that has prevailed in the United States (even though the costs of doing business have been higher because of it). What this has meant, though, is that workers some-

times break the social contract in wildcat strikes and other forms
of militance, and that in their assaults on unions, employers can
unwittingly provoke workers into a heightened trade union consciousness that *does* challenge and confront the individualism of
capitalist society.

In such confrontations, cultures of solidarity are created to cultivate the militance and solidarity that existing trade unions, with
their reliance on bureaucratic forms, do not express. These emergent cultures may represent trade union consciousness, but of a
sort that can break down status hierarchies between workers in
favor of a wider solidarity, that eschews bureaucratic responses in
favor of direct action, and that raises the language of worker mutuality and cooperation to a principle.

As fighting trade unionists, workers can be forced to see beyond
themselves, and hierarchies and authority structures that are evident in the workplace can be revealed in the wider community,
breaking down the sharp divide between work and community.
However episodic, solidarity and collective action can, for instance,
suddenly make traditional women's roles seem highly problematic,
creating an opening for change that might not have revealed itself
otherwise.

Oppositional initiatives in embryonic form are not easily incorporated by the dominant culture, as the hostility shown them by
dominant institutions attests.[12] At the same time, working-class
militance always has a certain episodic quality. Extra-institutional
activity creates insecurity among the participants. The disruption
of family life, finances, and emotional equilibrium can only be
sustained with some expectation that the result will be a more
stable existence.

On the local level, though, the case studies above suggest that
the vehicles of collective action, cultures of solidarity, are potentially durable associational forms that may shape reality beyond an
acute crisis. The emergent network of activists that arose out of the
wildcat strikes at Taylor Casting Company, the organizing committee whose character was tested and forged in conflict at Springfield
Hospital, and the labor community awakened by the Clinton Corn
strike represent nascent movements that could potentially have
reshaped local patterns of life in the aftermath of the crises that
gave rise to them.

But the important question is whether and how local struggles affect wider social structures at the national level. That is, are local collective actions handled by trade unions at the national level in a way that builds upon them to strengthen workers' institutional power, or are they marginalized, ignored, or actively opposed?

As I have shown, the character of the labor movement in the United States has been crucial in determining much of the shape and content of collective actions by workers. More generally, unions are a key factor in promoting or limiting opposition and dissent in societies in general. As Allen has argued:

> The actual practice of trade unionism has an important bearing on the facility to dissent. The closer trade union action is to the basic values of trade unionism then the more effective unions will be as vehicles for dissent. Or, the more they accommodate to the system of capitalism the less effective they will be for dissent. The unions are vital in this process because they alone amongst collectivities have the power to pursue and enforce dissent. They provide a protective forum for the discussion of dissenting views and a power base to enforce them. . . . The right of individuals to dissent is a cosmetic without the institutionalized means to pursue it. The most potent of those means are trade unions. [13]

If trade unions oppose or only minimally tolerate social dissidence, then the most potent institutional base of social opposition is effectively neutralized. But if trade unions themselves are centers or vehicles of opposition, the political configuration in the society can have a different complexion. This can be seen fairly clearly in Europe, where postwar unionism has shaped political allegiances and perspectives for large segments of working-class populations. For example, communist domination of the union movement in France and Italy has meant that postwar conditions were interpreted and assessed by militants, whereas in Belgium similar conditions were interpreted and assessed very differently by the moderates who controlled the key unions. [14] Moreover, when linked to radical political parties, as European movements often have been, the oppositional character of unionism can be translated into political action, providing a wider institutional base for dissent. [15]

The point is that while trade unionism may fall short of revolutionary consciousness, its character does shape consciousness in important ways, and there can be significant variations in its content. The social contract unionism practiced by the leadership of the foundry workers at Taylor Casting was different from the unionism of the militants who were willing to break that social contract; and the militancy demanded of Clinton workers during their strike caused a rupture with the more moderate, cautious national union leadership, suspicious of the militancy and radicalism of the strikers, rather than being fully supportive.

In Springfield, the organizing committee was affiliated with a union whose leadership is more militant than that of most other American unions. Though subject to the same legal, bureaucratic constraints, this leadership has generally been willing to support organizational activity that departs from the purely routine approach. This does not ensure victories over more powerful employers, who can use those legal and bureaucratic constraints effectively to their advantage, but it does mean that militant industrial action by workers is less likely to be discouraged or actively opposed by the leaders themselves.

But what can be achieved by workers acting independently of the dominant forms of unionism in these local struggles or by those few unions willing to devote institutional resources to militant activity is not the same thing as an overarching independent union *movement* fighting for working-class power at the national level. The CIO, in its formative years, was such a movement, and, had it been sustained in a similar form, America in the 1980s would arguably be a very different place, with a classwide, not a sectional, movement constructed along democratic rather than bureaucratic lines.

Instead, unions sought a measure of legitimacy and social standing in American society largely at the expense of what brought them into being in the first place—an ability and willingness to rely on workers' solidarity as the prime source of their power. The transmogrification of industrial unionism meant that the accepted bounds of unionism were largely those deemed acceptable by employers. After these changes were consolidated in the Taft-Hartley Act, the trade unionism that remained was one in which the ideologies of solidarity were discredited and banned, and their proponents reformed, eliminated, or frightened into submission. American unionism was shackled by the outlawing of traditional (and traditionally successful) forms of collective action and for the most part was to be dominated by union leaders willing to agree to these terms or unable to mount an effective opposition.

The essential irony is that in the face of the current management assault on unions, which has built up steam for well over a decade, the power of militance and solidarity necessary to withstand it has largely been traded away. Of course, through the relatively prosperous decades that followed the war, this bureaucratic contract unionism served union leaders well. With industry expanding and world markets prone to American corporate penetration, union leaders could promise and often deliver a steadily rising standard of living to their members, thus comfortably maintaining their positions atop the union hierarchy—with sporadic, but often easily repelled, opposition from the ranks—in exchange for a trade unionism that served corporate interests with virtually no political or economic independence from its general goals. This push-button unionism assured a steady membership through automatic dues transfers, routinized representation elections, and so on, while leaders maintained a safe distance from the problems and struggles of shop-floor life.

In contrast to the radicals who built the CIO, most of the current generation of trade union leaders have been schooled in the pragmatic ethos of the social contract, whereby independent rank-and-file activity and the mobilization of working-class solidarity have too often been seen as a threat to the ordered, bureaucratic machinery of the grievance process and the labor board. Though the language of solidarity is sometimes heard, it is as platitude rather than as manifesto, and it is usually confined to ceremonial occasions.

With the social contract increasingly violated by employers, however, the trade unionism it nursed into bureaucratic complacency is itself directly threatened. Flailing about and reeling from corporate blows, most union leaders have little knowledge about or experience in offering an effective response. Unions are, as one commentator has observed, "moving to fall-back positions in politics, public relations, pension power and organizing," though he notes rather bleakly that "their main significance at this point is that they are in place and are actively being pursued."[16]

But the problem is less tactical than it is substantive. The Taft-

Hartley legacy has meant that the solidarity of millions of workers has gone largely uncultivated, and rank-and-file initiative has been discouraged for more than forty years. The massive resources of the trade unions have not been devoted to mobilizing the source of labor's strength, and paradoxically (though not surprisingly), like a Faustian bargain, employers are now collecting their due from a movement that sold its soul by accepting the terms of the social contract. By abandoning effective repertoires of action and a political language that could articulate the dilemma, the union leadership now may be undercutting its own existence: "The labor movement, its militant traditions rusty from lack of use, is left with no way to protect its members' income . . . the employers mean to force a redistribution of wealth in their own favor, and to weaken the labor movement so that it can't redress the balance later."[17]

In many ways, this paradox makes it exceedingly difficult for the cultures of solidarity that emerge in local struggles to be realized at the national level or to gain strong support from it. Led largely by men whose careers as leaders were built upholding the postwar social contract through a bureaucratic unionism and the demobilization of militant rank-and-file initiative, the institutionalized union movement has not been maintained as a fundamental threat to capital or to the larger social order. But as long as labor remains unthreatening, there is little incentive for capital to cease its assault on gains labor has made since the 1930s, and indeed on the existence of unionism itself.[18]

In those local struggles where a threateningly militant national union presence could make an important difference—as in union-busting strikes like the one at Clinton—the paradox is often painfully felt. That existing networks of union solidarity, a generalized union consciousness, and the experience of militant collective action are often lacking means not only that these must be created "cold" in an environment where there is often minimal moral compunction about crossing picket lines, but also that there is generally little enthusiasm and leadership—and sometimes firm opposition—from above, where legal strategies predominate over strategies for mass mobilization.[19]

But it must be noted that in the midst of the current employer assault, Lane Kirkland, the president of the AFL-CIO, and other union leaders may now be beginning to at least question their faith in a legal system (and at least implicitly, the social contract on which it is based) that has done so much to aid employers in recent years. One labor lawyer who represents more than a score of unions has recently written:

> I agree fully with Mr. Kirkland's assessment. The act and the National Labor Relations Board have become a millstone around labor's neck and create a dangerous illusion that workers, unions, and the institution of collective bargaining are protected. Nothing could be further from the truth. . . . The labor movement must rely upon its own strength, as it did in earlier times. . . . It is in self-help, unity, allies, education and an end to internal squabbles that the labor movement will rebuild, not in legal stratagems and maneuvers.[20]

Such murmurs of dissatisfaction from the union hierarchy are hopeful signals that some revitalization of the union movement is possible, but whether or not union bureaucracies will be able and willing to follow it with the sort of wide-ranging actions that are, in my view, necessary is unclear.[21] Strategies and programs for aggressively organizing the mass of unorganized workers—particularly women, minorities, and service and technical workers—and uniting them in a "New Progressive Alliance" have been put forward and some unions have begun to take some initiative here.[22]

However, for more militance and solidarity (the ultimate basis of working-class power) to be structured into the workings of the union movement as a whole, a great deal more than this will have to be done. To begin with, at the local level, a thoroughgoing reform needs to be implemented, beginning with the aggressive organization of previously unorganized workers. Women, minorities, and workers from non-traditional areas of union strength (such as banking and the "high tech" industries) should be able to see unions as their own. They must be allowed to play a central role in union organization *and* maintenance, requiring the strict enforcement of union democracy and creative efforts to involve the membership in the life of the union.[23] The "atrophied, depoliticized state of shop-steward organization across the country," as Mike Davis has observed, needs to be reversed so that militance and solidarity could be organized and led at the level of the workgroup, rather than simply siphoned off through bureaucratic practices.[24] In general, the union presence at the local level must be experienced as more than a bureaucratic labyrinth through which grievances are channeled; the union hall should be a rich center of cultural life and education that cultivates traditions and practices of solidarity.[25]

At a wider level, regional and citywide labor councils, once important institutional mechanisms for labor solidarity, should be revived where they have ceased to exist and rejuvenated where they exist as largely ceremonial bodies. Labor councils could be effective in nourishing interunion connections and solidarity between periods of intense crisis and, if they represent unions with a membership that is mobilized, could be activated to support local strikes and other struggles in force. City and regional labor councils could serve to settle jurisdictional disputes between unions competing for members and could share strategies and resources in organizing activities, rather than allowing unions to work at cross-purposes. With statewide labor bodies engaged in political lobbying, regional and citywide central labor councils could be devoted full-time to forging solidarity at the local level, across industries, and could play a strong role in organizing campaigns with substantial union resources at this local level.

To begin to counter the massive internationalization of capital and the international worker disunity on which it thrives, the U.S. labor movement must overcome its reluctance and begin to forge strong links with unions abroad and to oppose a U.S. foreign policy that, among other things, creates havens for corporations seeking cheap labor and repressive anti-union governments abroad. Of course, where unions abroad have communist or socialist leaders, this would necessarily mean a modification of the rabid anticommunism that informs the relationship of the AFL-CIO and many individual unions to international labor federations. Clearly, international coordination and solidarity is becoming more and more essential for an effective union response to the activities of multinational corporations.

Given the legal sanctions against mass picketing, secondary boycotts, and solidarity strikes, the union movement will have to be prepared to break the law through such activities. Labor's failed attempt to modify the Taft-Hartley Act under the Carter administration and a Democratic Congress in 1978 suggests the futility of relying too heavily on legislative initiatives. Just as civil disobedience effectively prompted judicial changes for other groups, so labor must be prepared to mount similar campaigns of mass, illegal action to violate injunctions and assert rights of mutual solidarity.[26] Just as "illegal" factory occupations forced employers to recognize industrial unions in the 1930s, so unions should be prepared to mobilize workers in an effective way despite existing legal sanctions. Just as the right to strike has always and everywhere been won by striking, so the rights to effective collective action will most likely be won only by effective (thoughtfully planned, well-timed, well-organized) collective action.

These sorts of suggestions, however schematic, will doubtless be considered unrealistic or even utopian. Admittedly, it is unlikely that those who command the enormous resources of the American labor movement will fully break with past practices and transform their institutions to fully implement them. But, in my view, this has less to do with the utopian character of such reforms than with the threat they might pose to the system to which, generally, those leaders subscribe.

Though a trade unionism based on worker solidarity and the effective mobilization of collective action seems less than realistic in an American context, I have tried to show in part that, if anything, it is rather more utopian to try to base a union movement on anything else. While it is only a relatively small part of their reality, and while the forces that oppose them can be overwhelming, American workers are not as "exceptionally" or intrinsically averse to solidarity and collective action as we are sometimes led to believe. Workers in conflict, union organizers, and employers and their consultants know this very well and will continue to focus on solidarity in workplaces and communities where collective action, which has so often been misinterpreted or overlooked by academics, is a lived experience.

Appendix

The Measures Taken:
Some Notes on Methodology

In abandoning survey research as essentially inappropriate to a dynamic approach to working-class consciousness, I have had to be prepared to abandon the level of validity ensured by sophisticated statistical techniques and to expect that this may cause discomfort to those distrustful of less conventional "qualitative" approaches, as well as to those who would rightly question the validity of one's interpretation of data unconventionally compiled. There are certain costs and benefits associated with any methodological approach. Sterile debates between "quantitative" and "qualitative" methods aside (principled attachments to one or the other tend to provoke me to wish a plague on both their houses), though survey methodology is fraught with problems in the study of class consciousness, alternative approaches also contain difficulties of their own.[1] In outlining the methodological approaches taken in the case studies presented in this book, I want to highlight some of the problems I experienced and discuss my relationship to these events.

Generally speaking, I think it is important to consider two crucial elements inherent in studying collective action "on the ground." First, because it often takes place in a conflictual context, the researcher is directly confronted with the question of partisanship. Collective action, group solidarity, and militant protest tend to take place in a crisis-charged atmosphere where contending forces have a great deal at stake. Consequently, access to such settings can be enormously difficult, with both sides standing to lose by having been overly trusting of an "outsider" whose data may be used against them in some way. Workers and others with relatively little in the way of resources are, even in the most peaceful of times, often highly mistrustful of anyone with a notepad, tape recorder, or clipboard, as their experiences of manipulation on the job and in their communities rightly suggest that they should be. In general, I have been extremely fortunate in having been afforded the amount of access that I have to these communities of workers in conflict, but as I point out for each case below, in varying ways under varying circumstances, a level of partisanship was required as a pass-key to facilitate access.

The second important element in studying such actions is that they may be relatively ephemeral, limiting the collection of data. The sorts of conflicts I have examined seldom "stand still" long enough for a researcher to arrive on the scene and compile a record as detailed as one that might be compiled in the study of a settled community, for example. Moreover, once the dust has cleared from the conflict, the participants (indeed, the community itself) may be dispersed completely, making it more difficult to gain the sort of detail that ethnographic community studies often gather.[2] There are areas in my research that perhaps could have been strengthened in various ways, but, as Geertz points out, ethnography is not principally a matter of the *amount* of data collected, but an interpretive attempt to sort out the "structures of signification" in social and cultural processes.[3] Thus, although it is confined to emergent, rather than established, cultural formations, I would broadly characterize the approach I have taken in these studies as an ethnographic one, which variously combines participant observation, oral history through structured and open-ended interviews with participants, and extensive use of informants, as well as archival research.

In terms of the first of these studies (chapter 3), this sounds a good deal more elegant (and purposive) than it actually was in practice, for I began as a participant in the events before becoming a trained observer. I worked at Taylor Casting Company for more than ten months in 1975–76 at various jobs in the finishing department, and as a furnace operator during the period of the two wildcat strikes.

During the first of the strikes, I was fairly well placed to observe the strike as it developed because, out of a certain level of fear, I had "hung back" with others to assess the situation before making a material commitment to it. Had I not been in Group II in the initial stages (see diagram 1, p. 84), but rather among the most forceful strikers (Group I), I probably would not have been afforded a perspective that allowed me to observe the rather complex interactional dynamics that developed. Thus, although I was clearly a participant in the first wildcat strike, it probably aided my sociological analysis that I had not been one of the more fearless of the participants.

In the second wildcat strike, however, I was one of the four workers in the finishing department who had discussed the lack of heat in the break room, and the prospects of a work stoppage to protest it. When it was raised publicly in the break room the day before the strike, I was one of a group of workers who voiced support for the action and the next morning helped to persuade my co-workers to remain in their street clothes. Though others prompted the action, I agreed with it and actively supported it throughout, and I later attended the meetings with others attempting to challenge the union leadership in the subsequent election.

After the second wildcat strike, I began to take notes on the strikes and other developments with the thought that what was going on around me might be of some journalistic interest. Given that this was a period when union insurgencies were getting attention elsewhere, it seemed to me that being in the midst of an interesting example was a good reason to record the events. A couple of years later, as a student of sociology unhappy with much of the treatment afforded worker consciousness and action in the discipline, I returned to reexamine the wildcat strikes at Taylor. I dug out my ragged notebook and massaged my memory for as much detail as I could remember of my experience. The plant had closed down, and I could only contact two others who had worked there—one who had been very active in the events, the other a minor union official who had been involved only marginally. They confirmed the general flow of events in the plant, but they had not been present in the finishing department break room, and my notes and memory thus played an important part in reconstructing daily life in the finishing department. Quotations in the text have only been provided where I feel confident of their accuracy, but they have not all been independently confirmed by others present and thus may not always be verbatim.

After the plant had been closed for two years, I attempted to contact the Taylor Casting Company to seek assistance in my research. I sent a letter requesting access to the personnel files of workers (so that I might gain more systematic data on the workforce) and labor-relations files (to double-check for any history of plant militancy that workers at the time might have overlooked). Not surprisingly, my letter went unanswered, and in a subsequent phone call, I was told politely, but in no uncertain terms, that no company records would be made available. Though it is doubtful whether a private company would have obliged anyone in such a project, my having been an active participant most likely ensured this.

How reliable is my reconstruction, then? I think that there is always a danger in participant observation research that the subjectivity of the researcher may "construct," rather than simply "reconstruct," elements of the phenomenon being investigated. However, with the notes I originally compiled, subsequent additions, and the discussions with co-workers, I feel confident that I have been able to provide an accurate account, though of course in the final analysis the reliability of my interpretation must be assessed by the reader.

The Clinton research (chapter 5) was not a participant observation study. Intensive fieldwork was conducted over a period of several weeks in 1980 toward the end of the strike. Initially, I encountered a great deal of difficulty gaining access to the strike community. Despite being accompanied by a colleague who is a native of Clinton, and who, I had hoped, would help ease such problems, I found a strike community that was extremely mistrustful of outsiders like myself. It seemed as though the solidarity that strikers had mobilized against the employer might also serve to prevent me from collecting the data I needed in order to understand it.

After two frustrating days, in which I could manage only a cursory hour-long interview with a very cautious union official, and in which attempts to talk with rank-and-file strikers had failed, the strike community seemed impenetrable because of the distrust the conflict had aroused. However, after spending a day in the public library photocopying news clippings and other public documents related to the strike, my fortunes shifted dramatically on the fourth day.

A press conference was called in the city council chambers by a pro-labor "Ecumenical Task Force" of religious leaders from throughout the Midwest, who had been investigating the strike and its accompanying violence, to announce their findings. I attended along with about a dozen print and radio journalists from all over Iowa, a small group of strike leaders, and members of the public. My intention was to listen to the findings of the task force and secure a copy of the final report.

The findings read at the press conference were extremely critical of the corporation, accusing it of provoking the strike and attempting to break the union. At least implicitly, it was suggested that the picket-line violence was a direct result of the employment of strikebreakers. The Catholic priest from Indiana who presented the findings was then subjected to a barrage of questions from the assembled journalists, most of whom attempted to undermine the credibility of the task force by focusing on the attitudes of the priest that might have biased the report.

Fresh from having read scores of news clippings published throughout the strike, it seemed ironic to me that reporters from newspapers that had consistently editorialized against the conduct of strikers, often in the most one-sided fashion, were now relentlessly berating this priest for his lack of objectivity. After particularly vigorous questioning by a reporter from the *Clinton Herald*, I spontaneously decided to come to the aid of the by now beleaguered priest. I raised my hand and, when acknowledged, announced that I had come to Clinton to research the strike and had been finding reportage in the *Clinton Herald* consistently biased against the strikers. I then produced evidence from clippings I had collected as examples. The tone of the press conference shifted noticeably after this intervention, to the relief of the priest and the strike leaders present. The focus turned to the issues contained in the report, and the reporter from the *Clinton Herald* left the room soon after.

At the conclusion of the press conference, the strike leaders rushed over to thank me for my comments and invited me to join them for a drink. Thereafter, the strike community seemed to open up to me to an extraordinary degree. The word had gone out that my research needs were to be met, and I was then able to arrange interviews with strikers, their families, and their relatives, in addition to informal conversations with strikers in taverns and at the union hall, including some with those who had spurned my initial requests. I received invitations to attend church services and meetings of Concerned Citizens and other strike-related organizations, as well as being provided with access to church membership records, strike documents, and interviews with those outside of the immediate community.

Had I not intervened at the press conference, it is likely that I would have been "frozen out" of the strike community altogether and that I would have had to abandon research on the strike. Unpremeditatedly, I had taken a public, partisan stance on the strike that in the eyes of the strike leaders deserved reciprocation in the form of access to their community.

However, taking a partisan stance in the midst of conflict also means that areas of investigation may be closed off. Though they were never essential to the focus of this study (and I was able to use informants to gain a degree of access in any case), my pro-strike stance meant that anti-strike elements (the employer, strikebreakers) could not easily be approached. Thus, while partisanship may be necessary to facilitate research, it also hinders it, and future researchers would do well to consider the costs and benefits beforehand.

I had hoped to elude problems of this sort in my research for the Springfield case study. Chosen both because I had strong contacts within the union who I knew would aid my research and because the employer had retained the services of an anti-union management consultant, my original research strategy was to attempt to minimize the effects of my union sympathies in securing access to the management side, while using my ties to the union to create research opportunities among the workers.

The research was conducted over an eighteen-month period in 1983 and 1984. After a series of initial conferences with the union organizer, a meeting was arranged with a dozen or more workers who had been active in the union drive. There I spelled out my research needs and explained that before scheduling any interviews with union activists I would attempt to interview hospital administrators, supervisory staff, and anti-union workers. I wanted them to know why this research on "the other side" would be helpful, so that it would not jeopardize their willingness to aid the project.

After this meeting, I drafted a letter to the chief administrator of the hospital requesting permission to meet with him and asking if he would help me arrange interviews with supervisors and other members of the staff for my research on the union campaign. I explained that the union had agreed to speak with me and that I hoped he would do the same.

I was cordially informed in a phone conversation that it was felt not to be in the best interest of the hospital to participate in the study and that although individual workers were free to speak with me, the management would not do so. Though "on my own" in having to develop contacts among supervisors, at least it seemed possible to somehow accomplish this through contacts I might make through the organizing committee members.

But this possibility was soon effectively cut off when a memorandum was distributed to all supervisors in the hospital by the chief administrator, essentially warning them (and the workers in their departments) that if approached by this "agent of Smith College," they should proceed with caution. The memo read in full:

Please be advised that Springfield Hospital has been contacted by Smith College of Northampton, Massachusetts, regarding our desire to participate in an academic study as to the effects of unionization on a hospital and community. While the union has allegedly agreed to participate in and provide names of employees at Springfield Hospital that may want to take part in this study, Springfield Hospital cannot and will not participate or officially condone the study. The Hospital will continue to maintain the confidentiality of its employees and will not release the names of any employees to outside sources.

Aside from the confidentiality of the issue, Springfield Hospital refuses to participate in this academic study as this matter currently is under litigation and is expected to be under litigation for the next few years. Therefore, any employee wishing to take part in these interviews does so on his or her personal behalf. I would expect that a number of employees would be contacted by agents of Smith College in the near future and this information should be communicated by you to your departments and departmental employees immediately. If there are any questions, please contact me directly. Thank you.

Paradoxically then, despite my efforts to gingerly "work around" the conflict in organizing my research, the hospital management had used it as a weapon in the battle. By noting that the union had agreed to participate, while the management had not, the union was implicitly made to appear irresponsible. Moreover, the memo was used as an opportunity to demoralize union supporters further by emphasizing the lengthy legal delays that could be expected to forestall resolution of the election outcome.

The memo may have closed off access to supervisors in my research, a group who might have been an important source of data. Efforts to arrange meetings with supervisors and anti-union workers through my established contacts were unsuccessful, though it is hard to say whether this was owing to the memo or not. One reportedly anti-union worker who had agreed to an anonymous interview failed to turn up for scheduled meetings on two separate occasions; it is very likely that this was because she feared for her job, though I cannot be certain of this.

I was granted interviews with two workers who were not active in the union drive and who, at that point, considered themselves "neutral" in the conflict, but beyond this, an extensive set of management memoranda distributed throughout the campaign, and a substantial clipping file, the body of data for the Springfield case study came from interviews with organizing committee members and their spouses.

In the earlier stages, I relied heavily on two main informants, whose insights, culled from repeated taped interviews, informal discussions, and numerous phone conversations to check my factual accuracy, proved invaluable in reconstructing the dynamics of the organizing drive. In addition to helping me arrange interviews with the other members of the organizing committee, they furnished me with the "organizing charts" used by the committee to gauge union sympathies and antipathies in all departments and shifts over the course of the campaign. They and a larger group of participants also provided comments on, and corrections of, one draft of the study.

The interviews conducted in both this and the Clinton study were individual, family, and group interviews; in some cases individuals were interviewed separately, then with their spouse, and then with groups of other activists. The group interviews seemed particularly useful, as recall could be stimulated in dialogue with other participants. In cases where the proper names of persons and institutions may be found in the public record, I have generally used them in this book, though I have changed the names of some others to preserve their anonymity.

Retrospectively, I can see ways in which these studies might have been improved from a methodological standpoint. Studies more longitudinal in scope and with more systematic techniques can potentially yield a fuller data base than my approach has allowed. However, in studying collective action in a conflictual context, one cannot, I think, completely avoid similar methodological issues and difficulties.

Notes

References cited in abbreviated form in the notes may be found in full in the bibliography.

Chapter One

1. "Labor Takes to the Streets," *New York Times*, 7 September 1981.

2. Hugh C. Fetty, letter to the editor, *New York Times*, 9 September 1981.

3. Quoted in William Serrin, "Union Aid Abroad Laid to Traditions," *New York Times*, 7 September 1981.

4. See Selig Perlman, *The Theory of the Labor Movement*; John R. Commons et al., *History of Labor in the United States*; Daniel Bell, *The End of Ideology*; Seymour M. Lipset, *Political Man*; and Herbert Marcuse, *One Dimensional Man*.

5. Four general strikes were recorded in the United States before 1930: St. Louis, 1877; New Orleans, 1892; Philadelphia, 1910; and Seattle, 1919. There were at least ten general strikes from 1930 to 1947: San Francisco; Minneapolis; Terre Haute, Ind.; Pekin, Ill.; Wilmington, Del.; Lansing, Mich.; Stamford, Conn.; Lancaster, Pa.; Rochester, N.Y.; and Oakland, Calif. See Wilfrid H. Crook, *Communism and the General Strike*, 149–95; and George Lipsitz, *Class and Culture in Cold War America*.

6. Richard O. Boyer and Herbert M. Morais, *Labor's Untold Story*, 282.

7. Harold Wilensky, "Class Consciousness and American Workers," in *American Society, Inc.*, ed. M. Zeitlin. Despite some dispute over his findings, Richard Centers found that a study of class identification revealed that the "interest group theory of social classes" (class consciousness) was valid. This contradicted the results of an earlier *Fortune* survey which held that most Americans identified themselves as "middle class." See Richard Centers, *The Psychology of Social Classes*; Milton Gordon,

Social Class in American Sociology, 193–202; H. J. Eysenck, "Social Attitude and Social Class"; and Herman M. Case, "Marxist Implications of Centers' Interest Group Theory, A Critical Appraisal." Subsequent studies have continued to offer conflicting testimony on the existence of working-class consciousness: see Oscar Glantz, "Class Consciousness and Political Solidarity"; and Jerome G. Manis and Bernard N. Meltzer, "Attitudes of Textile Workers to Class Structure," for negative verdicts. See John C. Legget, *Class, Race and Labor*, for a more positive appraisal.

8. George Rudé notes in *Ideology and Popular Protest* that "inherent beliefs" often clash with or are mediated by "derived" or "outside" notions in history. And E. P. Thompson in "Patrician Society, Plebeian Culture" reveals an eighteenth-century "plebeian culture" that combined traditional values of deference with a revolutionary "leveling spirit." E. J. Hobsbawm describes early twentieth-century Russian peasants paradoxically announcing to the landlord as they pillaged his estate, "We aren't doing this in our name, but in the name of the Tsar" (*Primitive Rebels*, 186). Similar contradictions are found in contemporary working-class ethnographies as well; see the comments of a steelworker in William Kornblum, *Blue Collar Community*, 225; and the description of ideological disjuncture among British factory workers in Theo Nichols and Peter Armstrong, *Workers Divided*, especially part 2.

9. Quoted in Jeremy Brecher and Tim Costello, *Common Sense for Hard Times*, 232.

10. See Robin Blackburn and Michael Mann, "Ideology in the Non-Skilled Working Class," in *Working-Class Images of Society*, ed. M. Blumer, 155–56; as well as Jim Cousins and Richard Brown's "Patterns of Paradox Among Shipbuilding Workers" in the same volume. Also see Sidney Peck, *The Rank and File Leader*, for group interviewing techniques in which contradictory responses can be challenged and explored. Further, for an analysis of oscillations in consciousness among workers, see Michael N. Yarrow, "Exploring Fluctuations in Class Consciousness."

11. For an insightful review of the theories of "ambivalence" and "instrumentalism" in working-class consciousness, see Gordon Marshall, "Some Remarks on the Study of Working-Class Consciousness," 263–301.

12. Quoted in Marshall, "Working-Class Consciousness," 267. See Frank Parkin, *Class, Inequality and Political Order*, 92–93; and Howard Newby, *The Deferential Worker*.

13. The attempt of Commons et al. in *History of Labor in the United States* to account for oscillations in worker militancy was overly deterministic; see Bert Cochran's discussion of Commons in *Labor and Communism*, 343–44. See R. W. Connell's discussion of Sartre in "Class, Gender and Sartre's Theory of Practice," in *Which Way Is Up?* ed. Connell, 67. In

Everything in Its Path, Kai Erickson shows that cultural responses are not fixed and determined, but exist along an "axis of variation" in which oppositions are embodied within dominant cultural forms.

14. See "The Explosion of Consciousness," in Michael Mann, *Consciousness and Action Among the Western Working Class*, 45–54.

15. Charles Spencer, *Blue Collar*, 12–13.

16. John H. Goldthorpe et al., *The Affluent Worker in the Class Structure*. For a discussion of the events surrounding the Vauxhall uprising, see André Gorz, "Workers' Control." See also Mann, *Consciousness and Action*, 45–54, for a further analysis.

17. In "Workers' Control," Gorz identifies eruptions in various locations that contradicted the results of attitudinal surveys: a Firestone plant in Oslo, a Ford plant in Cologne, an Alfa Romeo plant in Milan, the shipyards at Genoa, the Pirelli factory in Turin, and among steelworkers in Dunkirk. In *Wartime Strikes* (121), Martin Glaberman analyzes the no-strike pledge voted by American workers during World War II, which was simultaneously contradicted by an unprecedented wave of wildcat strikes by those same workers. Moreover, the inability to make sense of collective action through surveys extends beyond the workplace. Lewis M. Killian, reviewing Gary T. Marx's *Protest and Prejudice*, noted that the book failed to predict the rebellions that swept through many black communities while it was being published because it was based on data from just a few years earlier. Marx's study of a representative sample of blacks could not have predicted the powerful influence that a few black militants would have on the many, as the statistical significance of such militancy would have appeared negligible in the survey data.

18. Marshall, "Working-Class Consciousness," 272, 288.

19. Stanislaw Ossowski, *Class Structure in the Social Consciousness*, 140; C. Wright Mills, *White Collar*, 325; and Legget, *Class, Race and Labor*, 40.

20. Karl Marx, quoted in *The Marx-Engels Reader*, ed. Robert C. Tucker, 218.

21. Karl Marx and Friedrich Engels, *The German Ideology*, 47.

22. Ibid., 21.

23. Shlomo Avineri, *The Social and Political Thought of Karl Marx*, 79.

24. Ibid., 141.

25. See Norman Geras, *The Legacy of Rosa Luxemburg*, 111–31; and Gerson S. Sher, *PRAXIS*, 62–63.

26. The following examples are illustrative: Ronald Aminzade, "The Transformation of Social Solidarities in Nineteenth-Century Toulouse," in *Consciousness and Class Experience in Nineteenth-Century Europe*, ed.

John Merriman; Mary Ann Clawson, "Brotherhood, Class and Patriarchy"; John Foster, *Class Struggle in the Industrial Revolution*.

27. See Frank Parkin, *The Marxist Theory of Class*, 44–54. While Parkin views "exclusion" and "usurpation" as two main forms of social action, "solidarity" represents one means by which subordinate groups act to usurp the power of the dominant group. Similarly, Wallerstein has argued that perhaps the Weberian triad (class, status, and party) ought to be viewed "as three existential forms of the same essential reality," with the key issue being the "conditions under which a stratum embodies itself as a class, as a status group, or as a party." See Immanuel Wallerstein, "Social Conflict in Post-Independence Black Africa," in *The Capitalist World Economy*, ed. Wallerstein. Although most American sociologists have failed to view class consciousness as more than the attitudinal responses to surveys, two notable exceptions are David Halle's *America's Working Man* and Susan A. Ostrander's "Class Consciousness As Conduct and Meaning."

28. See Erik Olin Wright's discussion of "gradational" versus "relational" conceptions of class in *Class Structure and Income Determination*, chap. 1.

29. Karl Marx, *Capital*, 1:309.

30. Duncan Gallie, *Social Inequality and Class Radicalism In France and Britain*, 12.

31. E. P. Thompson, *The Making of the English Working Class*, 9–11.

32. John Clarke et al., "Sub-Cultures, Cultures and Class," in *Culture, Ideology and Social Process*, ed. Tony Bennett et al., 53.

33. See B. Malinowski, *A Scientific Theory of Culture*, 38; Ruth Benedict, *Patterns of Culture*; and A. L. Kroeber, *Anthropology*, sections 122 and 125. For a full discussion, see Margaret S. Archer, "The Myth of Cultural Integration," 5.

34. Zygmunt Baumann, *Culture and Praxis*, 157–58.

35. Critical examples of cultural hegemony in American life are found in Richard Sennett and Jonathan Cobb, *The Hidden Injuries of Class*; see T. J. Jackson Lears, "The Two Richard Sennetts," for a good discussion of Sennett and cultural hegemony. See, too, Michael Lewis, *The Culture of Inequality*, especially his concept of the "individual-as-central sensibility"; and Christopher Lasch, *The Culture of Narcissism*.

36. See Michael Burawoy, *Manufacturing Consent*; and Paul Willis, "Shop-Floor Culture, Masculinity, and the Wage Form," in *Working-Class Culture*, ed. John Clarke, Charles Critcher, and Richard Johnson.

37. Ira Katznelson, *City of Trenches*; and Halle, *America's Working Man*.

38. See Pauline Hunt, *Gender and Class Consciousness*; also Heidi

Hartmann, "Capitalism, Patriarchy and Job Segregation by Sex," and Jane Humphries, "Class Struggle and the Persistence of the Working Class Family," both in *Classes, Power and Conflict*, ed. Anthony Giddens and David Held.

39. An exceptionally thoughtful survey research study of workers' consciousness is Erik Olin Wright's in *Classes*, 253, 279. He concludes that unions and political parties have undermined the development of working-class consciousness in the United States, a position I would agree with. In my view, however, Wright only weakly addresses the inherent problems with the method, though he does acknowledge them.

40. Victor Turner, *From Ritual to Theater*, 11.

41. B. Babcock, *The Reversible World*, 32, quoted in Peter Stallybrass and Allon White, *The Politics and Poetics of Transgression*, 20.

42. Lloyd W. Warner and J. D. Low, *The Social System of the Modern Factory*, 1.

43. Quoted in Connell, "Class, Gender and Sartre's Theory of Practice," 69.

44. Ibid. See also Marshall, "Working-Class Consciousness."

45. Clarke et al., "Sub-Cultures, Cultures and Class," 55.

46. Raymond Williams, *Marxism and Literature*, 114.

47. Clifford Geertz, *Local Knowledge*, 4.

48. Louise A. Tilly and Charles Tilly, eds., *Class Conflict and Collective Action*, 17, 233.

49. Quoted in John Foster, "The Declassing of Language," 44.

50. Henri Desroche, *The Sociology of Hope*.

51. See Art Preis, *Labor's Giant Step*, 24–30; and Jeremy Brecher, *Strike!* 161–66.

52. Brecher, *Strike!* 162.

53. Eric Leif Davin and Staughton Lynd, "Picket Line and Ballot Box," 54.

54. Preis, *Labor's Giant Step*, 25.

55. Quoted in Crook, *Communism and the General Strike*, 139.

Chapter Two

1. Georges Sorel, *Reflections on Violence*.

2. See E. P. Thompson, "Time, Work Discipline, and Industrial Capitalism," 56–97; and Sidney Pollard, "Factory Discipline in the Industrial Revolution," 254–71.

3. See Harry Braverman, *Labor and Monopoly Capital;* and Dan Clawson, *Bureaucracy and the Labor Process*.

4. David Montgomery, *Workers' Control in America*, 32.

5. Ibid., 32.

6. Allan Nevins and Frank Hill, *Ford*, 554–55.

7. U.S. Commission on Industrial Relations, *Centralizations of Industrial Control and Operation of Philanthropic Foundations*, 7627–29.

8. David Montgomery notes: "The impulse of peasant immigrants to work furiously when an authority figure was present and loaf in his absence (a tendency that persisted strongly in the steel mills) was soon exchanged in coal mines or car shops for the craftsmen's ethic of refusing to work while a boss was watching" (*Workers' Control in America*, 42).

9. Robert Ozanne, *A Century of Labor-Management Relations at McCormick and International Harvester*, 32–36.

10. See Irving Bernstein, *The Lean Years*, 158.

11. Richard O. Boyer and Herbert M. Morais, *Labor's Untold Story*, 190.

12. Bernstein, *Lean Years*, 159–60.

13. Quoted in Ozanne, *A Century of Labor-Management Relations*, 89.

14. Ibid., 116–17.

15. Quoted in Robert W. Dunn, *Company Unions*, 16.

16. Ibid., 27.

17. Ibid., 23, 22.

18. Quoted in ibid., 22.

19. See Ozanne, *A Century of Labor-Management Relations*, 118–20.

20. Ibid., 120.

21. Ibid., 122–23.

22. Ibid., 133–34.

23. Ibid., 135.

24. Ibid.

25. Dunn, *Company Unions*, 8.

26. Mike Davis, "The Barren Marriage of American Labor and the Democratic Party," 47; and Bert Cochran, *Labor and Communism*, 140.

27. See Thomas R. Brooks, *Toil and Trouble*, 169–70.

28. See James J. Matles and James Higgins, *Them and Us*, 63–64; and Frances Fox Piven and Richard A. Cloward, *Poor People's Movements*, 140.

29. See Ozanne, *A Century of Labor-Management Relations*.

30. See Richard Wilcock, "Industrial Management's Policies Toward Unionism," in *Labor and the New Deal*, ed. Milton Derber and Edwin Young, 312.

31. Ozanne, *A Century of Labor-Management Relations*, 56–57. Evidently, Harvester management anticipated the downturn, as they re-

placed Beeks with a new welfare officer whose "main aim was to block unionism" (ibid., 166).

32. Reinhard Bendix, *Work and Authority in Industry*, 268.

33. Montgomery, *Workers' Control in America*, 58–59.

34. Bendix, *Work and Authority*, 269–70.

35. See Foster Rhea Dulles, *Labor in America*, 226.

36. See Sydney Lens, *Left, Right and Center*, 156; and Melvyn Dubofsky, *We Shall Be All*, 376–97.

37. Boyer and Morais, *Labor's Untold Story*, 204.

38. See Dubofsky, *We Shall Be All*, 381; and Lens, *Left, Right and Center*, 157, 163.

39. Boyer and Morais, *Labor's Untold Story*, 209.

40. See Joseph G. Rayback, *A History of American Labor*, 287–90.

41. See James R. Green, *The World of the Worker*, 119–20.

42. See Davis, "Barren Marriage."

43. Ibid., 147; Boyer and Morais, *Labor's Untold Story*, 217.

44. Brooks, *Toil and Trouble*, 147–48.

45. Quoted in Boyer and Morais, *Labor's Untold Story*, 277–78.

46. Ibid., 278.

47. See Brooks, *Toil and Trouble*, 190.

48. Rayback, *History of American Labor*, 343.

49. Green, *World of the Worker*, 150.

50. See Preis, *Labor's Giant Step*, 97; Rayback, *History of American Labor*, 342; and Boyer and Morais, *Labor's Untold Story*, 291.

51. Quoted in Brooks, *Toil and Trouble*, 180.

52. Cochran, *Labor and Communism*, 114.

53. Louis Adamic, *Dynamite*, 408.

54. See Jeremy Brecher, *Strike!* 182.

55. Green, *World of the Worker*, 157.

56. Boyer and Morais, *Labor's Untold Story*, 295.

57. Green, *World of the Worker*, 158.

58. Boyer and Morais, *Labor's Untold Story*, 322.

59. Piven and Cloward, *Poor People's Movements*, 154.

60. Sidney Fine, *Sit-Down*, 69; also see Matles and Higgins, *Them and Us*, 57–58; Cochran, *Labor and Communism*, 105–6; and Davis, "Barren Marriage," 58–60.

61. Lens, *Left, Right and Center*, 163.

62. See Rayback, *History of American Labor*, 373–87; Dulles, *Labor in America*, 354; and Brooks, *Toil and Trouble*, 207.

63. Brooks, *Toil and Trouble*, 207.

64. Quoted in David Brody, *Workers in Industrial America*, 120.

65. Quoted in Cochran, *Labor and Communism*, 156–57.

66. Ibid., 157.

67. See Green, *World of the Worker*, 181.

68. CIO, "Convention Proceedings."

69. Cochran, *Labor and Communism*, 159–60. Cochran points out that the red-baiting campaign was aimed at local strikes where communists were prominent in either the local or the national leadership. In his review of the data, however, he shows that only 17 out of 109 strikes or strike threats certified by the National Defense Mediation Board were so led (ibid., 162–63).

70. Stan Weir, "Technology and the Absence of Labor's Ranks in Public Issue Politics."

71. Martin Glaberman, *Wartime Strikes*, 3.

72. Quoted in Cochran, *Labor and Communism*, 206, 214.

73. CIO, "Convention Proceedings," 145.

74. Boyer and Morais, *Labor's Untold Story*, 331.

75. As Glaberman has noted, though the wildcat strikes took place among workers who supported the war effort, the reality of the war was omnipresent in American factories as uniformed officers were stationed in all war production plants to intervene in strikes and threatened disputes (*Wartime Strikes*, 49).

76. See Sylvia Kopald, *Rebellion in Labor Unions*, 50–177; and Montgomery, *Workers' Control in America*, 91–101.

77. See Jerome F. Scott and George Homans, "Reflections on the Wildcat Strikes"; Joshua Freeman, "Delivering the Goods," 570–93; and Glaberman, *Wartime Strikes*, 49, 139. Glaberman notes the inaccuracy of "official" data on wildcat strikes, suggesting that government records sorely underestimated the actual number of such strikes.

78. See Green, *World of the Worker*, 183; Davis, "Barren Marriage"; August Meier and Elliot Rudwick, *Black Detroit and the Rise of the UAW*; and Nelson Lichtenstein, "Auto Worker Militancy and the Structure of Factory Life, 1935–1955."

79. Glaberman, *Wartime Strikes*, 119.

80. See Ed Jennings, "Wildcat!"

81. See Freeman, "Delivering the Goods," 583; and Jennings, "Wildcat!" Glaberman notes that Leonard Woodcock, a top UAW official, went so far as to recommend to an auto executive that he "get tough" with the wildcatters (*Wartime Strikes*, 38).

82. Nelson Lichtenstein, review of *Wartime Strikes*, by Martin Glaberman, 607–8.

83. Quoted in Glaberman, *Wartime Strikes*, 44.

84. Green, *World of the Worker*, 194. Also see George Lipsitz, *Class and Culture in Cold War America*, 37–86.

85. See Brody, *Workers in Industrial America*, 180.

86. Quoted in Neil W. Chamberlain, *The Union Challenge to Management Control*, 41.

87. Brody, *Workers in Industrial America*, 180.

88. Wilson is quoted in Boyer and Morais, *Labor's Untold Story*, 345.

89. O'Toole is quoted in ibid., 347. Senator Robert Taft himself remarked at the time that "the bill is not a milktoast [*sic*] bill. It covers about ¾ of the matters pressed upon us very strenuously by the employers." Moreover, one year before the passage of the Taft-Hartley Act, Senator Ball of Minnesota promised the National Association of Manufacturers at their convention that Congress would "deliver the goods." Both quoted in Matles and Higgins, *Them and Us*, 166.

90. See discussion of this provision in Lens, *Left, Right and Center*, 381.

91. See Green, *World of the Worker*, 198.

92. See Matles and Higgins, *Them and Us*, 167.

93. Green, *World of the Worker*, 198.

94. See Lipsitz, *Class and Culture in Cold War America*, 126.

95. Phillip Taft, "Understanding Union Administration," 252–53.

96. Matles and Higgins, *Them and Us*, 168.

97. See Davis, "Barren Marriage," 73. Lens points out that one hundred thousand workers marched against Taft-Hartley in New York City (*Left, Right and Center*, 379). It was also reported that half a million workers walked off their jobs in Detroit, and half of those took part in a massive protest march (*Guild Notes* [publication of the National Lawyers Guild], April 1978, 26).

98. Testimony of John L. Lewis before the U.S. Senate Committee on Labor and Public Welfare, "Taft-Hartley Act Revisions," 83rd Cong., 1st-2nd sess., 1953, pt. 4, 1898, 1918.

99. Davis, "Barren Marriage."

100. Matles and Higgins, *Them and Us;* and Robert Schatz, "The End of Corporate Liberalism."

101. See Matles and Higgins, *Them and Us;* Green, *World of the Worker*, 201.

102. See Lens, *Left, Right and Center*, 382; Lipsitz, *Class and Culture in Cold War America*, 153–72.

103. Davis, "Barren Marriage," 77. Also see Nelson Lichtenstein, *Labor's War at Home*, 239.

104. Boyer and Morais, *Labor's Untold Story*, 350.

105. Testimony of Harry Bridges before the U.S. Senate Committee on Labor and Public Welfare, "Taft-Hartley Act Revisions," 83rd Cong., 1st-2nd sess., 1953, pt. 4, 2277.

106. See Davis, "Barren Marriage," 79.

107. Green, *World of the Worker*, 201.

108. Daniel Bell, *The End of Ideology;* Seymour M. Lipset, *Political Man;* and Edward Shils, "The End of Ideology?"

109. Clark Kerr et al., *Industrialism and Industrial Man,* 225–26.

110. Barrington Moore, *Political Power and Social Theory;* Herbert Marcuse, *One Dimensional Man,* 11; and Robert Blauner, *Alienation and Freedom,* 181–82.

111. Bell, *End of Ideology,* 217; Harold Wilensky, "Class Consciousness and American Workers," in *American Society, Inc.,* ed. M. Zeitlin, 427; Arthur M. Ross and Paul T. Hartmann, *Changing Patterns of Industrial Conflict.*

112. Walter E. Baer, *Strikes;* James E. Cronin, "Theories of Strikes"; Douglas Hibbs, *Industrial Conflict in Advanced Industrial Societies;* and Charles Tilly, *From Mobilization to Revolution.*

113. Charles Tilly and James Rule, *Measuring Political Upheaval.*

114. Tilly, *From Mobilization to Revolution,* 159.

115. Stanley Aronowitz, *False Promises;* Barbara Garson, *All the Livelong Day;* and Charles Spencer, *Blue Collar,* 137.

116. Spencer, *Blue Collar,* 137.

117. Baer, *Strikes,* 68.

118. Everett M. Kassalow, "Labor-Management Relations and the Coal Industry"; and Jim Green, "Holding the Line."

119. John Lippert, "Fleetwood Wildcat," 9; and Frank Kashner, "A Rank and File Revolt at GE," 46.

120. Weir, "Technology and the Absence of Labor's Ranks"; and S. W. Kuhn, *Bargaining in Grievance Settlement,* 50–51.

121. See Stanley Aronowitz, *Working-Class Hero,* 93–94; and Richard Hyman, *Strikes,* 45, 53.

122. There are serious limitations in the Bureau of Labor Statistics' yearly strike data. The Bureau seeks to obtain complete coverage by a "census" of all strikes involving six or more workers and lasting a full shift or longer. But many wildcat strikes are less than a full shift long and consequently are not included in the data. It is impossible to determine the actual magnitude of the phenomenon using BLS data alone.

123. Sumner H. Slichter, James J. Healy, and E. Robert Livernash, *Impact of Collective Bargaining on Management.*

124. Garth Leroy Mangum, "Taming the Wildcat Strikes," 12–13.

125. Garth Leroy Mangum, "Wildcat Strikes and Union Pressure Tactics in American Industry," 24.

126. See Leonard R. Sayles, "Wildcat Strikes."

127. Herbert E. Meyer, "The Decline of Strikes," 66–70.

128. See Jane Slaughter, *Concessions and How to Beat Them,* 43–51;

and Barry Bluestone and Bennett Harrison, *The Deindustrialization of America*.

129. See Jack Barbash, "Trade Unionism from Roosevelt to Reagan," in *The Future of American Unionism*, ed. Louis Ferman, 15; and AFL-CIO, "RUB Sheet" ("Report on Union Busters"), no. 4 (May 1979).

130. See Robert Georgine, "From Brass Knuckles to Briefcases," in *The Big Business Reader*, ed. Mark Green and Robert Massie, Jr.; and Ron Chernow, "The New Pinkertons."

131. See "Labor Fights Back Against Union-Busters," *U.S. News and World Report*, 10 December 1979, 96–98; Dan Clawson, Karen Johnson, and John Schall, "Fighting Union Busting in the 8o's"; and John C. Anderson, Gloria Busman, and Charles A. O'Reilly III, "What Factors Influence the Outcome of Decertification Elections?"

132. See Slaughter, *Concessions*, chap. 1; and Thomas A. Kochan and Michael I. Piore, "Will the New Industrial Relations Last?" in *Future of American Trade Unionism*, ed. Ferman, 177.

133. See U.S. Congress, House, Subcommittee on Labor-Management Relations, "Pressures in Today's Workplace."

134. Ibid., 21.

135. Alan Kistler, "Union Organizing," in *Future of American Unionism*, ed. Ferman, 101.

136. Georgine, "From Brass Knuckles to Briefcases," 96.

137. Kistler, "Union Organizing," 102.

138. Quoted in Georgine, "From Brass Knuckles to Briefcases," 96.

139. Richard E. Walton, "From Control to Commitment in the Workplace," 77–84.

140. Kochan and Piore, "Will the New Industrial Relations Last?" 188.

141. Mark Grey, "Union Members Against Union Members," 16.

142. See "Behind GM's Labor Troubles," *New York Times*, 26 February 1982, D1. For an excellent comprehensive analysis of the problems of "participation" programs for workers, see Mike Parker, *Inside the Circle Game*.

143. Sar A. Levitan and Clifford M. Johnson, "The Changing Workplace," in *Future of American Unionism*, ed. Ferman, 123–24.

144. Kochan and Piore, "Will the New Industrial Relations Last?" 188.

Chapter Three

1. On the dynamics of class association and male bonding, see Mary Ann Clawson, "Brotherhood, Class and Patriarchy"; and Paul Willis, "Shop-Floor Culture, Masculinity, and the Wage Form," in *Working-*

Class Culture, ed. John Clarke, Charles Critcher, and Richard Johnson. Also see David Halle, *America's Working Man*, 180–85.

2. This sociability probably should not be overestimated; the fact that only "safe" issues were discussed may suggest the relative frailty of these social bonds. Although certain pairs of workers did develop close friendships, which probably allowed for the sharing of more personal issues as well as a range of controversial topics, many workers did not develop such intimate connections at work.

3. The processes of the two wildcat strikes were mainly observed in the finishing department, which is the focus of much of my analysis. On the day of the first strike there were eighteen or nineteen men working there. In general, the social cohesion of the department does not seem to have been particularly unique in relation to other departments at Taylor.

4. The process seems to conform to notions of a "threshold" where the number or proportion of potential participants must reach a certain point where the net benefit of participation exceeds the net costs for any given actor. See Mark Granovetter, "Threshold Models of Collective Behavior."

5. The notions of "keynoting" and "differential participation" are formulated by Ralph Turner and Lewis M. Killian in their book *Collective Behavior*. Also see Norris R. Johnson, "Collective Behavior as Group-Induced Shift."

6. Although not a member of a radical organization at the time, Gage was active in radical movements around the northern New Jersey area and was familiar with Marxist-Leninist ideology. He reportedly went on to join a Marxist organization later, as an auto worker, but at Taylor he was viewed largely as an articulate fighter for workers' causes, and this characterized much of his reputation in the plant.

7. Although there were occasional "shouting matches" between a worker and his foreman, this was nothing unusual at Taylor and did not lead to any sort of collective action. The tensions of work in a factory setting are often released through complaints and bickering with management. During the period after the first wildcat strike, there was neither an unusual amount of such bickering nor an unusual amount of formal grievance activity.

8. Interestingly enough, in a management booklet on how to deal with wildcat strikes, the author emphasizes the importance of formally informing the workers that their strike is illegal, so as to have it on the record for any litigation later on. He also suggests threatening workers with discharge and clearly noting who the "ringleaders" are. See Walter E. Baer, *Strikes*.

9. The clipping concerned ex-Black Panther leader Eldridge Cleav-

er's disillusionment with radical politics, socialism, and social change upon his return from exile. The emphasis of the article was his renunciation of radicalism. It seemed very out of context on the company bulletin board, and, as such, its potential impact was probably blunted.

10. This is mentioned only to note that George and Horace were "Bible-toting" Baptists who drank no alcohol. Although everyone showed respect for their religious habits and beliefs, they were occasionally the butt of jokes about their lack of vice. They seemed to combine a strong belief in the "rights of the working man" and in social justice with their commitment to the "word of God."

11. Clifford Geertz, *The Interpretation of Cultures;* Richard Centers, *The Psychology of Social Classes.*

12. Raymond Williams, *Marxism and Literature,* 139–40.

13. See John McDonald's "The Fruitful Errors of Elton Mayo," in *Readings in Industrial Sociology,* ed. William A. Faunce, 305–10.

14. Some examples of the former: Fred E. Katz, "Explaining Informal Work Groups in Complex Organizations"; Edward Gross, "Some Functional Consequences of Primary Controls in Formal Work Organizations"; and Stanley E. Seashore, "Group Cohesiveness in the Industrial Work Group"; all in *Readings in Industrial Sociology,* ed. Faunce, 290–348. Also see Donald F. Roy, "Banana Time," in *Life in Organizations,* ed. Rosabeth Moss Kanter and Barry A. Stein, 192–205; and Michael Burawoy, *Manufacturing Consent.* A notable exception to these is Stan Weir's "The Informal Work Group," in *Rank and File,* ed. Alice Lynd and Staughton Lynd, 179–200.

15. Burawoy, *Manufacturing Consent,* 142.

16. See Charles Tilly, *From Mobilization to Revolution,* 62–63.

17. See Lewis M. Killian, "Organization, Rationality and Spontaneity in the Civil Rights Movement," an analysis that minimizes the structured character of much spontaneous action and reaction, a point that will be explored further later in this book.

18. See Francis Fox Piven and Richard Cloward, *Poor People's Movements,* 19–23, on the dynamics of organizing. The authors' point underscores the potential influence Gage might have had by playing more of an activist than an ideological role.

19. Leonard R. Sayles, "Wildcat Strikes," 48; K.G.J.C. Knowles, "Strike-Proneness and Its Determinants," in *Labor and Trade Unionism: An Interdisciplinary Reader,* ed. Walter Galenson and Seymour M. Lipset, 35. For a similar managerial point of view on wildcat strikes, which emphasizes the necessity of "nipping them in the bud," see Garth Leroy Mangum, "Taming Wildcat Strikes."

20. This point is also suggested by other accounts of wildcat strikes,

such as Jim Green, "Holding the Line"; and Frank Kashner, "A Rank and File Revolt at GE."

21. In *Class and Culture in Cold War America*, George Lipsitz shows how the role of wildcat strikes and other "independent" worker activities prompted corporate capitalism to construct an industrial relations system to channel worker initiative; while Michael Schwartz argues in *Radical Protest and Social Structure* that all subordinate groups must act independently of dominant structures in order to realize their power, a point I pursue further in chapter 4.

22. Some wildcat strikes may actually be supported by local union leaders, though by virtue of their signatures on the contract, they are forced to take a public anti-strike stand. Even so, however, such strikes do break the contract, and rank-and-file workers must still mobilize the action.

23. Sayles, "Wildcat Strikes," 48–49.

24. See, for example, Stanley Aronowitz, *False Promises;* Jeremy Brecher, *Strike!;* Martin Glaberman, "Be His Payment High or Low"; Alvin Gouldner, *Wildcat Strike;* Jerome F. Scott and George Homans, "Reflections on the Wildcat Strikes"; as well as any of the other citations above concerning wildcat strikes, which will reflect the same thing.

25. See Dan Clawson, *Bureaucracy and the Labor Process;* and David Montgomery, *Workers' Control in America.*

26. Gouldner, *Wildcat Strike*, 66n, 52, 43–44.

27. This description refers to Horace and George, who met with a worker, and sometimes two or three, from other departments during the last ten or fifteen minutes of the lunch break to discuss the Bible. They would get together very unobtrusively in the locker room while everyone finished eating in the dining area.

28. Indeed, it is interesting to speculate how workers from particularly conservative backgrounds who nonetheless display strongly class-conscious behavior would respond to a survey dealing with job satisfaction, political voting patterns, etc. These people would probably not appear to be too different from less active workers, although it is hard to tell.

29. Gouldner, *Wildcat Strike*, 66.

30. Burawoy, *Manufacturing Consent.*

31. See Dan Clawson and Richard Fantasia, "Beyond Burawoy."

32. Montgomery, *Workers' Control in America*, 156.

33. Stan Weir, in "Technology and the Absence of Labor's Ranks in Public Issue Politics," offers an analysis of the pressures placed on "insurgent" unionists once they gain power. William Kornblum notes that union politicians may become more dependent on the administrative hierarchy of the union as their contact with the rank and file decreases because of time spent operating in the grievance system (*Blue Collar Community*, 29).

34. See Colin Crouch, *Trade Unions: The Logic of Collective Action*, 85.

35. See Samuel Bowles, David M. Gordon, and Thomas Weiskopf, *Beyond the Wasteland*, 108; and Barry Bluestone and Bennett Harrison, *The Deindustrialization of America*.

Chapter Four

1. "Plan to Save Vermont Factory Faces Several Big Obstacles," *Boston Sunday Globe*, 3 June 1984, 41.

2. Letter to the editor from "Concerned Staff," *Times-Reporter* (Springfield), 20 September 1972.

3. Beatrice Esther Manning examines the dynamics of professionalization and proletarianization among nurses in "Nurses on Strike."

4. See Stanley Aronowitz, *Working-Class Hero*, 113.

5. See Alan Kistler, "Union Organizing," in *The Future of American Unionism*, ed. Louis A. Ferman, 101.

6. William B. Gould, *A Primer on American Labor Law*, 43–50.

7. A recent ruling by the NLRB, which makes it more difficult to organize hospital workers, places limits on the number of bargaining units per hospital (for example, one unit for professional staff, one for nonprofessionals, etc.). This will likely force unions to focus their organizing on larger numbers of employees, which, in the context of employer intransigence and opposition, will make it more difficult to win elections and may give employers more of an opportunity to delay union certification by contesting the legality of bargaining units. See *Labor Notes*, no. 67 (23 August 1984), 4.

8. The law firm has been employed in numerous anti-union efforts throughout western New England. See Dan Clawson, Karen Johnson, and John Schall, "Fighting Union Busting in the 80s," 47.

9. See John Ehrenreich, "Hospital Unions," in *Prognosis Negative*, ed. David Kotelchuk, 255–66. For a solid, though somewhat dated, analysis of social versus business unionism in the United States, see Sydney Lens, *Left, Right and Center*.

10. Ron Chernow, "The New Pinkertons"; and AFL-CIO, "RUB Sheet" ("Report on Union Busters"), no. 3 (April 1979). MM was then referred to as 3M ("Modern Management Methods") and has since changed its name.

11. See review of MM's methods and tactics in Chernow, "The New Pinkertons."

12. Springfield Hospital memorandum, 8 June 1981.

13. Springfield Hospital memorandum, 11 June 1981.

14. Springfield Hospital memorandum, 25 June 1981.

15. Kistler, "Union Organizing," 103.

16. "Push for Union Recognition Goes On," *Eagle Times* (Springfield), 14 October 1981, 1. The hospital administration could have officially and legally recognized the union upon the presentation of a petition with more than 50 percent of the workers "showing interest" in union representation. However, few expected the administration to do so until ordered by the NLRB after a formal representation election.

17. Springfield Hospital press release memorandum, 30 October 1981.

18. "Union Supporters Escorted from Springfield Hospital," *Eagle Times* (Springfield), 24 November 1981.

19. See Paul Willis, "Shop-Floor Culture, Masculinity, and the Wage Form," in *Working-Class Culture*, ed. John Clarke, Charles Critcher, and Richard Johnson, for a provocative discussion of the ways in which masculine culture may hinder collective action in the workplace. Also see Theo Nichols and Peter Armstrong, *Workers Divided*.

20. Two brothers from this department who expressed some interest in the union at the outset were exceptions. Because of their strong personalities and outgoing characters, they wielded some influence. However, according to Richard Sanders, the organizer for District 1199 of the National Union of Hospital and Health Care Employees, as skilled workers occupying a traditional male role in the hospital, they were susceptible to management propaganda—their status set them apart, and they wanted to maintain this status. Sanders encouraged the organizing committee to keep trying to talk with these two workers, but he felt that a further obstacle may have been their resentment of the higher wages, standard of living, and comparative self-confidence of the men from Local 218 who were supporting the union drive.

21. Of the four switchboard operators for whom data were available (out of six altogether), two were actively anti-union, and the other two voted against the union, according to informants. The close proximity of the switchboard to administration offices would seem to have (at a minimum) provided support for anti-unionism and would have made pro-union sentiments difficult to maintain through the course of the campaign. The structuring of social networks has been found to be a key element in determining social movement participation. See David A. Snow, Louis A. Zurcher, Jr., and Sheldon Eckland-Olson, "Social Networks and Social Movements."

22. See Ehrenreich, "Hospital Unions," 198.

23. Eliot Friedson, *The Profession of Medicine*, 72, quoted in ibid.

24. See Barbara Melosh, *The Physician's Hand;* and Manning, "Nurses on Strike."

25. See Pauline Hunt, *Gender and Class Consciousness.*

26. Herbert Meyer, "The Decline of Strikes."

27. Robert Georgine, "From Brass Knuckles to Briefcases," in *The Big Business Reader,* ed. Mark Green and Robert Massie, 90.

28. Kistler, "Union Organizing," 101.

29. Ibid., 102–3. Also see "The NLRB: Help or Handicap to Labor?" *Labor Update* (newsletter of the National Labor Law Center, National Lawyers Guild) 2, no. 3 (March/April 1982); and "Labor Board Stirs Up a Storm," *New York Times,* 5 February 1984.

30. Shortly after the union election, Sanders left District 1199 for a position with another union. Workers in Springfield expressed frustration at the lack of regular contact with a union organizer after Sanders left.

31. See Jack Barbash, "Trade Unionism from Roosevelt to Reagan"; and Sar A. Levitan and Clifford M. Johnson, "The Changing Workplace"; both in *Future of American Unionism,* ed. Ferman.

32. Michael Schwartz, *Radical Protest and Social Structure,* 173.

33. Ibid., 189.

34. Lewis M. Killian, "Organization, Rationality, and Spontaneity in the Civil Rights Movement," 782.

35. Bert Klandermans, "Mobilization and Participation."

36. Kistler, "Union Organizing," 105.

37. See Kate Purcell, "Militancy and Acquiescence Among Women Workers"; Richard Brown, "Women as Employees"; Ian Watt, "Industrial Radicalism and the Domestic Division of Labour"; and Pauline Hunt, "Workers Side by Side"; all in *Women and the Public Sphere,* ed. Janet Siltanen and Michelle Stanworth.

38. See Purcell, "Militancy and Acquiescence Among Women Workers."

Chapter Five

1. Julie Jensen MacDonald, *Pathways to the Present in 50 Iowa and Illinois Communities,* 64.

2. See U.S. Department of Labor, "Area Wage Survey: Davenport–Rock Island–Moline (Iowa-Illinois) Metropolitan Area," Bureau of Labor Statistics Bulletin 3000–5 (February 1980).

3. MacDonald, *Pathways,* 66.

4. Concerned Citizens of Clinton, Iowa, "A Profile of Standard Brands," in *One Year of Our Lives: The Clinton Corn Strike, 1979–1980.*

In April 1981, Standard Brands and Nabisco merged to form Nabisco Brands. Based on 1980 results, this produced a corporation with sales (in the food industry) of $5.5 billion and 1980 earnings of $232 million ("Standard Brands, Nabisco to Merge," *Boston Globe*, 23 April 1981). See also "The New Food Giants," *Business Week*, 24 September 1984.

5. From *Milling and Baking News*, quoted in Concerned Citizens of Clinton, Iowa, "A Profile of Standard Brands."

6. See U.S. Department of Labor, "Productivity Indexes for Selected Industries," Bureau of Labor Statistics Bulletin 2002 (1978).

7. See U.S. Department of Labor, "Industry Wage Survey: Grain Mill Products, September 1977," Bureau of Labor Statistics Bulletin 2026 (1979), 2–3.

8. Ibid., 3.

9. See "Grain Millers Endorse Legislative Objectives," *AFL-CIO News* 22, no. 10 (9 July 1977).

10. See "Midwestern Grain Millers Vote to Return to Work," *Daily World* (New York), 6 October 1975, 2; and "Rank and File Sugar Workers Hit Takeaways," *Daily World* (New York), 27 March 1980, 4.

11. See the discussion of embezzlement and "taking rightful chips" among nineteenth-century workers in Dan Clawson, *Bureaucracy and the Labor Process*, 45–47.

12. Evidently, when the NLRB finally ruled on the unfair labor practice charge filed by the union, it suggested that the punishment had been extraordinarily harsh for such an offense, although the ruling upheld the company's right to punish workers for engaging in an "illegal" work stoppage.

13. See Concerned Citizens of Clinton, Iowa, *One Year of Our Lives*.

14. Quoted in "Clinco Workers Vote Strike," *Clinton Herald*, 30 July 1979.

15. The law firm of Robert Marsak had previously worked for the Delevan Corporation in Des Moines and had engineered the decertification of a United Auto Workers union local that had represented workers at Delevan for many years. See National Organizng Coordinating Committee, AFL-CIO, "Bargaining and the Busters," *Report on Union Busters* (*RUB*), no. 13 (February 1980), 4; and "Clinton, Iowa: Scarred Outpost in Labor War," *Des Moines Sunday Register*, 4 November 1979.

16. Jack Barbash ("Trade Unionism from Roosevelt to Reagan," in *The Future of American Unionism*, ed. Louis Ferman) seeks to place this sort of strike in the general context of industrial relations.

17. T. Lane and K. Roberts, *Strike at Pilkington's*, 105.

18. See E. T. Hiller's classic, *Strike*, for an interesting discussion of the dynamics of strike activity.

19. Quoted in "Peaceful Demonstration Staged at Clinton Corn," *Clinton Herald*, 27 September 1979; and *Iowa AFL-CIO News* 9, no. 2 (May 1980).

20. "Strike Erupts into Violent Melee," *Clinton Herald*, 4 August 1979, 1.

21. "City to Probe Police Harassment Charges," *Clinton Herald*, 19 April 1980.

22. Ibid.; and "Union Supporters Level More Charges," *Clinton Herald*, 23 April 1980.

23. "Union Leader's Home Fired at During Strike," *Des Moines Register*, 1 September 1979; and "Rifle Bullets Riddle Union Man's Home," *Clinton Herald*, 31 August 1979.

24. "Police Officer Was Man in the Middle," *Clinton Herald*, 7 June 1980.

25. "Seven Ordered to Jail in Labor Disorder," *Quad City Times* (Davenport, Iowa), 29 January 1980, 5.

26. There were numerous city council rulings related to the dispute. Among those that suggested city-company complicity to strikers were rulings clearing the police of brutality charges brought by the union and denying a request for the construction of wind-breaker sheds to shelter picketers in the winter months. See "Clinton Council Stays 'Neutral': Sheds for Pickets Denied," *Quad City Times* (Davenport, Iowa), 9 January 1980, 5; and "Clinton Mayor Clears Police of Charges," *Quad City Times* (Davenport, Iowa), 11 April 1980, 3.

27. "Introduction to Our Paper," *Voice of Labor* 1, no. 1 (March 1980).

28. Many of the taverns in Clinton became identified as pro-union or anti-union during the struggle. Bars that served strikebreakers or off-duty policemen were strictly boycotted by strikers, and certain bars were held to be off-limits to anti-union participants in the conflict. Some bar owners refused to serve known scabs in their establishments, but extended credit to strikers.

29. Gil Dawes, "Liberation Theology in the Bible Belt," 84.

30. Written account of Gil Dawes's role in the wildcat strike of 1975 from church records, St. Mark's United Methodist Church, Comanche, Iowa.

31. See C. Howard Hopkins, *The Rise of the Social Gospel in American Protestantism, 1865–1919*, 290–91.

32. Author's notes, 8 June 1980.

33. Ibid.

34. Analysis of church membership records.

35. See "Labor Controversy Returns to Pulpit," *Quad City Times* (Davenport, Iowa), 15 May 1980.

36. See David Halle, *America's Working Man*, 201.

37. "Black Militant to Visit Strikers," *Quad City Times* (Davenport, Iowa), 6 March 1980.

38. "Communist Party Support of Local 6 Is Denounced," *Clinton Herald*, 11 March 1980.

39. Ibid.

40. Tape recording of March union meeting.

41. "50 Wave Flags in Protest of Angela Davis Visit," *Des Moines Register*, 9 March 1980.

42. This notwithstanding that by 1979 the labor law reform initiative, supported by the AFL-CIO, had been defeated under a Democratic administration. See Barbash, "Trade Unionism," 21.

43. An article appeared in the *Washington Post* recounting the visit by Angela Davis to Clinton, giving this story, a source of potential embarrassment for the national union, exposure in the city that houses AFL-CIO headquarters.

44. Reportedly, officials of the national union had agreed to Local 6's request that a national boycott of Standard Brands be imposed by the AFL-CIO. The request was supposedly submitted by the American Federation of Grain Millers (AFGM) to the proper committee at the AFL-CIO's annual convention, but it apparently never reached the floor for a vote and was never implemented. The AFGM leadership reportedly blamed the lack of action on bureaucratic error by convention officials, but the strike community in Clinton tended to view it as deliberate sabotage by a national union leadership willing to defeat a strike they feared as a political threat.

45. Dawes, "Liberation Theology," 90.

46. Ibid., 90–91.

47. Raymond Williams, *Marxism and Literature*, 110.

48. Halle, *America's Working Man;* and Ira Katznelson, *City Trenches*.

49. See "Workers and Community Take on GM," *The Nation* 238, no. 5 (11 February 1984); "Can Communities Confiscate Closed Factories?" *Labor Notes*, April 1985, 8–10; "Corporate Ruthlessness and Community Despair," *Labor Update* (newsletter of the National Labor Law Center, National Lawyers Guild) 1, no. 4 (February 1981); "The Fight to Save Youngstown, Ohio," *Dollars and Sense*, no. 59 (September 1980), 14–16; "Men of Cloth Do Battle Over Steel," *New York Times*, 16 January 1985; "Community Coalition Wins Big Wage Increase for Non-Union North Carolina Auto Workers," *Labor Notes*, 26 July 1984, 5.

50. Indeed, Halle seems to clearly understand the volatile nature of working-class consciousness. He notes that "it is easy to stress an image of a nationalist worker while forgetting how quickly nationalism can turn into populism and how easily the ardor that fueled support of American hostages or athletes can change to anger at politicians who exploit the 'American people'" (*America's Working Man*, 292).

51. This seems to have been the case in the recent strike by Phelps-Dodge copper miners in Arizona, and it was certainly an issue in the long strike of metal workers in Massachusetts, in which I was involved. See Dan Clawson, Karen Johnson, and John Schall, "Fighting Union-Busting in the 80's"; "Phelps-Dodge Copper Miners Battle Police on Strike's First Anniversary," *Labor Notes*, 26 July 1984, 1; "The Strike Against Phelps Dodge Co. Continues—Barely," *In These Times*, 10–14 April 1984, 7; "Unionism Divided Against Itself," *The Nation* 237, no. 12 (22 October 1983), 262; and "Tri-State Coalition Fights to Save the Mon Valley," *Labor Notes*, April 1985, 9.

52. During the dispute various figures were offered by different sources on the number of union members crossing the line, but the approximate figure of 150 seems to be the most reasonable estimate. Similarly, the actual number of outside replacement workers hired was the subject of some dispute. The most reliable estimate of replacements was in the 400–450 range. The point that "scabs" were "outsiders" was made in separate conversations at different times with over a dozen strikers at the Labor Temple.

53. In many ways it made sense for the company to hire workers from outside, as they would not be as susceptible to community pressure and intimidation, thus ensuring that they would be better able to continue as replacement workers during the strike and after.

54. See Dawes, "Liberation Theology," 87.

55. After two strikers who had taken jobs during the strike at a nuclear power plant had been exposed to a potentially dangerous amount of radioactivity, a group of four or five women from the strike community got involved in a committee against nuclear power in a nearby city. Despite some criticisms that it was peripheral to the "real" issues of the strike—and despite significant opposition from one husband to his wife's involvement—the women remained committed to this activity.

56. Although there is no hard evidence, numerous anecdotes were told of the high incidence of divorce and separation among strike families. Severe marital tensions are to be expected in an eleven-month strike. One probable cause would be the pressure placed on "traditional" men through a sustained period of joblessness. The strike community attempted to ease pressures through various collective strike activities and

social events, but it was probably not enough to prevent some strikers from feeling threatened by the new-found activism and relative economic independence of their wives.

57. The women's support organizations in the British miners' strike of 1984–85 are one set of examples. See Jill Evans, Clare Hudson, and Penny Smith, "Women and the Strike: It's a Whole Way of Life," in *Policing the Miners' Strike*, ed. Bob Fine and Robert Miller, 188–203. For a negative example of women whose isolation was preserved because autonomous organization was not encouraged, see Clawson, Johnson, and Schall, "Fighting Union-Busting."

58. See Michael Schwartz, *Radical Protest and Social Structure*, 173.

59. See the account of the relationship of the metalworkers union and the membership in the strike detailed by Clawson, Johnson, and Schall in "Fighting Union-Busting."

60. Craig Calhoun, "The Radicalism of Tradition."

Chapter Six

1. See Craig Calhoun, *The Question of Class Struggle;* and Calhoun, "The Radicalism of Tradition."

2. On women's organization in the British miners' strike, see Maggi Wolton, "The Pit Props," *Guardian*, 1 April 1986, 17; Chris Salt and Jim Layzell, *Here We Go!;* Lynn Beaton, *Shifting Horizons;* and Loretta Loach, "We'll Be Right Here to the End . . . and After," in *Digging Deeper*, ed. Huw Beynon.

3. Jon Amsden and Stephen Brier, "Coal Miners on Strike," in *Industrialization and Urbanization*, ed. Theodore K. Rabb and Robert I. Rotberg, 138–39.

4. The "irrational crowd" is put forward in Gustave Le Bon, "The Mind of Crowds," in *Collective Behavior and Social Movements*, ed. Louis E. Genevie, 6–11; Eric Hoffer, *The True Believer;* and Kenneth Keniston, *Young Radicals*. The utilitarian model is best articulated by Mancur Olson in *The Logic of Collective Action*. Colin Crouch draws on Olson's basic model (with modifications) in his *Trade Unions*.

5. For example, Lewis Killian has argued the lack of planning of the 1956 Tallahassee bus boycott ("Organization, Rationality, and Spontaneity in the Civil Rights Movement"). Although Killian focuses on the emergence of new organizational forms, his data also indicate that the support of preexisting organizations was needed by Tallahassee CORE and that activities (testing the bus boycott and the color barrier at a white lunch counter, sit-in demonstrations, etc.) were planned and considered "ratio-

nally," even though they may not have been "part of a well-thought-out, ongoing strategy" (ibid., 777). While agreeing with Killian's criticisms of the utilitarian model of collective behavior, I think there is a danger in labeling all action with no direct links to national organizations or overall blueprints as "spontaneous."

6. Crouch has argued that, unless an employer must have a quick settlement, the longer a strike goes on, the weaker the workers' position will become relative to the employer, who commands more resources, and that "eventually the workers in a desperate strike will make the calculation that surrender is inevitable, and that the cost will never be made good" (*Trade Unions*, 78). His analysis is informed by the utilitarian perspective of Mancur Olson, but he recognizes, too, that both union and employer try to obscure the "calculations" of the other "by trying to give each other misleading information, bluffing and trying to call the other's bluff" (ibid., 85). The "spirit" of solidarity can, I would argue, stave off a drift back to work by those who might otherwise calculate that "the cost will never be made good," just as attempts by employers to manipulate the social psychological climate (as in the Springfield Hospital union drive) can influence workers to oppose unionization that may actually be in their own best interest.

7. V. I. Lenin, "What Is To Be Done?" in *The Lenin Anthology*, ed. Robert Tucker, 24. Although the limitations of union activity were paramount for Lenin, he also asserted that "the formation of a single trade union was of greater significance than the battle of Sadowa . . . and the first communist subbotnik organized by the workers of the Moscow-Kazan Railway in Moscow on 10 May 1919 was of greater historical significance than any of the victories of Hindenburg or of Foch and the British in the 1914–1918 imperialist war" (V. I. Lenin, "A Great Beginning," *Collected Works* 29:424).

8. V. I. Lenin, *What Is To Be Done?* 30–31.

9. Gordon Marshall, "Some Remarks on the Study of Working-Class Consciousness," 289.

10. Part of my objection has to do with the notion of a "revolutionary consciousness," which can probably never really exist except as an ideal-typical, utopian construct that can only be approached more or less empirically. Revolutions have certainly often included large numbers of workers, but what has made revolutions has had more to do with crises in the states concerned and the capacities of movements and parties than simply with the purposive intentions of workers. Similarly, the classification of intent seems less important in determining consciousness than collective actions and the ways workers organize and structure their lives. In criticizing John Foster's analysis of the class-conscious character of nineteenth-

century workers in *Class Struggle in the Industrial Revolution*, Stedman-Jones upbraids him for not outlining the content of workers' convictions and their subjective aims, when Foster has shown, in my view, that the "content" is revealed in their collective actions, marriages, housing arrangements (which broke down status barriers), and the practical organization of class consciousness. In his critique, Stedman-Jones seems to me to have been unduly concerned with subjective classifications. See Gareth Stedman-Jones, *Languages of Class*, 44.

11. V. L. Allen, "Dissent in the Appalachian Coalfields," 7, 30.

12. Fredric Jameson has drawn from Sartre to consider cultural production generally and, in an argument similar to my own, states that for those who "believe in an increasingly windless and all embracing total system[,] what shatters such a system . . . is . . . very precisely collective praxis or, to pronounce its traditional and unmentionable name, class struggle . . . [C]lass struggle, and the slow and intermittent development of genuine class consciousness, are themselves the process whereby a new and organic group constitutes itself, whereby the collective breaks through the reified atomization (Sartre calls it the seriality) of capitalist social life. At that point, to say that the group exists and that it generates its own specific cultural life and expression, are one and the same" ("Reification and Utopia in Mass Culture," 140).

13. Allen, "Dissent in the Appalachian Coalfields," 8.

14. R. F. Hamilton, *Affluence and the French Worker in the Fourth Republic*, 278.

15. Frank Parkin, *Class Inequality and Political Order*, 98–99, cited in Duncan Gallie, *Social Inequality and Class Radicalism in France and Britain*, 21.

16. Jack Barbash, "Trade Unionism from Roosevelt to Reagan," in *The Future of American Unionism*, ed. Louis Ferman, 19.

17. Jane Slaughter, *Concessions and How to Beat Them*, 51.

18. As mentioned earlier, there are some national unions, such as District 1199 of the National Union of Hospital and Health Care Employees, the United Electrical Workers Union, and the International Association of Machinists, who have at times placed the institutional weight of their organizations behind worker solidarity at the local level. But they remain on the left wing of the American union movement and are largely exceptions to the general tendency.

19. The Phelps-Dodge strike of copper miners in Arizona, which began in 1983 and lasted for almost two years, is a good example. Dr. Jorge O'Leary, who resigned as company doctor during the dispute to become a spokesperson for the strikers, offered the following criticisms of the United Steel Workers of America. His comments pointedly highlight how

the union's reliance on the legal and political system, rather than on militant unionism, misled the strikers. He begins by discussing the company's response when one thousand strikers met newly hired strikebreakers at the picket line, armed and prepared for a battle:

> At the time, I was still an employee of Phelps-Dodge, and I know that management was utterly terrified and shaken by the mobilization of the miners and their families. . . . I can say without fear of contradiction . . . they were within reach of a tremendous victory over the company. . . . Unfortunately, the union leadership forcefully intervened to stop the demonstration and persuaded the copper miners to place their trust in Governor Bruce Babbitt [liberal Democrat, re-elected with an AFL-CIO endorsement]. They were told to accept the 10-day "cooling-off" period and were assured that a settlement favorable to the union would soon be reached. The striking miners reluctantly accepted the advice of their leaders . . . and did not get the settlement that had been promised. Rather, we got the National Guard, the Department of Public Safety [state police], and a massive scabbing operation backed by the Government. What did the United Steel Workers do in response? First, they told miners that the company would not be able to operate with scabs. Then the union officials invited lawyers to Clifton in order to assure us that a brilliant "legal strategy" would force Phelps-Dodge to sign a contract. . . . Strikers and their families . . . gradually lost confidence in the ability and the determination of the unions—particularly the USWA—to win this struggle. . . . In the most recent weeks, the strikers were told that the company's attempt to decertify the unions would be defeated through the efforts of . . . lawyers. However, to the surprise of not a single striker, the NLRB ruled against the unions on every issue.

O'Leary urged the union (unsuccessfully) to mobilize workers widely through organized mass picketing, breaking the injunction limiting the number of pickets, and establishing a $10 million strike fund to sustain and organize such a battle. When the union declined, the vice president was asked what the union's strategy was, and he replied, "It's all in our Legal Department's hands." Quoted in Robert Roper, "Copper Strikers Refuse to Give Up, But Some Question Steel Workers' Strategy," in *Labor Notes*, 20 November 1984, 3, 14.

It should be noted that while union leaders' apparent squeamishness about militantly engaging the corporation was an important factor in the eventual defeat of the strike, a mass rally and a food collection drive were organized for the Phelps-Dodge strikers by thirty-five unions in the New York City area, an unusual, but encouraging, act of interunion solidarity.

20. I. Phillip Sipser, "Labor Relations Board Is No Friend," letter to the editor, *New York Times*, 1 July 1985.

21. Though I am skeptical of the ability and willingness of union leaders who preside over massive bureaucratic organizations to transform those organizations, union leaders who lead local unions and who are closer to the conflict "on the ground" are a different story. For example,

scores of local leaders from throughout the country regularly attend the yearly conferences in Detroit sponsored by the journal *Labor Notes,* which have been dedicated to revitalizing the labor movement. Many of the points in the brief set of recommendations I offer below derive from discussions I have had or workshops I have attended at these annual meetings.

22. Stanley Aronowitz has argued persuasively for such initiatives to reverse the decline of the labor movement and to develop a progressive "third force" in American politics (*Working-Class Hero*). The Service Employees International Union, District 1199 of the National Union of Hospital and Health Care Employees, the United Food and Commercial Workers Union, and several others have moved fairly decisively to organize in these areas, often aided by and aiding local minority and women's groups in the process. Aronowitz is absolutely correct in calling for vigorous organization among previously unorganized workers, but, in my view, he has minimized the potential strength inherent in the organization (or reorganization) of traditional union workers, who, as I have tried to show here, may be awakened to new conceptions, associations, and possibilities in defense of their unions.

23. Reportedly, the United Mine Workers Union of America has embarked on a program whereby active and laid-off union members serve as union organizers in addition to full-time professional staff. Although established to ease the financial burden on the union's treasury, it also seems an imaginative way to draw on the resources of the rank and file.

24. See Mike Davis, "The Lesser Evil? The Left and the Democratic Party," 26.

25. District 1199 of the National Union of Hospital and Health Care Employees sustains rich cultural programs for members. Theater projects, workers' art projects, and other initiatives have been introduced by Moe Foner, director of education. Similarly, but with fewer resources, the United Electrical Workers Union regularly sponsors political educational forums and discussions; in western Massachusetts, at least, these are often widely attended by members. In Britain, workers' culture and consciousness is still cultivated in the working-men's clubs (though this is severely limited by male-only admission policies that too often still operate). The British National Union of Mine Workers maintains an extensive system of welfare clubs and lodges, which serve as community centers in mining regions, with social activities such as lodge choirs, musical bands, lectures, and parties binding members and their families to a wider union culture.

26. Dan Clawson, Karen Johnson, and John Schall, in "Fighting Union

Busting in the 80's," have similarly argued the need for conscious violation of the Taft-Hartley Act.

Appendix

1. For an extremely insightful discussion of methodological problems and prospects in the study of class consciousness, see Gordon Marshall, "Some Remarks on the Study of Working-Class Consciousness."

2. See William Kornblum's *Blue Collar Community*, and, more recently, David Halle, *America's Working Man*, for excellent examples of social anthropologies of working-class communities.

3. Clifford Geertz, *The Interpretation of Cultures*, 5–10.

Bibliography

Adamic, Louis. *Dynamite: The Story of Class Violence in America*. New York: Viking, 1931.

Allen, V. L. "Dissent in the Appalachian Coalfields." School of Economic Studies, University of Leeds. March 1985. Typescript.

Aminzade, Ronald. "The Transformation of Social Solidarities in Nineteenth-Century Toulouse." In *Consciousness and Class Experience in Nineteenth-Century Europe*, edited by John Merriman. New York: Holmes and Meier, 1979.

Amsden, Jon, and Stephen Brier. "Coal Miners on Strike: The Transformation of Strike Demands and the Formation of a National Union." In *Industrialization and Urbanization: Studies in Interdisciplinary History*, edited by Theodore K. Rabb and Robert I. Rotberg. Princeton, N.J.: Princeton University Press, 1981.

Anderson, John C., Gloria Busman, and Charles A. O'Reilly III. "What Factors Influence the Outcome of Decertification Elections?" *Monthly Labor Review* 102, no. 11 (November 1979).

Archer, Margaret S. "The Myth of Cultural Integration." *British Journal of Sociology* 36, no. 3 (1985).

Aronowitz, Stanley. *False Promises*. New York: McGraw-Hill, 1973.

———. *Working-Class Hero: A New Strategy for Labor*. New York: Pilgrim Press, 1983.

Avineri, Shlomo. *The Social and Political Thought of Karl Marx*. Cambridge: Cambridge University Press, 1968.

Babcock, B. *The Reversible World: Symbolic Inversion in Art and Society*. Ithaca, N.Y.: Cornell University Press, 1978.

Baer, Walter E. *Strikes: A Study of Conflict and How to Resolve It*. New York: AMACOM, 1975.

Barbash, Jack. "Trade Unionism from Roosevelt to Reagan." In *The Fu-

ture of American Unionism, edited by Louis Ferman. Beverly Hills, Calif.: Sage, 1984.

Baumann, Zygmunt. *Culture and Praxis.* London: Routledge and Kegan Paul, 1973.

Beaton, Lynn. *Shifting Horizons.* London: Canary Press, 1985.

Bell, Daniel. *The End of Ideology.* Glencoe, Ill.: Free Press, 1960.

Bendix, Reinhard. *Work and Authority in Industry.* Berkeley and Los Angeles: University of California Press, 1974.

Benedict, Ruth. *Patterns of Culture.* London: Routledge and Kegan Paul, 1961.

Bernstein, Irving. *The Lean Years.* Boston: Houghton Mifflin, 1960.

Beynon, Huw, ed. *Digging Deeper.* London: Verso, 1985.

Blackburn, Robin, and Michael Mann. "Ideology in the Non-Skilled Working Class." In *Working-Class Images of Society,* edited by M. Blumer. London: Routledge and Kegan Paul/SSRC, 1975.

Blauner, Robert. *Alienation and Freedom.* Chicago: University of Chicago Press, 1964.

Bluestone, Barry, and Bennett Harrison. *The Deindustrialization of America: Plant Closings, Community Abandonment, and the Dismantling of Basic Industry.* New York: Basic Books, 1982.

Bowles, Samuel, David M. Gordon, and Thomas E. Weiskopf. *Beyond the Wasteland.* Garden City, N.Y.: Anchor Books, 1984.

Boyer, Richard O., and Herbert M. Morais. *Labor's Untold Story.* New York: United Electrical, Radio and Machine Workers of America, 1955.

Braverman, Harry. *Labor and Monopoly Capital: The Degradation of Work in the Twentieth Century.* New York: Monthly Review Press, 1974.

Brecher, Jeremy. *Strike!* Boston: South End Press, 1972.

Brecher, Jeremy, and Tim Costello. *Common Sense for Hard Times.* New York: Two Continents, 1976.

Brody, David. *Workers in Industrial America: Essays on the 20th Century Struggle.* New York: Oxford University Press, 1980.

Brooks, Thomas R. *Toil and Trouble.* New York: Dell, 1964.

Brown, Richard. "Women as Employees: Social Consciousness and Collective Action." In *Women and the Public Sphere,* edited by Janet Siltanen and Michelle Stanworth. London: Hutchinson, 1984.

Burawoy, Michael. *Manufacturing Consent: Changes in the Labor Process Under Monopoly Capitalism.* Chicago: University of Chicago Press, 1979.

Calhoun, Craig. *The Question of Class Struggle.* Chicago: University of Chicago Press, 1982.

————. "The Radicalism of Tradition: Community Strength or Venerable Disguise and Borrowed Language?" *American Journal of Sociology* 88, no. 5 (1983).

Case, Herman M. "Marxist Implications of Centers' Interest Group Theory: A Critical Appraisal." *Social Forces* 33 (March 1955).

Centers, Richard. *The Psychology of Social Classes*. Princeton, N.J.: Princeton University Press, 1949.

Chamberlain, Neil W. *The Union Challenge to Management Control*. New York: Harper, 1948.

Chernow, Ron. "The New Pinkertons." *Mother Jones*, May 1980.

CIO [Congress of Industrial Organizations]. "Convention Proceedings." Washington, D.C.: CIO, 1944.

Clarke, John, Charles Critcher, and Richard Johnson, eds. *Working-Class Culture*. New York: St. Martin's Press, 1979.

Clarke, John, Stuart Hall, Tony Jefferson, and Brian Roberts. "Sub-Cultures, Cultures and Class." In *Culture, Ideology and Social Process: A Reader*, edited by Tony Bennett, Graham Martin, Colin Mercer, and Janet Woollacott. London: Batsford, 1961.

Clawson, Dan. *Bureaucracy and the Labor Process*. New York: Monthly Review Press, 1980.

Clawson, Dan, and Richard Fantasia. "Beyond Burawoy: The Dialectics of Conflict and Consent on the Shop Floor." *Theory and Society* 12 (December 1983).

Clawson, Dan, Karen Johnson, and John Schall. "Fighting Union Busting in the 80's." *Radical America* 16, nos. 4 and 5 (July/August and September/October 1982).

Clawson, Mary Ann. "Brotherhood, Class and Patriarchy: Fraternalism in Europe and America." Ph.D. thesis, Department of Sociology, SUNY, Stony Brook, August 1980.

Cochran, Bert. *Labor and Communism: The Conflict that Shaped American Unions*. Princeton, N.J.: Princeton University Press, 1977.

Commons, John, David J. Saposs, Helen L. Sumner, E. B. Mittelman, H. E. Hoagland, John B. Andrews, and Selig Perlman, eds. *History of Labor in the United States*. 4 vols. New York: Macmillan, 1918–35.

Concerned Citizens of Clinton, Iowa. *One Year of Our Lives: The Clinton Corn Strike, 1979–1980*. Clinton, Iowa: n.p., 1980.

Connell, R. W. "Class, Gender and Sartre's Theory of Practice." In *Which Way Is Up? Essays on Sex, Class and Culture*, edited by R. W. Connell. London: George Allen and Unwin, 1983.

Cousins, Jim, and Richard Brown. "Patterns of Paradox Among Shipbuilding Workers." In *Working-Class Images of Society*, edited by M. Blumer. London: Routledge and Kegan Paul/SSRC, 1975.

Cronin, James E. "Theories of Strikes: Why Can't They Explain the British Experience?" *Journal of Social History* 12, no. 2 (Winter 1978).

Crook, Wilfrid H. *Communism and the General Strike*. Hampden, Conn.: Shoe String Press, 1960.

Crouch, Colin. *Trade Unions: The Logic of Collective Action*. London: Fontana, 1982.

Davin, Eric Leif, and Staughton Lynd. "Picket Line and Ballot Box: The Forgotten Legacy of the Local Labor Party Movement, 1932–1936." *Radical History Review*, no. 22 (Winter 1979–80).

Davis, Mike. "The Barren Marriage of American Labor and the Democratic Party." *New Left Review*, no. 124 (November/December 1980).

———. "The Lesser Evil? The Left and the Democratic Party." *New Left Review*, no. 155 (January/February 1986).

Dawes, Gil. "Liberation Theology in the Bible Belt." *Monthly Review* 36, no. 3 (July/August 1984).

Derber, Milton, and Edwin Young. *Labor and the New Deal*. Madison: University of Wisconsin, 1957.

Desroche, Henri. *The Sociology of Hope*. London: Routledge and Kegan Paul, 1979.

Dubofsky, Melvyn. *We Shall Be All: A History of the IWW*. New York: Quadrangle/New York Times Book Company, 1969.

Dulles, Foster Rhea. *Labor in America*. New York: Crowell, 1949.

Dunn, Robert W. *Company Unions*. New York: Vanguard Press, 1927.

Ehrenreich, John. "Hospital Unions: A Long Time Coming." In *Prognosis Negative*, edited by David Kotelchuk. New York: Vintage Books, 1976.

Erikson, Kai. *Everything in Its Path: Destruction of Community in the Buffalo Creek Flood*. New York: Simon and Schuster, 1976.

Evans, Jill, Clare Hudson, and Penny Smith. "Women and the Strike: It's a Whole Way of Life." In *Policing the Miners' Strike*, edited by Bob Fine and Robert Miller. London: Lawrence and Wishart, 1985.

Eysenck, H. J. "Social Attitude and Social Class." *British Journal of Sociology* 1 (March 1950).

Faunce, William A., ed. *Readings in Industrial Sociology*. New York: Appleton-Century-Crofts, 1967.

Ferman, Louis, ed. *The Future of American Unionism*. Beverly Hills, Calif.: Sage, 1984.

Fine, Bob, and Robert Miller, eds. *Policing the Miners' Strike*. London: Lawrence and Wishart, 1985.

Fine, Sidney. *Sit-Down: The General Motors Strike of 1936–1937*. Ann Arbor: University of Michigan Press, 1969.

Foster, John. *Class Struggle in the Industrial Revolution*. London: Weidenfeld and Nicolson, 1974.

————. "The Declassing of Language." *New Left Review*, no. 150 (March/April 1985).

Freeman, Joshua. "Delivering the Goods: Industrial Unionism During World War II." *Labor History* 12, no. 4 (Fall 1978).

Friedson, Eliot. *The Profession of Medicine*. New York: Mead, 1970.

Galenson, Walter, and Seymour M. Lipset. *Labor and Trade Unionism: An Interdisciplinary Reader*. New York: Wiley, 1960.

Gallie, Duncan. *Social Inequality and Class Radicalism in France and Britain*. Cambridge: Cambridge University Press, 1983.

Garson, Barbara. *All The Livelong Day*. Harmondsworth, England: Penguin Books, 1973.

Geertz, Clifford. *The Interpretation of Cultures*. New York: Basic Books, 1973.

————. *Local Knowledge*. New York: Basic Books, 1983.

Genevie, Louis E., ed. *Collective Behavior and Social Movements*. Hasca, Ill.: Peacock, 1968.

Georgine, Robert. "From Brass Knuckles to Briefcases: The Modern Art of Union-Busting." In *The Big Business Reader*, edited by Mark Green and Robert Massie. New York: Pilgrim Press, 1980.

Geras, Norman. *The Legacy of Rosa Luxemburg*. London: Verso, 1983.

Giddens, Anthony, and David Held, eds. *Classes, Power and Conflict: Classical and Contemporary Debates*. Berkeley and Los Angeles: University of California Press, 1982.

Glaberman, Martin. "Be His Payment High or Low." *Studies on the Left* 4, no. 3 (Summer 1964).

————. *Wartime Strikes: The Struggle Against the No-Strike Pledge in the UAW During World War II*. Detroit: Bewick Editions, 1980.

Glantz, Oscar. "Class Consciousness and Political Solidarity." *American Sociological Review* 23 (August 1958).

Goldthorpe, John H., David Lockwood, Frank Bechhofer, and Jennifer Platt. *The Affluent Worker in the Class Structure*. Cambridge: Cambridge University Press, 1969.

Gordon, Milton. *Social Class in American Sociology*. New York: McGraw-Hill, 1963.

Gorz, André. "Workers' Control." *Socialist Revolution* 1, no. 6 (November/December 1970).

Gould, William B. *A Primer on American Labor Law*. Cambridge: MIT Press, 1982.

Gouldner, Alvin. *Wildcat Strike*. Yellow Springs, Ohio: Antioch Press, 1954.

Granovetter, Mark. "Threshold Models of Collective Behavior." *American Journal of Sociology* 83, no. 6 (1978).

Green, James R. "Holding the Line: Miners' Militancy and the Strike of 1978." *Radical America* 102, no. 5 (May 1978).

———. *The World of the Worker*. New York: Hill and Wang, 1980.

Green, Mark, and Robert Massie, eds. *The Big Business Reader*. New York: Pilgrim Press, 1980.

Grey, Mark. "Union Members Against Union Members." *Workplace Democracy* 9, no. 4 (Summer 1982).

Gross, Edward. "Some Functional Consequences of Primary Controls in Formal Work Organizations." In *Readings in Industrial Sociology*, edited by William A. Faunce. New York: Appleton-Century-Crofts, 1967.

Halle, David. *America's Working Man*. Chicago: University of Chicago Press, 1984.

Hamilton, R. F. *Affluence and the French Worker in the Fourth Republic*. Princeton, N.J.: Princeton University Press, 1967.

Hartmann, Heidi. "Capitalism, Patriarchy and Job Segregation by Sex." In *Classes, Power and Conflict: Classical and Contemporary Debates*, edited by Anthony Giddens and David Held. Berkeley and Los Angeles: University of California Press, 1982.

Hibbs, Douglas. *Industrial Conflict in Advanced Industrial Societies*. Cambridge, Mass.: Center of International Studies, MIT, 1974.

Hiller, E. T. *Strike*. Chicago: University of Chicago Press, 1928.

Hobsbawm, E. J. *Primitive Rebels*. New York: Norton, 1959.

———. "The 1970s: Syndicalism Without Syndicalists?" In *Workers: Worlds of Labor*, edited by E. J. Hobsbawm. New York: Pantheon, 1984.

Hoffer, Eric. *The True Believer*. New York: Harper, 1951.

Hopkins, C. Howard. *The Rise of the Social Gospel in American Protestantism, 1865–1919*. New Haven, Conn.: Yale University Press, 1940.

Humphries, Jane. "Class Struggle and the Persistence of the Working-Class Family." In *Classes, Power and Conflict: Classical and Contemporary Debates*, edited by Anthony Giddens and David Held. Berkeley and Los Angeles: University of California Press, 1982.

Hunt, Pauline. *Gender and Class Consciousness*. New York: Holmes and Meier, 1980.

———. "Workers Side by Side: Women and the Trade Union Movement." In *Women and the Public Sphere*, edited by Janet Siltanen and Michelle Stanworth. London: Hutchinson, 1984.

Hyman, Richard. *Strikes*. London: Fontana, 1972.

Jameson, Fredric. "Reification and Utopia in Mass Culture." *Social Text* 1, no. 1 (Winter 1979).

Jennings, Ed. "Wildcat! The Wartime Strike Wave in Auto." *Radical America* 9, nos. 4 and 5 (July/August 1975).

Johnson, Norris R. "Collective Behavior as Group-Induced Shift." *Sociological Inquiry* 44, no. 2 (1974).

Kanter, Rosabeth Moss, and Barry A. Stein. *Life in Organizations*. New York: Basic Books, 1979.

Kashner, Frank. "A Rank and File Revolt at GE." *Radical America* 12, no. 6 (November/December 1978).

Kassalow, Everett M. "Labor-Management Relations and the Coal Industry." *Monthly Labor Review* 102, no. 5 (May 1979).

Katz, Fred E. "Explaining Informal Work Groups in Complex Organizations." In *Readings in Industrial Sociology*, edited by William A. Faunce. New York: Appleton-Century-Crofts, 1967.

Katznelson, Ira. *City Trenches: Urban Politics and the Patterning of Class in the United States*. New York: Pantheon, 1981.

Keniston, Kenneth. *Young Radicals: Notes on Committed Youth*. New York: Harvest, 1986.

Kerr, Clark, J. T. Dunlop, F. H. Harbison, and C. A. Myers. *Industrialism and Industrial Man*. Cambridge, Mass.: Harvard University Press, 1960.

Killian, Lewis M. "Organization, Rationality and Spontaneity in the Civil Rights Movement." *American Sociological Review* 49 (December 1984).

————. Review of *Protest and Prejudice*, by Gary T. Marx. *American Sociological Review* 33 (October 1968).

Kistler, Alan. "Union Organizing: New Challenges and Prospects." In *The Future of American Unionism*, edited by Louis Ferman. Beverly Hills, Calif.: Sage, 1984.

Klandermans, Bert. "Mobilization and Participation: Social-Psychological Expansions of Resource Mobilization Theory." *American Sociological Review* 49 (October 1984).

Knowles, K.G.J.C. "Strike-Proneness and Its Determinants." In *Labor and Trade Unionism: An Interdisciplinary Reader*, edited by Walter Galenson and Seymour M. Lipset. New York: Wiley, 1960.

Kochan, Thomas, and Michael I. Piore. "Will the New Industrial Relations Last? Implications for the American Labor Movement." In *The Future of American Unionism*, edited by Louis Ferman. Beverly Hills, Calif.: Sage, 1984.

Kopald, Sylvia. *Rebellion in Labor Unions*. New York: Boni and Liveright, 1924.

Kornblum, William. *Blue Collar Community*. Chicago: University of Chicago Press, 1974.

Kroeber, A. L. *Anthropology: Culture, Patterns and Processes*. New York: Harcourt, Brace, 1963.

Kuhn, S. W. *Bargaining in Grievance Settlement*. New York: Columbia University Press, 1961.

Lane, T., and K. Roberts. *Strike at Pilkington's*. London: Fontana, 1971.

Lasch, Christopher. *The Culture of Narcissism*. London: Abacus Sphere Books, 1980.

Lears, T. J. Jackson. "The Two Richard Sennetts." *Journal of American Studies* 19, no. 1 (April 1985).

Le Bon, Gustave. "The Mind of Crowds." In *Collective Behavior and Social Movements*, edited by Louis E. Genevie. Hasca, Ill.: Peacock, 1968.

Legget, John C. *Class, Race and Labor: Working-Class Consciousness in Detroit*. London: Oxford University Press, 1968.

Lenin, V. I. "A Great Beginning." In *Collected Works*, vol. 29. London: Lawrence and Wishart, 1965.

———. "What Is To Be Done?" In *The Lenin Anthology*, edited by Robert Tucker. New York: Norton, 1975.

———. *What Is To Be Done?* New York: International Publishers, 1902.

Lens, Sydney. *Left, Right and Center: Conflicting Forces in American Labor*. Hinsdale, Ill.: Henry Regnery, 1949.

Lewis, Michael. *The Culture of Inequality*. New York: Meridian, 1976.

Levitan, Sar A., and Clifford M. Johnson. "The Changing Workplace." In *The Future of American Unionism*, edited by Louis Ferman. Beverly Hills, Calif.: Sage, 1984.

Lichtenstein, Nelson. "Auto Worker Militancy and the Structure of Factory Life, 1935–55." Paper presented to the Organization of American Historians Meeting, New Orleans, April 1979.

———. *Labor's War at Home*. Cambridge: Cambridge University Press, 1982.

———. Review of *Wartime Strikes*, by Martin Glaberman. *Labor History* 21, no. 4 (Fall 1980): 605–8.

Lippert, John. "Fleetwood Wildcat: Anatomy of a Wildcat Strike." *Radical America* 11, no. 5 (September/October 1977).

Lipset, Seymour M. *Political Man*. Garden City, N.Y.: Doubleday, 1960.

Lipsitz, George. *Class and Culture in Cold War America: A Rainbow at Midnight*. South Hadley, Mass.: J. F. Bergin, 1982.

Loach, Loretta. "We'll Be Right Here to the End . . . and After: Women in the Miners' Strike." In *Digging Deeper*, edited by Huw Beynon. London: Verso, 1985.

Lynd, Alice, and Staughton Lynd. *Rank and File*. Boston: Beacon Press, 1974.

McDonald, John. "The Fruitful Errors of Elton Mayo." In *Readings in Industrial Sociology*, edited by William A. Faunce. New York: Appleton-Century-Crofts, 1967.

MacDonald, Julie Jensen. *Pathways to the Present in 50 Iowa and Illinois Communities*. Davenport, Iowa: Boyar, 1977.

Malinowski, B. *A Scientific Theory of Culture*. Chapel Hill: University of North Carolina Press, 1944.

Mangum, Garth Leroy. "Taming Wildcat Strikes." *Harvard Business Review* 38, no. 2 (March/April 1960).

———. "Wildcat Strikes and Union Pressure Tactics in American Industry." Ph.D. thesis, Harvard University, 1960.

Manis, Jerome G., and Bernard N. Meltzer. "Attitudes of Textile Workers to Class Structure." *American Sociological Review* 60 (July 1954).

Mann, Michael. *Consciousness and Action Among the Western Working Class*. New York: Macmillan, 1973.

Manning, Beatrice Esther. "Nurses on Strike: A Case Study." Ph.D. thesis, University of Connecticut, 1982.

Marcuse, Herbert. *One Dimensional Man*. Boston: Beacon Press, 1984.

Marshall, Gordon. "Some Remarks on the Study of Working-Class Consciousness." *Politics and Society* 12, no. 3 (1983).

Marx, Gary T. *Protest and Prejudice*. New York: Harper and Row, 1967.

Marx, Karl. *Capital*. 3 vols. New York: International Publishers, 1967.

Marx, Karl, and Friedrich Engels. *The German Ideology*. New York: International Publishers, 1970.

———. *The Marx-Engels Reader*. Edited by Robert C. Tucker. New York: Norton, 1978.

Matles, James J., and James Higgins. *Them and Us: Struggle of a Rank and File Union*. Englewood Cliffs, N.J.: Prentice-Hall, 1974.

Meier, August, and Elliot Rudwick. *Black Detroit and the Rise of the UAW*. Oxford: Oxford University Press, 1979.

Melosh, Barbara. *The Physician's Hand*. Philadelphia: Temple University Press, 1982.

Meyer, Herbert E. "The Decline of Strikes." *Fortune*, 2 November 1981.

Mills, C. Wright. *White Collar: The American Middle Classes*. New York: Oxford University Press, 1951.

Montgomery, David. *Workers' Control in America*. Cambridge: Cambridge University Press, 1979.

Moore, Barrington. *Political Power and Social Theory*. Cambridge, Mass.: Harvard University Press, 1958.

Nevins, Allan, and Frank Hill. *Ford: The Times, the Man, the Company*. New York: Scribner, 1954.

Newby, Howard. *The Deferential Worker*. Harmondsworth, England: Penguin Books, 1979.

Nichols, Theo, and Peter Armstrong. *Workers Divided: A Study in Shop Floor Politics*. London: Fontana, 1976.

Olson, Mancur. *The Logic of Collective Action: Public Goods and the Theory of Groups*. Cambridge, Mass.: Harvard University Press, 1977.

Ossowski, Stanislaw. *Class Structure in the Social Consciousness*. London: Routledge and Kegan Paul, 1963.

Ostrander, Susan A. "Class Consciousness as Conduct and Meaning: The Case of Upper-Class Women." *Insurgent Sociologist* 9, nos. 2 and 3 (Fall 1979 and Winter 1980).

Ozanne, Robert. *A Century of Labor-Management Relations at Mc-Cormick and International Harvester*. Madison: University of Wisconsin Press, 1967.

Parker, Mike. *Inside the Circle Game: A Union Guide to QWL*. Detroit: Labor Education and Research Project, 1985.

Parkin, Frank. *Class Inequality and Political Order*. London: MacGibbon and Kee, 1971.

———. *The Marxist Theory of Class: A Bourgeois Critique*. London: Tavistock, 1979.

Peck, Sidney. *The Rank and File Leader*. New Haven, Conn.: College and University Press, 1963.

Perlman, Selig. *The Theory of the Labor Movement*. New York: Macmillan, 1928.

Piven, Francis Fox, and Richard Cloward. *Poor People's Movements: Why They Succeed, How They Fail*. New York: Random House, 1979.

Pollard, Sidney. "Factory Discipline in the Industrial Revolution." *Economic History Review* 16, no. 2 (1963).

Pope, Liston. *Millhands and Preachers: A Study of Gastonia*. New Haven, Conn.: Yale University Press, 1942.

Preis, Art. *Labor's Giant Step*. New York: Pathfinder Press, 1972.

Purcell, Kate. "Militancy and Acquiescence Among Women Workers." In *Women and the Public Sphere*, edited by Janet Siltanen and Michelle Stanworth. London: Hutchinson, 1984.

Rabb, Theodore K., and Robert I. Rotberg. *Industrialization and Urbanization: Studies in Interdisciplinary History*. Princeton, N.J.: Princeton University Press, 1981.

Rayback, Joseph G. *A History of American Labor*. New York: Free Press, 1959.

Ross, Arthur, and Paul T. Hartmann. *Changing Patterns of Industrial Conflict*. New York: Wiley, 1960.

Roy, Donald F. "Banana Time: Job Satisfaction and Informal Interaction." In *Life in Organizations*, edited by Rosabeth Moss Kanter and Barry A. Stein. New York: Basic Books, 1979.

Rudé, George. *Ideology and Popular Protest*. New York: Pantheon, 1981.

Salt, Chris, and Jim Layzell. *Here We Go! Women's Memories of the 1984/85 Miners Strike*. London: London Political Committee Cooperative Retail Services, 1986.

Sayles, Leonard R. "Wildcat Strikes." *Harvard Business Review* 32, no. 6 (November/December 1954).

Schatz, Robert. "The End of Corporate Liberalism: Class Struggle in the Electrical Manufacturing Industry, 1933–1950." *Radical America* 9 (July/October 1975).

Schwartz, Michael. *Radical Protest and Social Structure*. New York: Academic Press, 1976.

Scott, Jerome F., and George Homans. "Reflections on the Wildcat Strikes." *American Sociological Review* 12 (June 1947).

Seashore, Stanley E. "Group Cohesiveness in the Industrial Work Group." In *Readings in Industrial Sociology*, edited by William A. Faunce. New York: Appleton-Century-Crofts, 1967.

Sennett, Richard, and Jonathan Cobb. *The Hidden Injuries of Class*. New York: Knopf, 1972.

Sher, Gerson S. *PRAXIS: Marxist Criticism and Dissent in Socialist Yugoslavia*. Bloomington: Indiana University Press, 1977.

Shils, Edward. "The End of Ideology?" *Encounter* 5, no. 5 (November 1955).

Siltanen, Janet, and Michelle Stanworth, eds. *Women in the Public Sphere*. London: Hutchinson, 1984.

Slaughter, Jane. *Concessions and How to Beat Them*. Detroit: Labor Education and Research Project, 1983.

Slichter, Sumner H., James J. Healy, and E. Robert Livernash. *Impact of Collective Bargaining on Management*. Washington, D.C.: Brookings Institution, 1960.

Snow, David A., Louis A. Zurcher, Jr., and Sheldon Eckland-Olson. "Social Networks and Social Movements: A Microstructural Approach to Differential Recruitment." *American Sociological Review* 45 (1980).

Sorel, Georges. *Reflections on Violence*. New York: Collier Books, 1961.

Spencer, Charles. *Blue Collar: An Internal Examination of the Workplace*. Chicago: Lakeside-Charter Books, 1977.

Stallybrass, Peter, and Allon White. *The Politics and Poetics of Transgression*. London: Methuen, 1986.

Stedman-Jones, Gareth. *Languages of Class*. Cambridge: Cambridge University Press, 1983.

Taft, Phillip. "Understanding Union Administration." *Harvard Business Review* 24, no. 4 (Winter 1946).

Thompson, E. P. *The Making of the English Working Class*. Harmondsworth, England: Penguin Books, 1963.

————. "Patrician Society, Plebeian Culture." *Journal of Social History* 7 (Summer 1974).

————. "Time, Work Discipline, and Industrial Capitalism." *Past and Present* 38 (1967).

Tilly, Charles. *From Mobilization to Revolution*. Reading, Mass.: Addison Wesley, 1978.

Tilly, Charles, and James Rule. *Measuring Political Upheaval*. Princeton, N.J.: Center for International Studies, 1965.

Tilly, Louise A., and Charles Tilly, eds. *Class Conflict and Collective Action*. Beverly Hills, Calif.: Sage, 1981.

Turner, Ralph, and Lewis M. Killian. *Collective Behavior*. Englewood Cliffs, N.J.: Prentice-Hall, 1972.

Turner, Victor. *From Ritual to Theater: The Human Seriousness of Play*. New York: Performing Arts Journal Publications, 1982.

U.S. Commission on Industrial Relations. *Centralizations of Industrial Control and Operation of Philanthropic Foundations*. Vol. 8 of *Industrial Relations: Final Report and Testimony*. Submitted to U.S. Senate, 64th Cong., 1st sess., 1916.

U.S. Congress. House. Subcommittee on Labor-Management Relations. "Pressures in Today's Workplace." 96th Cong., 2nd sess., December 1980.

————. Senate. Committee on Labor and Public Welfare. "Tart-Hartley Act Revisions." 83rd Cong., 1st–2nd sess., 1953.

Wallerstein, Immanuel. "Social Conflict in Post-Independence Black Africa: The Concepts of Race and Status Group Reconsidered." In *The Capitalist World Economy: Essays by Immanuel Wallerstein*. Cambridge: Cambridge University Press, 1979.

Walton, Richard E. "From Control to Commitment in the Workplace." *Harvard Business Review* 63, no. 2 (March/April 1985).

Warner, Lloyd W., and J. D. Low. *The Social System of the Modern Factory*. New Haven, Conn.: Yale University Press, 1947.

Watt, Ian. "Industrial Radicalism and the Domestic Division of Labour." In *Women and the Public Sphere*, edited by Janet Siltanen and Michelle Stanworth. London: Hutchinson, 1984.

Weir, Stanley. "The Informal Work Group." In *Rank and File*, edited by Alice Lynd and Staughton Lynd. Boston: Beacon Press, 1974.

————. "Technology and the Absence of Labor's Ranks in Public Issue Politics." 1980. Typescript.

Wilcock, Richard C. "Industrial Management's Policies Toward Unionism." In *Labor and the New Deal*, edited by Milton Derber and Edwin Young. Madison: University of Wisconsin Press, 1957.

Wilensky, Harold. "Class Consciousness and American Workers." In *American Society, Inc.*, edited by M. Zeitlin. Chicago: Markham, 1970.

Williams, Raymond. *Marxism and Literature*. Oxford: Oxford University Press, 1977.

Willis, Paul. "Shop-Floor Culture, Masculinity, and the Wage Form." In *Working-Class Culture*, edited by John Clarke, Charles Critcher, and Richard Johnson. New York: St. Martin's Press, 1979.

Wright, Erik Olin. *Classes*. London: Verso, 1985.

————. *Class Structure and Income Determination*. New York: Academic Press, 1979.

Yarrow, Michael N. "Exploring Fluctuations in Class Consciousness: Conversations with Militant Coal Miners." Paper presented at the annual meeting of the American Sociological Association, Toronto, August 1981.

Index

Activists: arrests of, 158–60; in strike, 109–10, 114, 117–18; and union organizing, 129, 133–56. *See also* Militance, workers'
Administration. *See* Management
AFL, 33, 40, 42, 46–51
AFL-CIO, 139, 183, 242, 274n.42, 274n.44; and international labor, 244
Air traffic controllers. *See* PATCO
Allen, V. L., 237
American Anti-Boycott Association, 40
American Federation of Grain Millers, 182–83, 210–11, 274n.44
American Legion, 42
American Liberty League, 45
American Management Association, 62
"American Plan," 42–43
Aminzade, Ronald, 11
Amsden, Jon, 232
Anticommunism, 40–42, 55–56, 103, 119, 209–14; and AFL-CIO, 244; and Taft-Hartley Act, 58–59
Anti-union consultants. *See* Consultants, anti-union
Anti-unionism, 138–40, 179; corporate, 20, 27, 29–30, 36–48, 59, 65–72, 119–20, 136, 188, 213, 241–42; government, 49–50, 55–56, 244. *See also* Open shop; Union-busting
Arbitration, 184–87
Armstrong, Peter, 256n.8
Aronowitz, Stanley, 280n.22
Arrests: of activists, 158–60, 172; of strikers, 198
Auto industry, 28–30, 80; strikes, 54, 64; unions, 48, 69; war production, 52

Babcock, B., 16
Baer, Walter E., 266n.8
Banking, unions in, 243
Barbash, Jack, 272n.16
Bargaining units, 130, 269n.7
Beeks, Gertrude, 29, 38
Belgium, 239
Bell, Daniel, 4, 60
Bendix, Reinhard, 40–41
Benefits, 66, 215
Bennett, Harry, 20
Bernstein, Irving, 30
Blackburn, Robin, 5
Black communities, 257n.17
Blacklists, 43, 216
Blauner, Robert, 60
Bonus system, 80–81
Boycotts, 274n.44, 276–77n.5; law against, 39–40, 56, 244
Boyer, Richard, 41, 44
Brecher, Jeremy, 21, 46
Bridgeport Brass Company, 32–33
Bridges, Harry, 51, 59
Brier, Stephen, 232
British miners' strike, 231, 276n.57, 276n.2
British workers, 5, 280n.25
Brooks, Thomas R., 43
Browne and Sharpe strike, 188
Burawoy, Michael, 15, 108, 114–16
Bureaucratization: of grievance system, 63, 71; of strikes, 62; of union leadership, 51–52, 55, 71; of unions, 55, 57, 60, 63–65
Bureau of Labor Statistics, 64, 112, 264n.122

297

Calhoun, Craig, 225, 231
Capital. *See* Management; Social contract
Capital flight, 119–20. *See also* Plant closings
Capitalism, 12, 237–38
Carter administration, 244
Centers, Richard, 107, 255n.7
Chamber of Commerce, U.S., 38, 42, 44, 49
Chrysler, 53
Church in strike community, 201–6, 212, 216–17; and strike support, 220–24, 236, 251
CIO, 26, 38, 46–47, 50–52, 57–59; formation of, 39, 240–41. *See also* AFL-CIO
City council. *See* Government: local
Civil disobedience, 244–45. *See also* Strikes: illegal
Class conflict, 18–20, 180
Class consciousness, 3–7, 12, 18, 114, 229, 237, 255–56n.7; ambivalence in, 5–6, 256n.11; and churches, 202–3, 217; and collective action, 8, 17, 228, 232, 236; and cultural process, 13–16, 22, 107; decline in, 60; development of, 22, 278n.12; and politics, 178, 205–6, 237, 275n.50; revolutionary, 9–10, 22, 256n.8, 277n.10; study of, 4–18, 22–23, 114, 258n.27, 259n.39, 281n.1; and union organization, 162–63; at workplace, 80, 114, 218, 265n.1
Class struggle, 14, 34, 60, 217, 224–25, 278n.12
Clawson, Dan, 272n.11, 276n.57, 276n.59, 280–81n.26
Clawson, Mary Ann, 11–12, 265n.1
Closed shop, 37; law against, 56
Cloward, Richard, 267n.18
Coal, 20, 232
Cobb, Jonathan, 258n.35
Cochran, Bert, 46, 262n.69
Cold War, 55–56
Collective action, 8, 10–11, 16–24, 25, 71, 96, 245, 277–78n.10; and grievances, 115–17; limits on, 26–27; local, 225, 239; motivation for, 91, 174, 225; and solidarity, 108, 174, 234, 237; study of, 23, 247–53, 257n.17; and union organization, 121, 132, 143–44, 172. *See also* Class consciousness; Strikes
Collective bargaining: channels for, 64, 92–93, 126, 128; right of, 131, 231, 232; routinization of, 60–65, 72, 115, 228–30; and works councils, 33

Colorado Fuel and Iron Company, 30
Commons, John R., 6, 256n.13
Communist Party, 20, 22, 51
Communists: in strikes, 209–14, 224; suspected, 41–42, 103, 104, 118–19; and union leadership, 239, 244, 262n.69. *See also* Anticommunism; Red-baiting
Communities, traditional, 225, 231. *See also* Strike community
Company unions, 30–40, 68–70, 128, 204
Concessions in bargaining, 66, 116–17, 183
Congress, 67, 244, 263n.89
Connell, R. W., 17
Consultants, anti-union, 71, 120, 131, 135, 138, 139, 152–53, 157, 167, 168, 172, 188, 233, 251
Contracts, labor-management, 153, 214; and grievances, 63; negotiation of, 82, 103, 168, 187; and strikes, 62, 83, 89, 96
Corporations. *See* Anti-unionism: corporate; Management
Courts, 41; and strikes, 198, 201, 206, 218, 236
Crouch, Colin, 277n.6
Culture: of strike community, 217–18; work-group, 78–79, 108; working-class, 14–15, 218, 257n.13, 258n.35. *See also* Class consciousness
Cultures of solidarity: defined, 17–22, 25, 48; formation of, 19–22, 107–12, 225, 228–29, 233–38; opposition to, 55–59, 112; scope of, 176, 179, 242; in strikes, 120, 224, 238; and union organization, 122, 174–77

Darcy, Sam, 22
Davin, Eric Leif, 22
Davis, Angela, 209–13, 274n.43
Davis, Mike, 58, 243
Dawes, Gilbert, 201–4, 212, 217, 273n.29, 273n.30, 274n.45
Decertification of union, 66, 69, 180, 214–17, 229, 272n.15, 279n.19; election for, 180, 215, 229
Demonstrations, 191–92, 201, 223
Desroche, Henri, 20
Detroit, strikes in, 52, 263n.97
Discharge. *See* Firing of workers
Disciplinary action, 113, 147, 187. *See also* Firing of workers
Dunn, Robert W., 36

Education: and strikes, 221; and unions, 244, 280n.25

Elections, union, 45, 56, 101–6, 118; for decertification, 180, 215, 229; for organization, 68, 122, 130–32, 139, 141, 146, 152–60, 167–68, 269n.7, 270n.16; for representation, 56, 101–6, 229, 249, 270n.16, 271n.30
Electrical industry, 38, 59; strikes in, 64
Employer associations, 39–43. *See also* National Association of Manufacturers
Employers. *See* Management
England, 7; industrialism in, 12, 27. *See also* British miners' strike; British workers
Erikson, Kai, 6, 257n.13
Espionage, 40, 43–46, 67, 70
Ethnic divisions, 12, 43, 70, 79, 100–101, 218

Factory occupations, 70, 227, 245. *See also* Strikes
Families: of strikers, 190–91, 193, 200–201, 208, 219–21, 238, 275n.56; of union organizers, 161–66, 174–76. *See also* Marriage
Farm Equipment Workers Union, 38
Fielde, George, 38
Firing of workers, 58, 67, 68, 147, 171, 184; conditions of, 119; threat of, 144, 173, 266n.8; and wildcat strikes, 82, 98, 113
Ford, Henry, 28–29
Ford Motor Company, 28–30, 69, 257n.17
Foreign competition, 55, 66, 69
Foster, John, 12, 19, 277–78n.10
France, 239
Fraternal orders, 11–12

Gallie, Duncan, 13
Geertz, Clifford, 18, 107, 248
Gender roles, 231; during strikes, 190–91, 221–22; traditional, 166, 200, 238; and union organizing, 163–66, 175, 270n.19, 270n.20. *See also* Families; Marriage; Women
General Electric Corporation, 55
General Motors, 54, 62
General strikes, 4, 10, 71, 226, 255n.5; in Poland, 3; in San Francisco, 20, 22; in Seattle, 41; against Taft-Hartley Act, 57
Glaberman, Martin, 257n.17, 262n.71, 262n.75, 262n.77, 262n.81
Goldthorpe, John H., 7–8, 16
Gorz, André, 257n.16, 257n.17

Gouldner, Alvin, 113–14
Government: and industrial relations, 51, 71; local, 198–200, 201, 206, 218–19, 221, 236, 273n.26. *See also* National Labor Relations Board; Taft-Hartley Act
Grain mill industry, 182. *See also* American Federation of Grain Millers
Gramsci, Antonio, 10
Green, James R., 47, 54
Grievance resolution, 75, 81, 85, 112, 171; system for, 62, 71, 82, 115–17, 129, 185–86, 241, 268n.33; and Taft-Hartley Act, 180; and wildcat strikes, 117, 185, 223, 229–31
Grievances, 94, 244, 266n.7; accumulation of, 62–63; and union leaders, 95, 102–3. *See also* Grievance resolution

Halle, David, 15, 208, 218–19, 275n.50, 280n.2
Hartmann, Paul T., 60
Health care industry, 123, 146. *See also* Nursing
Health insurance, 128, 135, 177
Hegel, G. W. F., 9
Hicks, Clarence, 31
High-technology industries, 243
Hill, Frank, 28
Hiller, E. T., 273n.18
Hiring: and seniority, 184–85; and strikes, 113
Hobsbawm, E. J., 256n.8
Homans, George, 52
Hormel strike, 188
Hospital and Health Care Employees, National Union of, 128–29, 278n.18, 280n.22, 280n.25
Hospital workers, organization of, 269n.7. *See also* Union organizing
Humor: ethnic, 79–80; at workplace, 108

Immigrants as workers, 27–28, 42, 260n.8
Incentive system, 89
Independent Labor League of America, 40
Industrial council plan. *See* Works council
Industrial relations. *See* Collective bargaining; Labor relations
Industrial Revolution, 12, 27
Industrial Workers of the World, 41–42
Injunctions, court, 40, 47; against mass picketing, 180, 198, 279n.19; violation of, 245
International Harvester, 29–38, 192, 260–61n.31. *See also* Works council

Iowa, 47, 215
Iowa Beef strike, 188
Iron and steel industry, 36–37
Italy: strike in, 226–27; unions in, 239

Jameson, Fredric, 278n.12
Job loss, threat of, 69, 206–7. *See also*
Firing of workers
Job transfers, 171
Johnson, Clifford, 70
Johnson, Karen, 276n.57, 276n.59, 280–
81n.26

Katznelson, Ira, 15, 218–19
Kerr, Clark, 59, 62
Killian, Lewis M., 173, 257n.17, 266n.5,
267n.17, 276n.5
King, McKenzie, 31
Kirkland, Lane, 242–43
Klandermans, Bert, 173–74
Knowles, K.G.J.C., 111–12
Kochan, Thomas, 69
Kornblum, William, 256n.8, 268n.33,
281n.2
Ku Klux Klan, 42

Labor: foreign, 244; fragmentation of, 12;
history of, 26; proletarianization of,
152; supply of, 34. *See also* Unions;
Workers
Labor board, 241
Labor Congress, 202
Labor councils, 244
Labor law reform, 274n.42
Labor movement, 4, 11–12; postwar, 26;
revitalization of, 280n.21, 280n.22
Labor relations: government and, 49–51,
54–59 (*see also* Taft-Hartley Act);
routinization of, 115, 229; and strikes,
7, 116, 178–79, 188; structures of,
227–28. *See also* Anti-unionism; Collec-
tive bargaining; Union-busting
Lane, T., 189
Lay-offs, 69, 119, 177, 280n.23; and se-
niority, 184–85
Lears, T. J. Jackson, 258n.35
Legal system. *See* Courts
Lenin, V. I., 237, 277n.7, 277n.8
Lens, Sydney, 263n.97, 269n.9
Levitan, Sar A., 70
Lewis, John L., 57–58
Lewis, Michael, 258n.35
Lichtenstein, Nelson, 53
Lipset, Seymour M., 4
Lipsitz, George, 268n.21

Lockout, 186
Longshoremen, 51
Loyalty oaths, 58
Ludlow Massacre, 30–31, 38
Lumber industry, 181–82
Luria, A. R., 19
Luxemburg, Rosa, 10
Lynd, Staughton, 22

McCormick, Cyrus H., II, 31, 33
McCormick, Cyrus, III, 33
Machinists, International Association of,
40, 43, 47–48, 191, 278n.18
Male workers, 15; bonding among, 80.
See also Gender roles
Management: access to, 252–53; control
of, over labor, 34, 54–56, 111, 113,
132, 170, 214–15; and strikes, 39–41,
233; and worker organization, 26–27,
33, 233. *See also* Anti-unionism: corpo-
rate; Labor relations; National Associa-
tion of Manufacturers; Strikebreaking,
corporate; Union-busting; Union orga-
nizing
Mangum, Garth Leroy, 63–64, 267n.19
Mann, Michael, 5
Manning, Beatrice Esther, 269n.3
Marches, 39, 191, 223, 235, 263n.97
Marcuse, Herbert, 60
Marriage, 12, 278n.10; strains on, 200,
209, 275–76n.56. *See also* Families
Marshall, Gordon, 8, 237, 281n.1
Marx, Gary T., 257n.17
Marx, Karl, 8–10, 13–14
Marxism, 17, 178, 266n.6
Mass-production industries, 42–49, 167
Meetings, workers', 34, 37, 45, 81, 127–
28
Memorial Day Massacre, 44
Men. *See* Gender roles; Male workers
Metalworkers' union, 276n.59
Militance, workers', 7, 22–24, 70, 175,
232, 236, 238, 243; decline of, 60; of
strikers, 119, 213, 223–24. *See also*
Activists
Military force, 39, 41
Miners: British, 231, 280n.25; coal, 30–
31, 63, 231–32; copper, 188, 275n.51,
278–79n.19; and Taft-Hartley Act, 57
Miners for Democracy, 105
Minimum wage, 125–26
Minneapolis, 22, 25
Minority groups, 243, 280n.22
Mohawk Valley Formula, 44–47

Montgomery, David, 28, 39–40, 117, 260n.8
Moore, Barrington, 60
Morais, Herbert, 41, 44
Murray, Phillip, 50

Nabisco Brands, 272n.4
National Association of Manufacturers, 38–44, 56, 263n.89
National Defense Mediation Board, 50
National Industry Recovery Act, 36, 45
National Labor Relations Board, 45; protection by, 58, 243; rulings by, 187, 269n.7, 272n.12, 279n.19; and strikers, 206, 272n.12. *See also* Elections, union
National Metal Trades Association, 40–41, 43
National unions: leadership of, 224, 240; and local actions, 213–14, 224, 239, 278n.18. *See also* Union leadership; Unions
Nevins, Allan, 28
Newby, Howard, 6
New Deal, 45, 49
Newspapers and strikes, 199, 218, 219
Nichols, Theo, 256n.8
No-strike policy, 51–53, 62, 257n.17
Nursing, 122–25; professionalization of, 151–52; proletarianization of, 124, 152; 269n.3

Occupational groups, 137, 151
O'Leary, Dr. Jorge, 278–79n.19
Olson, Mancur, 174, 277n.6
Open shop, 27–39; campaigns for, 40–48, 70
O'Toole, Donald, 56
Overtime, 33, 113, 144
Ozanne, Robert, 31–35

Parker, Mike, 265n.142
Parkin, Frank, 6, 258n.27
PATCO, 3, 4, 167, 226
Paternalism, corporate, 28–29, 121, 176
Peck, Sidney, 256n.10
Perlman, Selig, 4
Personnel managers, 28
Phelps-Dodge strike, 188, 275n.51, 278–79n.19
Picketing, mass, 22, 39; injunctions against, 56, 180, 198, 244, 279n.19
Picket lines, 21, 90–91, 189–90, 223, 273n.26; strikebreakers crossing, 4, 40, 194–95, 198, 214, 219–20, 242, 275n.52; violence on, 194–95, 250

Pinkertons, 39
Piore, Michael, 69
Piven, Francis Fox, 267n.18
Plant closings, 45, 69, 106–7, 119, 120, 122, 168, 231
Poland, 3, 226
Police, 45; strike by, 41; strikers', 201; and strikes, 20, 21, 46, 158–60, 172–73, 194–99, 206, 218–19, 227, 236, 273n.26, 273n.28, 279n.19
Political parties, 17; and class consciousness, 259n.39
Politics, 177–78, 225, 280n.22
Polls of union members, 6, 52, 257n.17
Pope, Liston, 202
Populism, 206, 275n.50
Preis, Art, 22
Production, 13; loss of, 187; rate of, 113
Productivity, 29, 89, 182
Professionalization of nursing, 123–24, 151–52, 269n.3
Profits: corporate, 7, 89; wartime, 52
Progressive Era, 32, 36, 38
Proletarianization of nursing, 124, 152, 269n.3
Property, private, 197, 208–9, 227
Purcell, Kate, 175–76

Racial divisions, 42–43, 79, 100–101
Rand, James R., 44
Rand, Remington, Jr., 47
Rank and file, 243; discipline of, 63; independent action of, 11, 112, 131–32, 241; interests of, 90; and union leadership, 55–57, 276n.59. *See also* Union leadership; Wildcat strikes
Reagan, Ronald, 3, 167
Red-baiting, 21, 40, 42, 47, 213, 224, 262n.69. *See also* Anticommunism
Religion, 80, 267n.10. *See also* Church in strike community
Remington Rand Corporation, 44
Replacement workers. *See* Strikebreakers
Republic Steel, 44
Research: interviews in, 253; management participation in, 252–53; participant, 250; partisanship in, 250–51; survey, 5–8, 16, 236, 247, 257n.17, 258n.27, 259n.39; union participation in, 251–53
Revolutionary consciousness, 9–10, 225, 237, 256n.8, 277n.10. *See also* Class consciousness; Trade union consciousness
Right-to-work states, 119–20, 180, 215

Roberts, K., 189
Rockefeller, John D., 30, 38
Roosevelt, Franklin D., 45, 49, 55
Ross, Arthur, 60
Roy, Donald F., 108
Rubber industry, 53, 64
Rudé, George, 256n.8

Safety standards, 89, 113, 214–15
Sanctions: against strikes, 113, 244–45;
    and unfair labor practices, 68. *See also*
    Injunctions, court
Sanders, Richard, 128–29, 131–32, 135,
    141–43, 156–58, 270n.20
San Francisco, strike in, 22, 255n.5
Sartre, Jean-Paul, 6, 16–17, 278n.12
Sayles, Leonard R., 111, 113
Scabs, 42, 46, 56, 161, 207, 208, 219,
    223, 273n.28, 275n.52. *See also* Strike-
    breakers
Schall, John, 276n.57, 276n.59, 280–
    81n.26
Schwartz, Michael, 170–71, 268n.21
Scott, Jerome F., 52
Seattle, general strike in, 41, 255n.5
Seniority: departmentwide, 77, 89; loss
    of, 184–87
Sennett, Richard, 258n.35
Service workers, 243, 280n.22
Shop stewards, 53–56, 96–99, 243
Sit-down strikes, 20, 48, 167
Skilled workers, 77–78, 175
Skill levels, 43, 48, 70
Slowdowns, 63
Social contract, 67–68, 92, 112, 115, 119,
    243; breaking of, 183–88, 217–18, 223,
    225; postwar, 75, 115, 180, 186–87,
    228, 237–38; and union leadership,
    224, 240; wartime, 49–53; and wildcat
    strikes, 120
Socialism, 224
Socialization of production, 8
Solidarity: and American labor move-
    ment, 3–4; class, 48; community, 177;
    corporate, 31–32; expression of, 25,
    47, 64–65, 188, 227; formation of, 11,
    88–89, 108–9, 233; and general strikes,
    3, 22–23; limit on, 19; opposition to,
    26, 70–72, 233; rank-and-file, 32, 71,
    230; strikers', 88–93, 99–100, 108–9,
    113, 174, 250, 277n.6; of subordinate
    groups, 258n.27; among unions, 191–
    92, 223, 244, 279n.19. *See also* Cul-
    tures of solidarity; Solidarity, workers';
    Solidarity strikes

Solidarity, workers', 7–8, 12–13, 26, 32,
    49, 113–14, 240; expression of, 64–65,
    145; local, 278n.18; obstacles to, 27,
    39, 48, 55–56, 68, 70; and union organi-
    zation, 131, 245. *See also* Cultures of
    solidarity; Solidarity
Solidarity strikes, 20, 45, 244
Sorel, Georges, 25
South: capital flight to, 107–8; unions in,
    59, 119
Spencer, Charles, 6
Spontaneous collective action, 111, 173,
    234, 267n.17, 277n.5. *See also* Wildcat
    strikes
Spying. *See* Espionage
Standard Brands Incorporated, 182,
    272n.4, 274n.44
Standard of living, 65, 241, 270n.20
Standard Oil Company, 30–31
Status groups, 12–13, 137, 151, 238,
    278n.10
Stedman-Jones, Gareth, 278n.10
Steel industry, 6, 38, 54, 75–76, 81; griev-
    ances in, 62–63
Steel Workers Organizing Committee, 44
Stimson, Henry, 50
Strike, miners', 30–31, 188, 275n.51,
    278–79n.19
Strike, right to, 50, 245
Strikebreakers, 40, 45, 46, 70, 189, 194,
    198, 236, 273n.28, 275n.52, 275n.53,
    279n.19; contempt for, 207–8; hiring
    of, 20–21, 71, 233; permanent, 214–
    15; and union elections, 56; and vio-
    lence, 194–95, 250. *See also* Scabs
Strikebreaking, corporate, 39–46, 66, 70,
    180. *See also* Consultants, anti-union
Strike community, 21, 194–209, 216–22,
    273n.28, 274n.44, 275n.55; access to,
    250–51; counterinstitutions in, 230,
    233, 236; partisanship in, 205; politics
    in, 255; post-strike, 216–18, 222
Strike fund, 190, 192, 200, 204, 208–9,
    279n.19
Strikers: and labor leaders, 54; and po-
    lice, 194–99. *See also* Families: of strik-
    ers
Strikes: during contract term, 57, 62; de-
    cline in, 60–62, 65; fear of, 146, 154–
    55, 172; illegal, 95–96, 272n.12; inten-
    sity of, 61; length of, 277n.6; limits on,
    47, 56, 230; mass, 25, 70; morale in,
    191; moral issues in, 206–9; official, 62,
    66, 183; participation in, 266n.5; pro-
    test, 187–88, 227; rates of, 60–61,

264n.122; routinization of, 61–62, 66; sit-down, 46; solidarity, 11, 20–22, 39, 40, 45, 56, 244; supporters of, 21, 193, 201–5, 244; union-busting, 188–89; wartime, 51–52. *See also* General strikes; Wildcat strikes
Supervisors: access to, 252–53; anti-unionism of, 135–38, 146–55, 168, 171–72; confrontation with, 230–31
Survey research, 5–8, 16, 236, 247, 257n.17, 258n.27, 259n.39

Taft, Phillip, 57
Taft, Robert, 263n.89
Taft-Hartley Act, 55–66, 186, 244, 263n.89; and collective action, 26, 60, 71, 75, 178–79, 188, 198; and decertification, 66, 214; effect of, 60–62, 120, 121, 167, 240–43; and griev-ance system, 62, 71, 180; opposition to, 57–58, 263n.97, 280–81n.26; and union solidarity, 192, 242
Taylor, Frederick W., 27
Teamsters, 20–21
Textile industry, 59
Textron Corporation, 122
Thompson, E. P., 14, 256n.8
Tilly, Charles, 18, 62, 110
Tilly, Louise, 18
Trade associations, 39
Trade union consciousness, 237. *See also* Class consciousness; Revolutionary consciousness
Trade unionism. *See* Unionism
Truck drivers, 20
Trusteeship of local union, 210
Tugwell, Rexford, 49
Turner, Ralph, 266n.5
Turner, Victor, 16

Ulman, Lloyd, 3
Unemployment, 42, 47, 218; fear of, 34
Unemployment benefits, 168
Unfair labor practice charges, 184, 224, 272n.12
Union cards, 131, 136, 141–42, 154, 171, 235
Union dues, 154, 186
Union elections. *See* Elections, union
Unionism, 19, 128, 237; bureaucratic, 13, 75, 110–12, 117–19, 222–25, 227, 238, 241–43, 278–79n.19; business, 131, 269n.9; democratic, 243–45; in Eu-rope, 239; fear of, 154–55; militant,

151, 231, 279n.19; and professionalism, 151; and seniority system, 184–85; so-cial, 131–32, 269n.9; and wildcat strikes, 111, 116, 229. *See also* Anti-unionism
Unionization. *See* Union organizing
Union leadership, 49, 50, 66, 241–43; and anticommunism, 212; communists in, 57–58, 262n.69; elections for, 101–6, 110, 249; and grievances, 85, 89, 95, 117; local, 211, 279–80n.21; and man-agement, 40; and militance, 241, 279n.19; national, 224, 240; and rank and file, 45, 56, 71, 75, 90, 92, 116, 268n.33; and strikes, 21, 50–57, 63, 89, 187–88, 210, 274n.44, 279n.19; and Taft-Hartley Act, 56–58; and union organizing, 143; and wildcat strikes, 100, 112–13, 116, 268n.22
Union membership: decrease in, 43, 59, 69–70; growth of, 49, 67; maintenance of, 120, 186. *See also* Rank and file
Union organizers, 128–37, 238, 240, 245, 252, 271n.30
Union organizing, 27, 35, 122–79, 219, 230, 233, 235, 252–53; community sup-port in, 176–77; and consultants, 139; management countermobilization to, 140–42, 146–60, 168, 173, 175, 233, 277n.6; procedures for, 130, 269n.7; re-sistance to, 44–45, 120, 129–30
Union-busting, 65–72, 188, 197; consul-tants for, 135; and national leadership, 211, 224, 242; and strikes, 188–89, 198. *See also* Anti-unionism: corporate; Decertification of union
Unions: and class consciousness, 17, 259n.39; contracts among, 192; dis-putes between, 58, 244; foreign, 244; formation of, 38, 67, 130; postwar, 49, 54; and racism, 42–43; recognition of, 168–69; routinization of, 60; threat to, 58–59, 225. *See also* AFL; AFL-CIO; Anti-unionism; CIO; Company unions; Decertification of union; National unions; Rank and file; Unionism; Union leadership; Union organizing
United Auto Workers, 52, 57, 191, 272n.15
United Electrical Workers Union, 54, 57, 58, 122, 278n.18
United Food and Commercial Workers Union, 280n.22
United Mine Workers Union, 30, 31, 105, 280n.23

United Steel Workers of America, 278–79n.19

Unskilled workers, 77–78; organization of, 42

Vauxhall strike, 7, 16, 257n.16

Violence: during a strike, 194–95, 250; threat of, 155, 158, 172, 220

Wage cuts, 32–36, 47, 66

Wage freeze, 50, 52

Wage increases, 35, 125

Wages, 28, 146, 215, 270n.20; base, 80, 125–26; minimum, 125–26

Wagner Act, 45, 47, 55–56

Wallerstein, Immanuel, 258n.27

War Labor Board, 50

Warner, Lloyd W., 16

War production, 51–53, 262n.75. *See also* World War II

Washington, D.C., 49, 274n.43

Weir, Stan, 50, 268n.33

Welfare, corporate, 29–32, 36, 38, 39, 48

Wildcat strikes, 60–61, 82–120, 202, 219, 232, 248–49, 266n.3, 266n.7; and bureaucratic unionism, 112–13, 178, 229–30, 268n.22; and grievances, 63, 115, 230–31; intensity of, 61, 233; management response to, 98–100, 184–85, 266n.8, 267n.19, 268n.21; number of, 63–64, 262n.77, 264n.122; prohibition of, 180; and social contract, 75, 238;

and solidarity, 108, 113, 234; wartime, 52–57, 257n.17, 262n.75

Wilensky, Harold, 60, 62

Williams, Raymond, 17, 107

Willis, Paul, 15, 265–66n.1

Wilson, Charles E., 55

Wobblies, 41–42

Women: and domestic roles, 162–63, 176; as shop stewards, 175–76; supporting strikes, 220–22, 231, 276n.57, 276n.2; as union organizers, 133, 166, 175–76, 232, 280n.22; in workforce, 122, 125, 149–50, 243. *See also* Gender roles; Nursing

Workers: anti-union, 253; unorganized, 117, 243

Workforce: age of, 215; changing of, 169; elements of, 27–28, 76–77; gender differences in, 149–50. *See also* Solidarity, workers'

Working class, 9, 16–17. *See also* Class consciousness; Culture

Working conditions, 93–94, 113, 124, 126, 152, 168–69

"Working to rule," 230

Works council, 33–35, 38. *See also* International Harvester

Work stoppages. *See* Strikes

World War II, 47–55, 257n.17, 262n.75

Wright, Erik Olin, 258n.28, 259n.39

Yarrow, Michael N., 256n.10

Young, Arthur H., 31–35

Compositor:	Huron Valley Graphics
Printer:	Maple-Vail Book Mfg. Group
Binder:	Maple-Vail Book Mfg. Group
Text:	11/13 Caledonia
Display:	Caledonia